THANKS, JOHNNERS

JONATHAN AGNEW

Thanks, Johnners

An Affectionate Tribute to a Broadcasting Legend

blue door

Blue Door
An imprint of HarperCollins*Publishers*
77–85 Fulham Palace Road,
Hammersmith, London W6 8JB

www.harpercollins.co.uk

Published by Blue Door 2010
1

This edition produced for The Book People, Hall Wood Avenue,
Haydock, St Helens WA11 9UL

A catalogue record for this book is available from the British Library

ISBN 978 0 00 788107 9

Typeset in Minion by Palimpsest Book Production Limited,
Falkirk, Stirlingshire

Printed and bound in Great Britain by
Clays Ltd, St Ives plc

This book is dedicated to my friends and colleagues on Test Match Special, and to our many loyal listeners

CONTENTS

THANKS, JOHNNERS

FOREWORD

by Stephen Fry

Whenever I worry that the growing vulgarity, coarseness, ignorance, roughness, meanness, pessimism, miserabilism and puritanical stupidity of England will get me down, I invent a certain kind of Englishman to put all that right. He is entirely a fantasy figure of course. He must be charming, gallant, funny, courteous, kindly, perceptive, soldierly, honourable and old-fashioned. But old-fashioned in the right way. Not in terms of intolerance, crabbiness or contempt for the new, but in terms of consideration, amiability, attention and open sweetness of nature. Able to walk with kings nor lose the common touch, as Kipling put it. On top of that, this paragon must also, to please me, have a love of laughter, theatre and the world of entertainment. He should, of course, know, understand and venerate cricket.

Impossible that such an ideal could ever exist in the real world; and yet he did, and his name was Brian Alexander Johnston. Gallant? Certainly: the Military Cross is more than just a 'he turned up and did his bit' medal; it is an award only ever given for 'exemplary acts of gallantry'. Johnners won his in 1945 after taking part in the Normandy landings. Naturally, if you ever tried to talk to him about it, he gently glanced the subject to leg. Funny? You don't need me to remind you of that. I have his 'Stop it, Aggers!' moment as a phone ringtone, and I turn to it whenever I feel homesick or unhappy.

The fact is, Brian Johnston was the most perfect and complete Englishmen I ever met. His education at Eton and New College, Oxford, and his commission in the 2nd Battalion, the Grenadier

Guards might mark him out in your mind as one of a class who expected to rule and to be respected and obeyed as a matter of course, as a birthright. He had no such pompous expectations. Life was good to him, but it dealt him hardships too. Aggers will take you through those; they tested him as few of us would want to be tested.

I first met him when I was invited to appear on the Radio 4 quiz game *Trivia Test Match*.

'Ah, Fryers!' he cried as I entered the pavilion of the cricket club where the show was to be recorded. 'Welcome. This is your first time, so perhaps we ought to have a net.'

'Fryers'? Only he could convincingly abbreviate my name by doubling its letter-count.

Within seconds of meeting him, I felt we were . . . not friends, that would be silly . . . we were the kind of warm acquaintances who would always be glad to see each other again. We spoke of Billy 'Almost a Gentleman' Bennett, Sandy Powell, Robb Wilton, George Robey and other music-hall stars, most of whom he had seen many times, and some of whom he knew personally from his old *In Town Tonight* days. The greatest light came into his eyes when he told tales of the Crazy Gang, his favourites from the golden age of British stage comedy. It was a mystery to many of his *TMS* listeners as to why he always referred to a Pakistani cricketer called Mansur as 'Eddie'. Only aficionados of the Crazy Gang would know that the craziest of the gang was always called 'Monsieur' Eddie Gray.

To bump into Brian at Lord's, in the part of London I shall always think of as St Johnners Wood, was the greatest pleasure of a British summer. With him passed something of England we shall never get back.

Introduction

There are many people who have had an impact on my life – while I was growing up, as a professional cricketer, as a journalist and a commentator. But, my father apart, none has been as significant as Brian Johnston.

One of the most natural communicators and broadcasters there has ever been, the man known around the world simply as 'Johnners' was a seasoned entertainer on a wide range of programmes on the BBC. He began his career at a time when up to twenty million people would crowd around their radios every Saturday evening. Whether he was spending the night in the Chamber of Horrors at Madame Tussaud's, lying beneath a railway track as an express train thundered overhead, or gently interviewing a nervous resident of a sleepy village on *Down Your Way*, Brian Johnston's decades of broadcasting made him a household name, and every one of his listeners felt as if they knew him, even those who had never met him and were never likely to. But he was best-known as the legendary friendly, welcoming voice of *Test Match Special.*

Brian was more than merely the presenter of *TMS*; he was the heartbeat of the programme. He brought to it humour, colour, drama, the ability to establish personal contact with an audience, and, of course, a deep love of cricket that lasted a lifetime; ingredients that made his commentary burst into life in a way that no one had ever quite managed before. Listeners knew, too, that lying just beneath the surface the spirit of a schoolboy was bursting to get out. Be it deliberately waiting until his colleague had stuffed his mouth full of cake before asking him a question on air, or sniggering at even the most contrived *double entendre*, Johnners was a big kid at heart. And yet, at the age of only ten, he had watched helplessly from a Cornish beach as his father drowned in front of him, while during the Second World War his bravery under enemy fire was such that he was awarded the Military Cross.

Brian was nearly fifty years older than me when I joined *Test Match Special* in 1991, following in his footsteps as the BBC's fourth cricket correspondent. We had never met before, but as with many who knew him, something immediately clicked. For someone of my age, Brian was like a kindly old grandfather who the youngsters can quietly tease, but who never loses his temper. Within a few weeks of starting to work together we inadvertently created the notorious broadcasting cock-up now known simply as 'the Leg Over', which is still replayed as much today as it was when it first brought much of the nation to a standstill.

Johnners and I will always be linked as a double act because of those ninety seconds of madness, but the impact that living and working alongside him left on me was far greater than the effects of just one giggling fit, however famous it may subsequently have become. I, and many others in commentary boxes around the world, continue to seek to emulate Brian's relaxed and informal description of cricket, and his ability to make everyone who is either listening or working with him feel welcome.

This book is not a biography of Brian Johnston. The journalist Tim Heald has written the authorised story of Brian's life, while Brian's eldest son Barry beautifully recorded every aspect of his father's full and varied time at the crease in *The Life of Brian*. I am especially grateful to Barry, and all the Johnston family, for their help and support in the writing of this book.

Thanks, Johnners is a tribute written from the perspective of a man who was fortunate enough to work alongside such a talented and genuinely warm-hearted individual at a key time in his life. Brian Johnston liberated me as a broadcaster, and gave me the confidence to commentate without apprehension or nerves. He showed me how easy and welcoming communication ought to be. Now, in a world governed by brief soundbites, *Test Match Special* can sometimes seem to stand virtually alone in the broadcast media in allowing conversation, good company and colourful description to flourish in a way that still makes radio intimate in a way that television can never be.

For some who read this book, 'the Leg Over' may be their only memory of Brian Johnston. If that is so, well, it is a start at least. But if today's *Test Match Special* brings the wonderful game of cricket alive for you, makes you feel involved and, through gentle humour and leg-pulling, puts a smile on your face, then we have succeeded in preserving Johnners' legacy.

Jonathan Agnew
June 2010

ONE

The Guest Speaker

I can remember the first time I heard *Test Match Special.* I was aged eight or nine, and enjoying another idyllic summer of outdoor life on our farm in Lincolnshire when I became aware of my father carrying a radio around with him. It was not much of a radio, certainly not by the standards of today's sleek, modern digital models, but was what we would have called a transistor. It was brown in colour and, typical of a farmer's radio, was somewhat beaten up and splattered with paint. The aerial was always fully extended. Dad would often laugh out loud as he carried it about, the programme echoing loudly around the barns and grain silo as he stored the freshly harvested wheat and barley. It is the perfect summer combination, the smell of the grain and the sound of the cricket, and whenever I think of it the sun always seems to be shining, although that is probably stretching things a bit. When he had finished work for the day, we would play cricket together in the garden, Dad teaching me with tireless patience the basic bowling action. He so wanted me to become an off-spinner like him.

Soon the unmistakable voices became very familiar: Arlott, Johnston, Mosey and the others who with their own different and individual styles helped the summers pass all too quickly with their powerful descriptions and friendly company. The programme sparked an interest in me, in the same way it has in so many tens of thousands of children down the years, igniting a passion that lasts a lifetime. Whether it be playing the game, scoring, watching, umpiring or simply handing down our love of cricket to the next generation, listening to *Test Match Special* is how most of us got started.

Thanks to that programme, and Brian Johnston's commentary in particular, I have always associated cricket with fun, banter and friendship. As a boy, if there was cricket being played, I would be following it either on the television or on the radio. Brian was always incredibly cheerful, and it was impossible not to listen with a smile – even if England's score was really terrible and Geoffrey Boycott had just run somebody out again. Dad's enjoyment of the humour within the cricket commentary was infectious, and made me appreciate everything that sets *Test Match Special* apart from other radio sports programmes.

I became rather obsessed with the game, even to the point of blacking out the windows of our sitting room and watching entire Test matches on the television. Until I was ten Brian commentated more on the TV than on the radio, but in 1970, when he was dumped by BBC television with no proper explanation, he moved to radio's *Test Match Special* full time. So I joined the legions of cricket nuts who watch the television with the sound turned down and listen to the radio commentary instead. I actually lived the hours of play, with Mum appearing a little wearily with a plate of sandwiches at lunchtime, and some cake at tea. I would not miss a single ball on that black-and-white television, and while my parents recognised how much of a passion I was developing for cricket, I think they felt I needed to get out more. I remember a cousin of mine, Edward, being invited to stay during a Test match. I was furious, and felt this was clearly a plot to get me out of the house and into the fresh air. But Edward sat quietly beside me in the dark for the next five days. By the end, I think he was even starting to like it a little.

At the end of the day's play it was out into the garden, where I would bowl at a wall for hours on end, trying to repeat what I had seen, and imitating the players, whose styles and mannerisms were etched in my mind. I developed quite a reasonable impersonation of the England captain Ray Illingworth, even down to the tongue sticking out when he bowled one of his off-spinners, and I loved John Snow's brooding aggression and moodiness. How did Snow bowl so fast from such an ambling run-up? Little could I have imagined that Illingworth would become my first county captain, and that when I moved to journalism Snow would be my travel agent. Then there was the captivating flight and guile of Bishen Bedi, wearing his brightly coloured turbans, and the trundling, almost apologetic run-up of India's opening bowler, Abid Ali. And Pakistan's fast bowler Asif Masood, who seemed to start his approach to the wicket by running backwards, and who Brian Johnston famously – and, knowing his penchant for word games and his eye for mischief, almost certainly deliberately – once announced as 'Massive Arsehood'.

I loved the metronomic accuracy of Derek Underwood, who was utterly lethal bowling on the uncovered pitches of that time, and still have a vivid memory of the moment he bowled out Australia in 1968 – helped, I am sure, by the fact that Johnners was the commentator when the final wicket fell. It was an extraordinary last day of the final Test at The Oval, where a big crowd had gathered in the hope of seeing England secure the win they needed to square the series. A downpour in the early afternoon seemed to put paid to the game, but when it stopped the England captain, Colin Cowdrey, appeared on the field and encouraged the spectators to arm themselves with whatever they could find – towels, mops, blankets and even handkerchiefs – and get to work mopping up the vast puddles of water. On they all came, to the absolute dismay, I imagine, of the Australians, and in contravention of just about every modern-day 'health and safety' regulation in existence. Before long, with sawdust scattered everywhere, 'Deadly Derek' was in his element. With only three minutes of the Test left, and with all ten England fielders crouching around the bat, he snared the final wicket: the opener John Inverarity, who had been resisting stubbornly from the start of Australia's innings. Inverarity was facing what was almost certainly the penultimate over, with the number 11, John Gleeson, at the non-striker's end.

'He's out!' shouted Johnners at the top of his voice. 'He's out LBW, and England have won!'

This was my first memory of the great drama and tension that cricket can conjure up, and it came as a result of watching heroes and epic contests on television. This is the reason for my disappointment that most of today's children do not have the same opportunity. How can you fall passionately in love with a sport you cannot see?

At Taverham Hall, the prep school just outside Norwich that I attended as a boarder from the age of eight, there was a small television in the room in which you sat while waiting to see matron in the adjoining sick bay. She was a big one for dispensing, twice per day for upset tummies, kaolin and morphine, which tasted utterly disgusting, and then, as a general pick-me-up, some black, sticky, treacly stuff which was equally foul. Despite that, my best pal, Christopher Dockerty, and I would rotate various bogus ailments on a daily basis in order to get a brief look at the cricket on her telly – even just a glimpse of the score was enough. Matron never twigged that Christopher and I were only ever under the weather during a Test match. Incidentally, Chris was a brilliant mimic who could bowl with a perfect imitation of Max Walker's action while commentating in a more than passable John Arlott. He was also the most desperately homesick little boy in the school. His later life would take an unexpected and ultimately tragic turn. As Major Christopher Dockerty he became one of the most senior and respected counter-terrorism experts in the British Army. Posted to Northern Ireland, he was a passenger on the RAF Chinook helicopter that crashed on the Mull of Kintyre in June 1994, killing all twenty-nine people on board.

My first cricket coach at school was a woman. Eileen Ryder was married to an English teacher, Rowland Ryder, whose father had been the Secretary of Warwickshire County Cricket Club in 1902, when Edgbaston staged its first Test match. The R.V. Ryder Stand, which stood to the right of the pavilion before the recent redevelopments, and where I used to interview the England captain before every Test match there, was named after him. Mrs Ryder was patient and kindly, and along with my father was the person who really taught me how to bowl at a tender age. Like him, she reinforced the image I already had of cricket as a happy and friendly occupation.

A couple of years later we had our first professional coach when Ken Taylor, a former Yorkshire and England batsman, professional footballer and wonderful artist, moved to Norfolk. A gentle and quiet man, he might well have played more than his three Tests had he been more pushy and enjoyed more luck. It has been said that he was an exceptional straight driver because of the narrowness of the ginnells – those little passageways that run between the terraced houses of northern England – in which he batted as a child. I suspect some of the ginnells might even have been cobbled, which would have made survival seriously hard work.

The privileged boys of Taverham Hall, in their caps and blazers of bright blue with yellow trim, must have been quite an eye-opener for Ken. I saw him for the first time in the best part of forty years when Yorkshire CCC held a reunion for its players in 2009, and one of his paintings was auctioned to raise money for the club. It was the most lifelike image one could imagine of Geoffrey Boycott playing an immaculate cover drive. I regret not buying it now, given my close connections to both men. In any case, I managed to encourage Ken onto *Test Match Special*, and memories of hours spent in the nets with him at Taverham came flooding back.

A trip to London in those days was considered by my dad to be quite an outing, but he booked tickets for the two of us to watch Lancashire play Kent in the 1971 Gillette Cup final at Lord's. He was still reeling from a disastrous attempt to find Heathrow airport by car at the start of our recent family summer holiday. Utterly lost and desperate, he flagged down a passer-by who kindly offered to take us there, but instead directed us to his house somewhere in London, whereupon he jumped out, leaving us stranded. We opted for the train this time.

The whole occasion had a profound impact on me. The smell and sound of Lord's was captivating, and it was a good match. I was thrilled by the sight of Peter Lever, the Lancashire fast bowler, tearing in from the Nursery end from what seemed to me an impossibly long run-up. Sitting side-on to the pitch in the old Grandstand, I had never seen a ball travel so fast, and Peter immediately became my childhood hero. The Lancashire captain Jack Bond took a brilliant catch in the covers, and David 'Bumble' Lloyd scored 38; these ex-players are all now friends of mine. Dad took his radio, but with an earpiece so I could listen and gaze up at the radio commentary box high to my right in the nearest turret of the Pavilion. All the usual suspects were on duty, and it is surprising to remember now that Brian Johnston, then aged fifty-nine, was only one year away from compulsory retirement as the first BBC cricket correspondent. I suppose I might have wished that one day I would also be commentating from that box, with its wonderful view of the ground. Twenty years later, I would be doing just that.

I moved on to Uppingham School in Rutland in 1973, and one year there was great excitement amongst the boys because Brian Johnston was coming to give a talk. These events usually took place in one of the smaller assembly rooms, which were commonly used for concerts and such things, or in the school theatre. Guest speakers did not normally arouse much excitement among the boys at Uppingham, and those who did come were usually untidily bearded professors and the like. But this was different, and any boys who were not aware of who Brian was, would have been told firmly by their fathers to attend. In the end, such was the demand that Brian addressed us in the vast main hall, which spectacularly dominates the central block of the school's buildings and which could seat all the pupils and staff – a total of close to nine hundred people. It was almost full. I remember Johnners wearing a grey suit, and standing very tall at a lectern in the middle of the enormous stage. If he had any notes, they can have been little more than a few scribbled jottings. He certainly did not read from a script.

I was sitting about a third of the way down the room, and assumed that Brian would talk purely about cricket, but this was the moment I started to realise that there was more to his life than just cricket commentary. Typically, he was more interested in getting laughs during his well-honed speech than he was in telling us about the more interesting and intimate aspects of his life. That would also be the case when we worked together, because for Johnners everything simply had to be rollicking good fun; almost excessively so. Significant and poignant events in his life, such as the unimaginable horror of watching his father drown off a Cornish beach at the age of ten, or being awarded the Military Cross in the Second World War for recovering casualties under enemy fire, were absolutely never mentioned. Is it possible that his almost overpowering *bonhomie*, which some people could actually find intimidating rather than welcoming, had been a means of coping with the impact of his father's sudden and tragic death when Brian was a youngster?

The annual summer trip to Bude was a Johnston family tradition that had been started by Brian's grandmother, and even extended to their renting the same house every year. The Johnstons were a large family with a very comfortable background as landowners and coffee merchants. Reginald Johnston, Brian's grandfather, was Governor of the Bank of England between 1909 and 1911, and his father, Charles, had been awarded both the Distinguished Service Order and the Military Cross while serving as a Lieutenant Colonel on the Western Front in the First World War. At the end of the war he returned to the family coffee business, which required him to work long hours in London. As a result Brian, the youngest of four children, saw little of his father, and consequently they did not enjoy a close relationship. Brian's early childhood was, nonetheless, a happy time, spent on a large farm in Hertfordshire, and with the war over, he and his family had every reason to feel optimistic about the future.

All this was destroyed in the summer of 1922, when the Johnston clan, together with some family friends who were holidaying with them, settled down for a day on the beach at Widemouth Sands in north Cornwall. Ironically, Brian's father had been due to return to London that morning, but had decided to stay on. At low tide, they all went for a swim. The official version of events is that Brian's sister Anne was taken out to sea by the notoriously strong current and, seeing that she was in trouble, the Colonel and his cousin, Walter Eyres, swam out to rescue her.

Anne was brought to safety by Eyres, but Brian's father, who was not a strong swimmer, was clearly struggling as he battled against the tide to reach the shore. A rope was found, and one end was held by the group on the beach while another member of the party, Marcus Scully, took the other end, dived into the water and desperately swam out in an attempt to save Colonel Johnston. But the rope was too short. Scully could not reach the Colonel, who was swept out to sea and drowned at the age of forty-four.

The tragedy was clearly a devastating moment in Brian's life, and neither he nor his brothers and sister could ever bear to talk about it. To the ten-year-old Brian, his father, a highly decorated army officer, must have been an absolute hero. How can the young boy have felt as he stood helplessly on the shore and watched his father drifting slowly out to sea? A few weeks after the Colonel's death, his own father – Brian's grandfather – died from shock.

The whole dreadful saga was made even more complicated by an extraordinary turn of events. Only a year later, Brian's mother, Pleasance, remarried. Her second husband was none other than Marcus Scully, whose rescue attempt had failed to save Brian's father. There had been some gossip about the pair having been on more than friendly terms before the Colonel perished. However, it seems more likely that Scully, who was the Colonel's best friend, suggested that he take on the family in what appeared, to the children at least, to be a marriage of convenience. In the event, it did not last long, and when they divorced Brian's mother reverted to being called Mrs Johnston.

Interestingly, Brian's recollection of his father's death in his autobiography differs from this, the official account, in one crucial respect. As Brian told it, it was Scully who found himself in trouble, not Brian's sister Anne, and it was a heroic attempt to rescue Scully by the Colonel that cost him his life. This version of events appears to have been a typically charitable act by Brian in order not to distress his sister, who, the family privately agreed, was at fault for ignoring warnings not to swim too far away from the beach, and got into difficulties. Brian could not bring himself to blame her for their father's death in print, and so concocted a different story for his book.

Brian's education had started at home with a series of governesses, then at the age of eight he was sent away to boarding school. Temple Grove, located in Eastbourne in Brian's day, sounds rather an austere establishment, with no electricity or heating. Brian, who was a rather fussy and predictable eater throughout his life, found the food particularly awful, and supplemented his diet with Marmite. Years later, I remember him asking Nancy, the much-loved chef whose kitchen was directly below our commentary box in the Pavilion at Lord's, for a plate of Marmite sandwiches as a change from his usual order of roast beef, which he used to collect from her every lunchtime. Brian appears to have remembered Temple Grove for two reasons: the matron had a club foot, and the headmaster, the Reverend H.W. Waterfield, a glass eye. How did he know he had a glass eye? 'It came out in conversation!'

Although cricket was Brian's first love, it seems that he might have been more successful at rugby, in which he was a decent fly-half. He kept wicket for the first XI in his final two years at Temple Grove – he always referred to wicketkeepers as standing 'behind the timbers' – and was described in a school report as 'very efficient' and unfailingly keen. His batting appears to have been rather eccentric, and he was a notoriously poor judge of a run. This might explain his excitement during commentary on *Test Match Special* at the prospect of a run-out, and especially at the chaos invariably created by overthrows, which he always referred to as 'buzzers'. This appears to be very much, although not exclusively, an Etonian expression. Henry Blofeld, like Johnners an Old Etonian, remembers 'buzzers' rather than 'overthrows' being the term of choice in matches involving the old boys, the Eton Ramblers. Like Johnners, Henry always describes buzzers with particular relish.

From Temple Grove, Brian went on to Eton, which he loved, and remembered as being like a wonderful club. It was there that he discovered he could make people laugh, and also where it is believed he started his unusual habit of making a sound like a hunting horn from the corner of his mouth. We often heard this from the back of the commentary box, usually in the form of two gleeful 'whoop whoops' whenever he detected even the faintest whiff of a *double entendre* in the commentary, or just to amuse himself. 'It's amazing,' Trevor Bailey observed once of an excellent delivery from the Pakistani fast bowler Waqar Younis, 'how he can whip it out just before tea.' *Rear of commentary box: 'Whoop whoop!'*

As was the case at prep school, cricket was Brian's particular love at Eton, although he still seemed to be more successful at rugby. He proudly told the story of being surely the only player in the history of the sport to score a try while wearing a mackintosh. This occurred while he was at Oxford. He lost his shorts while being tackled, and had retired to the touchline and put on the coat 'to cover my confusion', as he put it. The ball was passed down the three-quarter line and Brian outrageously reappeared on the wing, mackintosh and all, to score between the posts. Oh, to have seen that.

Inevitably, Brian's dream in his final summer at Eton in 1931 was to represent the first XI and to play against the school's great rivals, Harrow, in the traditional two-day showpiece at Lord's. This was almost as much of a date in the calendar of the social elite as it was a cricket match, and it was the ambition of every cricketer at both schools to make the cut. But Brian never did, and as would be the case with his sacking from the BBC television commentary team many years later, he deeply resented the fact, and often spoke quite openly about it. He laid the blame firmly at the feet of one Anthony Baerlein, who had kept wicket for the Eton first XI for the previous two years. Brian always held the firm belief that Baerlein should have left school at the end of the summer term, allowing Brian a free run at his place behind the timbers in his final year. But according to Brian, Baerlein, with an eye on a third appearance at Lord's, decided to stay on an extra year, and dashed Brian's hopes. (Records show that Baerlein was indeed nineteen and a half years old when he, rather than Johnners, played against Harrow in the summer of 1931, but also that he had arrived at Eton in 1925, and was therefore in the same year as Brian. He would go on to become a novelist and journalist before joining the RAF in the Second World War. He was killed in action in October 1941, at the age of just twenty-nine.)

During his time at the famous old school Johnners made many lifelong friends, and the Eton connection would provide him with invaluable contacts later on; not least – and most conveniently – Seymour de Lotbiniere, who happened to be head of Outside Broadcasts when Brian applied for his first job at the BBC. Brian was late for the interview, which was very unusual for a man who in my experience was a fastidious timekeeper. It turns out that he had been given the wrong time for his appointment, but the Old Etonian 'Lobby' gave him the job anyway.

At the time Brian left Eton, everything seemed to be pushing him towards the family coffee business, but he already knew this was not for him. He was not particularly enthusiastic about university, but managed to secure a place at New College, Oxford. He claimed this was achieved more on the back of his father having been there than because of any academic merit or even potential. At least it meant delaying the apparently inevitable career in coffee, which would also mean a lengthy spell living in Brazil. He read History at Oxford, gained a third-class degree and very obviously had a good time. Cricket featured highly, but so too did practical jokes, which usually involved his partner in crime William Douglas-Home, who had been at Eton with him and whose older brother Alec would later become Prime Minister. The pair would dress up, often disguising themselves, and cause various degrees of mayhem, not least when Douglas-Home lost his driving licence and, as an emergency, hired a horse and carriage and appointed Brian his groom. (Douglas-Home's offence, incidentally, was no more than parking without sidelights, suggesting, possibly controversially, that traffic wardens have mellowed over the years.)

What a sight it must have been as the mischievous pair steered this contraption through the middle of Oxford. The first proper outing involved being taken by 'Lily' – named after the Lady Mayor of Oxford – to buy a newspaper; it ended in chaos when they found it impossible to turn the carriage around, and caused a major traffic jam. In time and with practice, Brian and Douglas-Home became adept at handling Lily and the carriage, and they even travelled to lectures in this manner. Lily became a familiar figure in Oxford, and the police gave her precedence at crossroads.

The comical image this conjures up is Brian to a T: larger than life, outrageous and definitely slightly ridiculous, but also more than sufficiently confident to pull it off. These traits would all manifest themselves when it came to performing in his regular live radio slot in *Let's Go Somewhere* in the late 1940s and early 1950s, when Brian was much more widely known as an entertainer than as a cricket commentator, and was involved in such pranks as hiding in a postbox and startling members of the public who had been urged to post their Christmas cards early, and even carrying out a robbery on a jeweller's shop in Nottingham. Looking back, it beggars belief that Brian was able to convince the powers that be that he should be allowed actually to stage a burglary, live on radio. The Chief of Nottingham Police was in the know, but nobody else. Of course, Brian kept up a running commentary throughout the entire madcap adventure, even while smashing the shop window and stealing a silver cup, and right up to the point of his eventual arrest by a humourless constable after a lengthy car chase. In typical Brian fashion, he was able to pass off the whole exercise as a demonstration of how wonderful our police force is, when in fact it was an absurd piece of almost childish escapism.

It seems that Brian's only disappointment at Oxford was, once again, falling short on the cricket front. He was playing up to four times a week, for the Oxford Authentics, which is the university club team, for I Zingari, a nomadic team very much for the well-heeled, and for the Eton Ramblers. This must have affected his studies, but he did not come close to earning a much-coveted blue. Although he captained his college team for two seasons from behind the timbers, it seems that he was not good enough to play for the university.

The three years at Oxford passed all too quickly, and once again the question of Brian's career was thrust into the spotlight. One of his school friends, Lord Howard de Walden, had suggested to Brian during their teens that he should become a broadcaster – almost entirely due to the fact that he never stopped talking. Bearing in mind that the BBC was only founded in 1922, when Brian was ten, and that broadcasting was pretty rudimentary while the boys were growing up, this showed remarkable foresight and perception. But Brian apparently shrugged it off. If he was moved towards anything – and that is debatable – he wanted to be an actor. What he did not want to do was to pursue a career as a coffee merchant in the family business.

Nevertheless, within two years he was indeed despatched to Santos, an island port off the Brazilian coast with a dreadful reputation for yellow fever. He had at least learned the art of coffee-tasting during a brief apprenticeship in London, which included a short posting to pre-war Hamburg, where he was taken to listen to a tub-thumping speech by Josef Goebbels. He was based in Kensington, staying with his uncle, Alex Johnston, in a house that sounds like something out of *Upstairs, Downstairs.* Certainly there was a substantial staff that Brian was quick to befriend, a particular favourite being the butler, Targett. Brian and Targett would meet below stairs for games of cribbage which included Edward the footman and a one-legged tailor, who would remove his wooden leg and carefully lodge it under the table for the duration. Edward reappeared after the war when Brian married Pauline, working as Brian's valet and ironing his shirts once a week. Brian's son Barry tells me that he also served the drinks at the Johnstons' much anticipated annual summer parties before he was fired for becoming incapably drunk in the course of one such event, and was last seen being bundled unceremoniously into the back of a taxi.

Much more significant in this brief interlude while he was learning about coffee beans was that Johnners fell passionately in love with music-hall comedy. He devoted much of his time in London to the theatre, watching the best comedians on stage. His favourites were Flanagan and Allen, who as well as being a double act in their own right were also members of the Crazy Gang, and Max Miller, whose risqué brand of humour particularly appealed to Brian. It was during these often solitary evenings that Brian's love of word-play developed, and while in Brazil he took to amateur dramatics, probably for the first time; there is no evidence of his having performed in so much as a single school play either at Temple Grove or at Eton, which is something of a surprise considering he was such a natural showman, and hardly the shy and retiring type. These productions, which Brian essentially ran himself, were far and away the highlight of what was clearly a miserable experience. Brian admits to having been pretty useless at his job: he could hardly tell the coffee beans apart, and consequently was never given a position of any authority or responsibility. Within eighteen months he was struck down by peripheral neuritis, a nasty-sounding illness affecting the nervous system which all but paralysed him. So serious was his condition that his mother had to travel to Santos and take him home. A poor diet, and a lack of vegetables in particular, is believed to be one of the primary causes of peripheral neuritis, so Brian's fussy eating may have played its part. Unlike at prep school, there was no supply of Marmite to fall back on.

Brian's convalescence saw him reunited with William Douglas-Home for more pranks and more cricket. He saw the 1938 Australians, including the innings of 240 by Wally Hammond for England in the second Test at Lord's which, during those inevitable commentary box discussions when rain stopped play, Brian always determinedly advocated as being one of the greatest Test innings of all time. He was soon back at work as assistant manager in the coffee business, and although he still hated the job he was now twenty-six, and much as he resented it, the prospect of a lifetime in coffee trading loomed realistically large. Indeed, had it not been for the outbreak of the Second World War the following year, that might very well have been his destiny.

With a group of fellow Old Etonians, Brian signed up with the Grenadier Guards shortly after Germany invaded Czechoslovakia in March 1939 – his cousin happened to be in command of the 2nd Battalion. He was drilled at Sandhurst, although it tests the imagination somewhat to imagine Johnners marching and saluting with absolutely razor-sharp military precision. But, back in the 'boys together' environment he had so enjoyed at school and at university, Brian felt liberated and able to express himself in a way that he never could in an office. He was clearly excellent entertainment in the officers' mess, where he would often sing 'Underneath the Arches', perhaps the most famous song of Flanagan and Allen, just about accompanying himself on the piano. The song would remain a lifelong favourite of his: he sang it live on *Test Match Special* with Roy Hudd, the comedian and music-hall singer, who he was interviewing for 'A View from the Boundary' in the final Ashes Test of 1993. I remember it well: the unaccompanied duet drifting through the open window of the old commentary box at The Oval in a passable impersonation of Flanagan and Allen, their mutual heroes. Poignantly, this would be Brian's last match on *Test Match Special*. He died five months later.

In May 1940 Brian was preparing to join the 2nd Battalion in France when it was evacuated from Dunkirk. After a brief period in charge of the motorcycle platoon, which he led from a sidecar brandishing a pistol – I suspect he loved this enormously – he became Technical Adjutant in the newly formed armoured division. Brian was not the least bit technically minded, and his first challenge was to learn about the workings of a tank engine. With two of his fellow trainees – one of whom was the future Conservative Deputy Prime Minister and Home Secretary William Whitelaw, the other Gerald Upjohn, later the Lord Justice of Appeal, Lord Upjohn – Brian was given an engine and told to strip it down and reassemble it. The first task was a good deal easier than the second, but finally their engine was apparently rebuilt, although there remained several pieces that they simply could not account for. Looking around the room, Brian and Whitelaw could see the inspecting officer seriously reprimanding any trainees who had attempted to hide surplus engine parts or nuts and bolts, so at Brian's instigation they decided to pop their leftovers into Upjohn's pocket. Come the inspection, Brian and Whitelaw duly turned out their pockets with absolute confidence, while the unfortunate Upjohn found himself handing over an unfeasible number of redundant nuts and bolts to an increasingly agitated inspector. It fell to Upjohn to find homes for all the remaining parts while Brian and Whitelaw were given leave to retire to the NAAFI.

Action for Brian started three weeks after the Normandy landings on 6 June 1944. His battalion had been due to sail with the main force, but bad weather delayed their departure. His first encounter with the Germans was on 18 July, and in his autobiography he wrote powerfully and graphically about the experience.

> *The heat and the dust, the flattened cornfields, the 'liberated' villages which were just piles of rubble, the refugees, the stench of dead cows, our first shelling, real fear, the first casualties, friends wounded or killed, men with whom one had laughed and joked the evening before, lying burned beside their knocked-out tank. No, war is* not *fun, though as years go by one tends only to remember the good things. The changes are so sudden. One minute boredom or laughter, the next, action and death. So it was with us.*

Essentially, Brian's job was to rescue and recover the tanks that had been damaged on the battlefield. In practice this meant physically pulling burning and horribly injured colleagues from their wrecked machines as battle raged around him. So dismissive was Brian of the Military Cross he was awarded towards the end of the campaign that he would claim it was more or less given out with the rations. In fact, the MC is the third-highest military decoration, awarded to officers in recognition of 'an act or acts of exemplary gallantry during active operations against the enemy'. To treat it as a sort of handout was typical of Brian, who would genuinely have been embarrassed to have dwelt on his own acts of bravery, and certainly would in no way consider himself to be a hero. Unusually, although not uniquely, Brian's MC was awarded not for a single incident, but more for his consistent attitude and contribution throughout what was clearly a ghastly situation. His citation included the words: 'His own dynamic personality, coupled with his untiring determination and cheerfulness under fire, have inspired those around him always to reach the highest standard of efficiency.'

Just as Brian chose not to talk about the tragic and distressing circumstances of his father's death, his time in the army was a topic of conversation we never shared. In his talk at the school when I was at Uppingham, and later in his supposed retirement when he toured the country's theatres with *An Evening with Johnners*, his entire army career of six years was more or less dispensed with in three jokes.

When the war ended, it is fair to say that Brian had no idea what to do with his life. He was now thirty-three years old, and knew that a return to the coffee trade was out of the question. The trouble was that while he wanted to be involved in 'entertainment', nothing particularly interested him. A chance reunion with two BBC war correspondents, Stewart MacPherson and Wynford Vaughan-Thomas, who Brian had met during the war, led to his interview with the Old Etonian Seymour de Lotbiniere at Outside Broadcasts. Although Brian did not seem to be entirely convinced, he agreed to take part in two tests that can hardly be described as taxing. In the first, he simply had to commentate on what he could see going on in Piccadilly Circus; the second involved interviewing members of the public in Oxford Street about what they thought of rationing. It is fair to say that his performances did not set the world alight, but he was nevertheless regarded as promising enough to be offered a job, starting on 13 January 1946. So began a career in broadcasting that was to last almost fifty years.

At the time Brian joined the BBC, the flagship Saturday-evening programme *In Town Tonight* attracted a staggering twenty million listeners or more every week. Entire families would crowd around the radio to listen to the studio-based magazine programme featuring interviews and music, including a brief three-and-a-half-minute live segment. This was the slot that Brian inherited from John Snagge, but now made his own, and his off-the-cuff, unscripted and often daring broadcasts to millions of people earned him his fame and his reputation.

Many of these live broadcasts have passed into folklore, although I do think the naïvety of the audience in those early days did give Brian a sizeable opportunity for hamming things up a bit – something he certainly would not have shied away from. There was the night he spent in the Chamber of Horrors at Madame Tussaud's, during which he claimed to be terrified as he cowered amongst the waxworks of mass murderers, executioners and their victims. Yet this was a man who had only recently been under fire, winning the Military Cross. And there would certainly have been BBC technicians with him in the Chamber of Horrors. The whole episode was surely skilfully laced with Brian's love of dramatics. A rather braver episode was lying beneath the track outside Victoria Station in a pit about three feet deep, and commentating as the Golden Arrow, en route from Paris, thundered overhead. Unfortunately, the Golden Arrow was running a few minutes late that evening, so after quite a build-up Brian had to make do with a comparatively dull suburban electric train, which nonetheless sounded very impressive as it passed over him, with Brian barely audible as he described the impressive shower of sparks. In *An Evening with Johnners* he would claim that when the delayed Golden Arrow finally rattled overhead, someone happened to flush the toilet and absolutely soaked him, although I suspect this was another case of entirely harmless Johnston creativity.

Live broadcasting in those days must have been a hairy business of poor communications, failed live crossings and all manner of technical mishaps. The best presenters would have been those who could remain calm, or lucid at least, when everything was falling down all around them. Maybe the post-war attitude, as famously expressed by the great Australian cricketer and fighter pilot with the Royal Australian Air Force, Keith Miller, was a contributing factor. When asked about handling the pressure of a situation in a particular cricket match, Miller scoffed: 'Pressure? Pressure's having a Messerschmitt up your arse!'

It was in 1946, during his first year at the BBC, that Johnners was first approached to commentate on cricket. This began as little more than a gentle enquiry from an old friend, Ian Orr-Ewing, who was now head of Outside Broadcasts at BBC television, which in those days was little more than a fledgling operation. Only four Test matches had been broadcast on television before the war, but Orr-Ewing was now planning to show the 1946 series against India. Brian was a staff man at Outside Broadcasts, and was known to love cricket; those credentials proved to be more than enough to get him the job.

It must have been a terribly exciting time – these were the pioneering days of television commentary, with no rules or experience to fall back on. Brian's colleagues in the box included the former Surrey and England captain Percy Fender, whose nose was equally prominent as Brian's, and R.C. Robertson-Glasgow, who had played for Somerset and was one of the leading writers on cricket of the time. I suspect this environment was not unlike that of my early days on the new digital television networks. All the equipment was in place, but only a tiny audience was watching, so it was a perfect way to learn the trade without too many people witnessing one's mistakes.

BBC Radio had been broadcasting cricket reports since 1927, and Howard Marshall began providing commentary in short chunks in 1934. He was joined by E.W. (Jim) Swanton, and later by Rex Alston, and in 1946, the same year that Brian started in the television commentary box, John Arlott was recruited by BBC Radio. Despite the BBC having the personnel to broadcast a full day's play, there were still only short periods of commentary until 1957, when for the first time an entire Test match, against the West Indies, was broadcast. A new programme needed a new name: *Test Match Special.* It was not until he became the BBC's cricket correspondent in 1963 that Brian started to appear occasionally on *Test Match Special*, sharing his radio duties with television, despite regularly touring overseas for BBC Radio from the winter of 1958 until he retired as cricket correspondent in 1972.

Despite often living on the edge, in broadcasting terms at least, Brian was always capable of laughing at himself. He absolutely adored cock-ups, and in those early days of broadcasting these must have been many and often. One I distinctly remember him mentioning in his Uppingham speech all those years ago involved Wynford Vaughan-Thomas rather than himself, but he told the story with tremendous enthusiasm, and as was his wont, he could not help but laugh along too.

This gaffe occurred when Queen Elizabeth, later to become the Queen Mother, launched HMS *Ark Royal* at Birkenhead in 1950. Vaughan-Thomas was reporting the event for BBC television, and was briefed by the producer that there were three cameras. The first would show the Queen officially naming the ship, breaking the bottle of champagne against the hull. He was not to speak at this stage, or indeed during the second shot, which would be of the Marine band playing and the crowd cheering. Camera three would then show the *Ark Royal* slipping slowly down the ramp, and only when it finally entered the water could Vaughan-Thomas start his commentary. Everything went perfectly until the third shot, when, with the *Ark Royal* sliding down the ramp, the producer saw that camera one had a lovely picture of the Queen smiling serenely and waving to the crowds, so he switched the picture from camera three to camera one. Vaughan-Thomas failed to check his monitor as the *Ark Royal* hit the water, and with televisions all around the country showing a full-sized frame of a beaming Queen, Vaughan-Thomas said: 'There she is, the huge vast bulk of her!'

That story brought down the Uppingham School hall, and would later feature in Brian's theatre show. Little did he know that sitting in the audience that day was a schoolboy with whom, almost a quarter of a century later, he would combine to create an even more notorious broadcasting cock-up. Johnners would then always use what has become known as 'The Leg Over' as the climax to his speeches, as indeed I do today. But that afternoon in the mid-1970s, as I walked back to my boarding house with my mates chuckling at the stories we had just heard, I had no idea that this wonderful entertainer and I would one day be colleagues.

TWO

A Radio Man

Brian Johnston was a major influence on my career. Sitting and watching him communicate with his listeners with such ease and warmth was an object lesson in broadcasting. Most of what I learned from Johnners came purely from example – he was the most natural broadcaster I have ever met. He only ever directly gave me one firm piece of advice.

We were sitting together in the commentary box high in the left-hand turret of the Lord's Pavilion before the start of a day's play in a Test match. Bill Frindall settled down beside us as we relaxed with a cup of tea at the commentators' desk, while Peter Baxter, the producer, was constantly on the move preparing for *Test Match Special* to go on air. Backwards and forwards he rushed between the commentary box and the engineers' room, which was little more than a small glory hole to our left, full of tangled wires and electronic equipment. There was no direct communication between the two. Beyond the engineers was an even smaller booth, at the end of the run of three semi-permanent boxes which was where the BBC reporting position used to be located before the arrival of the spectacular Media Centre which now dominates the Nursery End. Its shape has been compared variously to a spaceship, a gherkin and even Cherie Blair's smile. The old reporters' box was barely wide enough for two people to sit and watch the game. I remember interviewing the actor, comedian and my fellow Old Uppinghamian Stephen Fry and the former Archbishop of Canterbury, Robert Runcie, in there, but not at the same time. Shame: it would have made a great combination.

That old commentary box at Lord's, which has since been torn down, was Brian's favourite. Shortly before he died, when he was very poorly indeed following a serious heart attack, his wife Pauline took him to Lord's in the hope that it might spark some memories. Slowly they walked around the ground, arm in arm. Brian clearly did not recognise his surroundings until he gazed up at the commentary box at the top of the Pavilion and said, '*Test Match Special*.'

It was not merely the spectacular view directly down the pitch that made that commentary position so special. To get to it one had to go through the Pavilion, which is strictly the domain of the MCC members, who before the start of play would be rushing about trying to grab the best vantage point. We retraced the steps of all the greatest cricketers the game has known as we walked through the Long Room, with its musty smell of stale cigar smoke, its wonderful collection of paintings of revered figures from the past, and cricketing memorabilia from a bygone age. How could one not feel thoroughly excited about the day ahead? It still gives me goosebumps just thinking about it now. We passed the umpires' dressing room on the way up the creaking old wooden staircase, and I would often pop my head through the door and say good luck to David Shepherd, Dickie Bird or whoever was on duty. Another staircase, which was decorated by framed scorecards of memorable Test matches, and we were at the very top of the Pavilion, where after turning left and squeezing past the members who had already taken their seats, a couple of steps took us to an unpromising wooden door that was probably once white. It was rather battered and badly in need of a coat of paint, but this was home to *Test Match Special*.

The box was far from luxurious. Running its entire length was a purpose-built shelf at which the broadcasters and scorer perched on tall stools. There were a few chairs at the back of the box for visitors and off-duty commentators, and, bizarrely, an ugly metal pillar almost directly in the middle, which always got in the way but presumably stopped the roof from falling in on us. The large wooden-framed windows could only be opened by using some force to slide them down, but the effort was worth it, because the box would then come alive with the unique sound of Lord's – a satisfied murmur of contentment made by 29,000 people enjoying themselves. One could not help but be lifted when one sat at the open window and started commentating.

These days our old turret is home to an MCC members-only champagne bar, and very nice it is too. One day, when I am firmly retired, that is where I have every intention of watching my cricket from, while I fondly remember our old box and all those friends who worked in it.

On that particular morning, in the television studio, BBC TV was also preparing for another day. This involved setting up the in-vision studio, and particularly getting the presenter, Tony Lewis, and his guests into position. Rather than having televisions tuned in to BBC 1, which was prone to breaking off from the cricket for the news or a horse race, our radio commentary boxes are kitted out with monitors which constantly relay everything that is being filmed within the ground by the TV rights holders. This includes the setup shots at the start of the day, which invariably includes the front man meticulously sorting out his hair. (That may sound mundane, but believe me, it makes for great television. Mark Nicholas, formerly of Channel 4 and now of Channel 5 fame, is indisputably the current world champion. Countless little flicks and minute adjustments while staring with increasing approval at his monitor in the studio create hours of entertainment for the rest of us, who are invariably a little 'dressed down' in radio land. Richie Benaud was more of a gentle hair-teaser, carefully manoeuvring a grey curl over his right ear to conceal his earpiece. David Gower, on Sky, does not have to bother much these days, but Tony Lewis, who was always meticulously groomed, liked to ensure that he had a neat and crisp parting in his jet-black hair.)

On this day, as he and I were watching Tony preparing himself for the nation's viewers, Johnners announced: 'Aggers, whatever you do, don't go to telly.' I assumed the reason for this observation was the amount of time and effort required just to get one's hair ready, and I nodded in a non-committal sort of a way. 'No, Aggers, I mean it,'

Johnners said. 'For a start, you are a radio man. But also because television doesn't treat you nearly so kindly.' This was the prelude to him telling me about the time he was dropped as a television commentator in 1970, after twenty-four years, without so much as a letter or telephone call of explanation. It was unusual to see Brian anything other than jovial and light-hearted, but although this had happened over twenty years previously, it was clear that the bitterness still ran surprisingly deep. Not only does the episode seem to have been rudely and thoughtlessly handled by the corporation, but for Brian, who remained the BBC cricket correspondent, it was a public humiliation. For a man who until then had led a largely charmed life, rejection was a new and unpleasant experience.

I heeded Brian's advice when, in 1998, Channel 4 surprised everybody by securing the rights to televise cricket ahead of the BBC, starting the following season. I was approached by Channel 4 and Sunset + Vine, the production company that would revolutionise the coverage of cricket in this country, and asked if I would resign as the BBC's correspondent and join them for the 1999 season. This was a huge decision, and one to which I gave serious and considerable thought. Financially, it was no contest: television pays much better than radio, and even before they had broadcast a ball, this promised to be an exciting and groundbreaking venture. That had huge appeal, besides which, the move might set my family up for life. My wife Emma, who works in television news, felt that I should take the plunge. But I was not convinced. Radio felt like home to me; not in an easy, unchallenging, job-for-life sort of way, but because I felt much more comfortable on the radio than I had when I had covered one-day matches on television in previous years for the BBC. Television commentary was fine, but it was more restrictive than radio, and offered less opportunity for my style of banter. I also found the work 'to camera' quite awkward. For me, the whole television thing lacked the fun and spontaneity of radio.

In the end, after much soul-searching, I stuck with my instincts. These were endorsed by Brian's view of me as a radio man, and I also felt a deep-seated sense of loyalty to *Test Match Special*. Many people in the industry told me during the course of that summer that I was mad, but I knew I had made the right decision. So too did Ian Botham, who still takes great delight in telling me that I have the perfect face for radio.

The sudden appearance of Channel 4 caught the BBC on the hop, and started quite a stampede of commentators who now found themselves having to find work either with Channel 4 or Sky, which were both simultaneously broadcasting cricket live. To complicate matters further, England was due to stage the 1999 cricket World Cup, which was to be televised on the BBC. It really was quite a mess.

Eventually, and presumably because there was nobody else, I was asked to present the BBC television coverage of the World Cup. Richie Benaud was still available to work alongside me, but everyone else had flown the nest. I really had no option but to agree to do it, despite my reservations about working in television. Coming so quickly after my decision to stay on the radio, this was quite an irony.

I was given one day of training in some BBC studios at Elstree. My tutor was Peter Purves, a dapper and kindly man who with Valerie Singleton and John Noakes had been a member of the best-known trio of presenters on *Blue Peter* when I religiously watched the programme in the late 1960s. Peter taught me the basics of television presentation, in particular handling the talkback from the director, the producer and the myriad other voices that television front men have to deal with while maintaining an expressionless face to camera. Although I can happily talk to the precise second on the radio by using a stopwatch, it is a different thing altogether to have a robotic voice in your ear counting the seconds down from one minute to zero, at which point you have to say goodbye.

I did not find that easy at all, and when the tournament got underway the end of the programme was always a terribly tense time for me. Richie and I would be sitting together in the studio, and we would talk about the match we had just watched until it was time for me to close the programme. But I made a real hash of it after one of the early games in Cardiff, and it was clear that I needed some help. In Richie, I had the coolest, most experienced and professional cricket presenter there has ever been on our television screens, and I asked him to give me a hand. Very kindly, he suggested a plan which we then employed for the rest of the World Cup: as soon as the count started in our earpieces I would ask him a question, and he would talk until the count reached eight seconds to go. I would then thank him, turn to the camera and tell the audience briefly about the next game to be televised. Miraculously, for the rest of the tournament I always heard 'zero' in my ear at the moment I said goodbye. Richie is seriously good, but the whole experience served to confirm my belief that my decision to stick with *Test Match Special* was the right one.

Brian had become the BBC's first cricket correspondent in 1963, and while this inevitably reduced his appearances in the world of general entertainment, and therefore his public profile, it did establish him as the country's leading voice on cricket. He commentated mostly on the television during home Test matches, and on radio during England's winter tours and also on Saturday afternoons, when BBC Radio Sport spent considerably more time covering county cricket than it does now. It was, apart from anything else, how new commentators used to cut their teeth.

The demands placed upon the BBC cricket correspondent have changed enormously in recent years, particularly with the arrival of twenty-four-hour rolling news channels and Radio 5 Live. There were also fewer tours in those days. Although Brian did tour Pakistan briefly, where he appeared to spend more time commentating on rioting students than on cricket, the only time he ever went to India was for three weeks as a spectator in 1993, when he lived exclusively on eggs. This, and a shot of whisky every evening, was necessary, he claimed, to stave off what he called Delhi-belly. He was an old man by that time – in fact he was eighty, and he died less than a year later – but he and Pauline had a colourful holiday, of which a trip to the Taj Mahal was clearly the highlight.

'Six hours in the car each way, Aggers,' he told me, 'and I still don't know what side of the road they drive on over here.'

He popped into the commentary box in Bombay to say hello at the end of a particularly hot day's play, just at the time that I was rattling off my reports, interviews and two-way conversations with the studio in London. Brian, whose commitments in his time would have been little more than one close-of-play report, sat quietly behind me until I had finished. 'Goodness me, this job has changed,' he said.

Because Brian was never told why he was removed from television commentary, different theories have emerged over the years. One was that the authorities, in other words the Test and County Cricket Board, wanted a more serious image of its product than that which was being presented by Brian's jokey style and brand of humour, and the BBC, keen to protect its position as rights holders, complied. This was vehemently denied by Brian Cowgill, who had recently arrived as the new head of television sport, and was believed by some to be the man who was determined to get Brian off the nation's screens.

A more likely reason was the desire to introduce more former cricketers, with their expert knowledge and insight, to the microphone. Jim Laker, the England off-spinner who still has the best-ever match analysis in Test history, was introduced to the team in 1970. However, that theory is complicated by the fact that Denis Compton, one of the all-time great batsmen and a regular television commentator at the time, was shown the door with Johnners, while Peter West, who had never played first-class cricket in his life, was promoted to present the programme. But if this really is the true version of events, Brian was the first casualty in what has since become a procession of retired Test cricketers into television commentary boxes the world over, to the point that Test experience is now seen as a necessary requirement for a commentator. It helps, of course, but television also needs colourful and interesting commentary, just as radio does.

A third theory, and perhaps the least plausible, was nevertheless the one favoured by Compton. Both Brian and Denis, who could be outspoken and who had much stronger right-wing views than Brian, were of the belief that sport and politics should not mix. In the late 1960s the question of apartheid South Africa continuing to compete in international sport was the biggest off-field issue Brian had to deal with in his time as BBC cricket correspondent. While mass protests forced the abandonment of the proposed tour of England by South Africa in 1970, Brian and Denis were not alone in supporting the view that a sporting boycott of South Africa was not the answer to the political problems there. Peter Dimmock, the general manager of BBC Outside Broadcasts at the time, denied that their stance on South Africa had anything to do with their being fired.

Whatever the reason, it was a huge blow to Johnners. At the time, his disappointment prevented him from appreciating quite what a godsend it would turn out to be, because he was immediately approached by Robert Hudson, the head of BBC Outside Broadcasts, to join *Test Match Special* full time. Two years later, aged sixty, he was forced by BBC regulations to retire from his position as cricket correspondent. Now a freelance, he took over as the presenter of *Down Your Way*, a weekly interview-based radio programme that he fronted for the next fifteen years.

Just as *In Town Tonight* had encouraged Johnners to show his extrovert side, so *Down Your Way* tapped perfectly into his ability as a communicator. He would visit a different town, village or community every week, and talk to some of the more interesting locals he encountered along the way. Since he always had a very kindly and welcoming manner with people, this helped make members of the public who had never appeared on the radio before feel at ease when faced by a microphone – brandished by an imposingly tall man – for the first time. It was his warm, fun and friendly presence on those classic radio programmes that firmly established Brian Johnston as a national institution, and those were the qualities he brought to freshen up *Test Match Special*. Now, with cricket in the summers and *Down Your Way* to occupy him in the winters, Brian really was in his heaven.

This was the time many *Test Match Special* stalwarts consider to have been the programme's golden age. After John Arlott retired in 1980, Johnners was indisputably the leading character, but I rather lost contact with the programme when I left Uppingham School and joined Leicestershire County Cricket Club as a young fast bowler. From the age of sixteen I had been playing second-XI cricket at Surrey CCC, and my dream of becoming a professional cricketer was finally realised when Leicestershire offered me a contract while I was still at school. For an eighteen-year-old bowler I was unusually fast, and enjoyed terrorising our opponents, be they schoolboys (8 wickets for 2 runs and 7 for 11 stick in the memory) or, better still, the teachers in the annual staff match. This, I gather, used to be a friendly affair until I turned up, and I relished the chance to settle a few scores on behalf of my friends – for whom I was the equivalent of a hired assassin – as well as for myself.

Within only a few weeks of leaving school, a sudden injury crisis at Leicestershire propelled me into the first team for a county championship match against Lancashire at Grace Road – something for which I was not very well prepared. For a start, I had been a dedicated Lancashire fanatic ever since Dad had taken me to Lord's for that Gillette Cup final when I was eleven, and suddenly I found myself playing against my heroes. Merely watching them walk out to practise in the nets before play began felt quite bewildering. I remember Ray Illingworth, who I had met only once, briefly, when I was signed by the club, and who was now my captain, laughing as I produced my plastic-soled bowling boots from my bag in the dressing room. Illy had played with, and led, some of the best fast bowlers England has ever produced, and clearly he did not rate the equipment which up to now had served me perfectly well at school. He was right, of course. We had to field for 130 overs in that match, and I could barely walk at the end.

Another problem was the serious lack of protective equipment I possessed, and this was brought sharply into focus when I saw Lancashire's giant West Indian fast bowler Colin Croft mark out his run-up and proceed to bowl at a speed and hostility I had never imagined to be humanly possible. I noticed that even my experienced colleagues were rather subdued by the prospect of facing him, but they produced thigh guards and carefully moulded foam padding which they meticulously strapped all over their bodies. I had none of these, and very few batsmen wore helmets in 1978. While my pads had provided sufficient protection against schoolboy bowling at Uppingham, they were hopelessly inadequate for the missiles Croft was now hurling down, increasingly angrily, it seemed, at our batsmen. Thankfully, in that year the rule in county cricket was that all first innings had to close after a hundred overs, and although things looked very ugly indeed for us at 126 for 5, a fighting innings by Jack Birkenshaw, for which I will always be grateful, spared me from my date with Croft. 'Crofty' has since reinvented himself as a surprisingly genial, entertaining and hospitable colleague on the radio, but he was anything but friendly that day.

So, with plastic boots firmly strapped on, I walked out into the late-afternoon sunshine to bowl my first over in first-class cricket. Illy set the field for Lancashire's opening batsmen, David Lloyd and Andy Kennedy, both wearing the slightly faded blue caps bearing the red rose of Lancashire that I had so coveted as a child; at one point I had written cheekily to Lancashire CCC while I was at Taverham Hall to ask if they could post me one. I was sent a sheet of the players' autographs instead.

Nervously I paced out my run-up, and down the hill I rushed, with my head swimming. Because of the massive adrenalin surge, the first delivery was a huge no-ball, called by a startled umpire David Constant, who I know wanted to be kind to an eighteen-year-old lad in his first match, but simply could not ignore the fact that I had overstepped by at least two feet. It was not the most auspicious of starts, but the fourth ball swung sharply from a full length and shattered Lloyd's stumps. I remember leaping about all over the place in sheer delight, and Illy trotting up with his hand outstretched to offer his congratulations while Bumble turned and plodded forlornly towards the pavilion.

Since that initial, brief encounter when he was such a senior cricketing figure and I was a complete novice, Bumble has become a very good friend. Exactly twenty-five years later to the day, on 19 August 2003, my telephone rang at home. I picked up the receiver:

'Hello?'

'What were you doing twenty-five years ago?'

'Er, I'm not sure. Is that you, Bumble?'

'Yes, and twenty-five years ago today you got me out, you bastard.' Bang: the telephone went dead.

By then Bumble and I had enjoyed several summers together on *Test Match Special*, and he was my partner in crime in many a wind-up of Johnners. Henry Blofeld also suffered cruelly before Bumble left us to become England coach, and finally moved to Sky television.

I quickly learned that Illy was right about most things. There were some amusing stories doing the rounds about him never accepting that he was out when he was batting. Like the time he was facing the Glamorgan fast bowler Alan Jones, who always released an explosive grunt to rival Maria Sharapova's when he let the ball go. On one occasion Jones beat Illingworth all ends up and demolished his stumps, only for Illy to claim, when he returned in high dudgeon to the dressing room, that he had mistaken Jones's grunt for the umpire calling 'No-ball,' and naturally changed his shot.

It was a great shame that he and Mike Atherton never hit it off when Illy was the England manager in 1994. Illy's tough and uncompromising style of management was hopelessly out of date by then, but he remains the best reader of a cricket match I have ever met. I remember one match against Lancashire when he brought himself on to bowl to the towering and massively destructive figure of Clive Lloyd. Illy was concerned about the position of Chris Balderstone at deep square leg. 'Come on, Baldy!' he scolded. 'I'm bowling uphill and into t'wind on a slow pitch. You should be ten yards squarer.' Balderstone duly moved ten yards to his right as directed, Lloyd played the sweep shot and the ball went absolutely straight to him: he took the catch without moving a muscle. A fluke? I do not know, but boy, was I mighty impressed.

Illingworth was a blunt character, brought up in the old-fashioned way and as canny in his regular bridge school whenever rain stopped play as he was on the field. Thanks to him, I was sent to Australia that first winter on what was called a Whitbread Scholarship. My dad and I went down to London to be given the good news by one of his great heroes, Colin Cowdrey, and before I knew it I was on my way to Melbourne. I was picked up by the legendary fast bowler Frank 'Typhoon' Tyson.

Like his predecessor Harold Larwood, Frank had been welcomed to Australia when he moved there after his playing days were over, despite having blown away the Aussie batsmen in a spell of fast bowling at the Melbourne Cricket Ground in 1954–55 that is still talked about in reverential terms. Frank took 7 for 27 in a furious spell to skittle Australia, and now he was the coach of Victoria. He was also, as I discovered when I moved into his house, still very competitive, especially after a surprisingly small amount of beer. 'Reckon you're fast, then?' he would suddenly announce, putting down his can and grabbing a tennis ball, which he would then proceed to hurl quickly and comically all around his back garden until it vanished into the hedge.

Frank was great. He despatched me all over Victoria to coach in small towns and rural communities. I was only eighteen, and this was a whole new world to me. On the weekends I played for Essendon, a top-grade club in north Melbourne, and experienced at first hand the strength and competitiveness of club cricket in Australia. Three years later I played in Sydney for Cumberland Cricket Club, where John Benaud, Richie's brother, was captain. If Richie is quiet, measured and immaculately turned out, then John – fourteen years Richie's junior – is a veritable party animal. He was a highly successful journalist in his own right, becoming editor-in-chief of the now defunct *Sydney Sun*, and his colourful nature is best illustrated by the ban from cricket that he received in 1970, when he was captain of New South Wales, for insisting on wearing a certain type of ripple-soled cricket shoe that had been outlawed by the authorities. He played the first of his three Tests two years later, his top score being 142 against Pakistan. The twenty-year gap between John and Richie's Test debuts is surpassed by only one pair of brothers, Johnny and Ernest Tyldesley, whose great-great-nephew is one Michael Vaughan.

It was hardly surprising that Ray Illingworth was infuriated, albeit affectionately, by the distinctly laid-back approach of the youthful, curly-haired David Gower, who would also captain Leicestershire and England. There is an argument that had Gower had the dedication to fitness and practice of, say, Graham Gooch, he might have scored more than his eighteen hundreds for England. But he would not have batted with the carefree elegance that made him one of cricket's greatest attractions, and the criticism he so often received for perishing to apparently casual shots was born of onlookers' frustration at knowing his innings was over long before they wanted it to be. It is fair to say that I was also from the Gower school of training and invariably he and I would be some distance behind the rest of the pack, chatting as we jogged along the canal towpath from Grace Road to what used to be Leicester Polytechnic for pre-season training every April.

Although there was always keen competition for places in the Leicestershire first team, the dressing room was usually a friendly place. There would always be a disgruntled player or two who was not in the side, and who would sit chuntering on the fringes, but if you were playing well, and scoring runs or taking wickets, county cricket was about as pleasant an occupation as you could possibly find. My career could be divided up into two sections: the first being when I was an out-and-out fast bowler and played for England when I probably should not have done; and the second being when I slowed down a bit, learned how to swing the ball and did not play for England when I probably should have done.

My first Test, against the West Indies in 1984, was the final game of a five-match series of which the Windies had already won the first four. Let us say that when I joined the England camp, morale was a little on the low side. There was humour all right, but it was of the death-row variety, with everyone apparently bowing to the inevitable before a ball was bowled. Graeme Fowler and Chris Broad, the opening batsmen, who had every right to be shell-shocked after the ferocious and downright dangerous bowling they had faced that summer, went about their preparations cheerfully, if resignedly. The pride in playing for one's country burned strongly, and the effort put in would be absolute, but despite that, it seemed everyone knew realistically that we would not win.

I did not know many of the other players very well, including Ian Botham, who was a massive presence in the dressing room. I found him very intimidating – not physically or in an unpleasant way, but because he was a superstar, and totally out of my league. It helped me that David Gower was captain, and that I knew him well. But I felt rather sorry for Richard Ellison, who made his debut alongside me, as he not only had the Botham factor to deal with, but also Gower, whose status was every bit as lofty as Beefy's, if a little more understated. It must be easier these days, with the England team having a much more settled look to it – too much so, some would argue. In fact, there cannot be many players in the current England set-up who do not know their international team-mates better than they know their colleagues back at their counties. This must help enormously. By contrast, at the time I made my debut, England players reported for duty on the morning before the Test, and had a quick net and fielding practice in the afternoon. The selectors, wearing suits, would watch knowingly from a distance, and then it was back to the hotel to prepare for the evening team get-together.

I was curious to experience the eve-of-Test dinner, for this really was entering the inner sanctum. Ever since those days of the blacked-out sitting room at the farm I had dreamed of playing for my country, and although I had not been told that I would definitely fulfil my ambition the following morning, I was at least sitting at the table. To my right was Alec Bedser, the former great Surrey and England seam bowler and a previous chairman of selectors. To my left was Peter May, another legend of the game and the current chairman. How I wished Dad could see me now.

Bedser and I had an interesting, if unusual, eve-of-Test-debut conversation, not about bowling, but about the potatoes he had recently planted in his allotment. He spoke at length about the variety involved, although I cannot now remember what they were. May was polite but very reserved. It dawned on me all too late that the experienced old hands – Botham, Gower, Allan Lamb and co. – had all dashed for the other end of the table. Down there, there was much laughter and banter. Finally, after May had said a few words of welcome, the selectors left the room. It was now Gower's turn to give the captain's team talk. This was taken very seriously, with the players chipping in with their thoughts on how to dismiss each opposition batsman. After a short debate amongst the bowlers about the batsman's weaknesses, Botham would announce that he would bounce him out. It became apparent that he would finish with all ten wickets in each innings, and the West Indies batsmen would be lucky to make double figures between them. It was funny, of course, but just like Fred Trueman, Ian had absolute, unswerving conviction in his own ability: he meant it.

Ian did actually feature in both of the wickets I claimed in the match. First, he caught Gordon Greenidge at third slip. Then, as his great friend Viv Richards sauntered to the crease, Botham said: 'Right. Don't pitch a single ball up at him. Have two men back for the hook, and bowl short every ball.' This I did for three overs or so, by which time Viv was looking a little exasperated, but was definitely on the back foot. Finally I pitched one up, the great man missed it and umpire David Constant ruled that Richards was LBW for 15. If I am honest, had the umpires' Decision Review System been in place at The Oval that day, Viv might have had the decision overturned by technology: it looked a little on the high side.

I remained in the team for the Test that followed; a one-off encounter with Sri Lanka at Lord's which was a terribly disappointing match from an England perspective. Again, the team dinner was dominated by Botham's plan to bounce out every batsman, but when he executed this theory against Sri Lanka's captain, Duleep Mendis, the ball kept disappearing several rows back into the Mound Stand. Mendis hammered 111 in the first innings, and 94 from only 97 balls in the second as his team dominated the match, and we all fared badly. The Test began in unusual fashion when, just as I was about to bowl the first ball, some demonstrators ran onto the field and Dickie Bird, the umpire, panicked. 'Terrorists!' he shouted, flapping his arms about. 'They're terrorists!' In fact they were supporters of the Tamil Tigers in Sri Lanka, and after a few minutes they had made their point and quietly left the ground.

I took only a couple of wickets in Sri Lanka's first innings of 491, and preparing to leave the dressing room to bowl in their second, I heard a discussion on the television between the commentators, who were agreed that this was make or break for me. I do not blame them – it was our fault for having the sound up, and besides, they were right. Unfortunately, I went out to bowl with my head full of negative thoughts, bowled a load of no-balls, and although I was called out as a replacement, I failed to make the original selection for the winter tour of India.

My final opportunity with England came the following summer, in the fourth Test against Australia at Old Trafford. I might have played in the previous game at Trent Bridge, but Arnie Sidebottom – father of Ryan – got the nod despite not being fit. Arnie knew he would probably not get through the Test, but such was his determination to win an England cap that he declared himself fit. He managed to bowl eighteen overs before hobbling off, and was never chosen again.

The Test was played in miserable weather, with a howling gale blowing straight down the ground throughout, and too much time was lost for either team to force a result. I failed to get a wicket in my twenty-three overs, finished with match figures of 0 for 99 and lost my place to Richard Ellison, who bowled magnificently in the next two Tests to win the Ashes.

I was surprised to receive, a few weeks later, an invitation from the Prime Minister's office to attend a celebration at Number 10 Downing Street, but set off anyway full of curiosity. I suspected that the incumbent, Margaret Thatcher, was not much of a cricket fan when she shook my hand at the top of the famous staircase in Number 10 and warmly congratulated me on my performance. But she was a very generous hostess, and gave a small group of us a guided tour of the building.

That was it for me on the international front; just a taster, and it is hard to avoid the feeling that I should have done better. Still, my England cap remains one of my proudest possessions.

One thing my brief experience of Test cricket did teach me is that it cannot be easy to be England captain and then go straight back to one's county and lead that team as well. But that is what David Gower had to do. It certainly would not happen today. Although there is now much more international cricket than there used to be, I refuse to accept that being captain of England against Australia in 1985 was any less stressful than it was in 2009. We knew in the Leicestershire dressing room that David would return from Test duty exhausted, and that taking us onto the field in a comparatively dull championship match was probably the last thing he felt like doing. It did lead to some amusing incidents, however, like the time he lost the toss and we found ourselves in the field against Surrey.

'Bowl the first over then,' he said to me rather wearily as we approached the middle. 'And set your own field.'

David wandered off to second slip, while I did the rest: point, mid-off, short leg, fine leg, third man . . . Hang on. Third man? A quick headcount revealed that we had twelve players on the field: David had forgotten to tell one of our squad that he was not playing in that match. In the end my old sparring partner Les Taylor, who was profoundly deaf in one ear, was despatched from the field after a great deal of long-range shouting and arm-waving from the skipper in the slip cordon.

I loved playing under David's captaincy, and he remains a regular dinner companion when we are commentating on England's winter tours. He always allowed bowlers to think for themselves and work at their own plans. If he was not happy with the way things were going, he would suggest a change, but he was nothing like as pernickety as modern captains, who seem to make fielding changes after every delivery.

Peter Willey, who led Leicestershire when David was absent and for one complete season when David took a breather, also played a huge part in my development as a cricketer. Peter was as hard as nails, and his legendary bravery at the crease meant he was regularly pushed out to do battle with the terrifying West Indian fast bowlers of the late 1970s and 1980s. He could not tolerate anything other than total commitment, and hated what he called 'namby pambies', of whom I would certainly have been one. He would exact his revenge for my gentle dressing-room teasing by making me nightwatchman whenever possible. This has to be the worst job in cricket. Having bowled for most of the day, the victim is then ordered to go out and bat against opposition fast bowlers who have only a few overs in which to give it everything they have. The theory is that a tail-ender is more dispensable than a front-line batsman, but it is a no-win situation, the cricketing equivalent of being blindfolded, having your hands tied and being given a last drag on a cigarette.

The situation is far worse when one is also a complete coward, a weakness I cannot deny, and which Willey knew only too well. It always disappointed me that I was not braver as a batsman, but the sight of a huge West Indian fast bowler hurtling in to bowl at me turned my knees to jelly, while at the same time not rendering me incapable of retreating with an impressive turn of speed towards the square-leg umpire just as the bowler let the ball go. Jack Birkenshaw, who became an umpire after his playing days, once held up play when I was batting against Michael Holding. The problem was that I was stepping to leg to give Holding a good view of the stumps which, hopefully, he would then aim at and hit. But Holding, armed with a new ball, thought there was some sport to be had, and fired bouncer after bouncer at me as I moved further and further away from the pitch. In the end Birkenshaw had to inform the fielding captain that he was moving from square leg and would take up his position on the other side of the wicket, because he believed he was in danger of either being trampled on by me, or being struck on the head by a Holding thunderbolt. A cricket ball hurts, as is a recurring theme amongst the celebrity guests I interview on Saturday lunchtimes on *Test Match Special*; they all love the game, but many of them were put off playing it because they were hit as youngsters.

I remember Willey gleefully sending me out to bat as nightwatchman against Hampshire when only a few overs remained in the day, and the great West Indian fast bowler Malcolm Marshall was in full cry. It always took me by surprise, after my time came to pick up my bat and leave the sanctuary of the dressing room, to discover that, against my better judgement, I had actually managed to transport myself to the pitch. Rather like getting from the dentist's waiting room to his surgery chair, you know you do not want to do it, but something overrides your anxiety and you make the walk. It is hardly surprising that I was particularly hesitant on this occasion, because Marshall bowling at full tilt gave you less than half a second to see the ball, let alone hit it or, more important still, stop it from hitting you.

I once had the sort of view that money cannot buy when I was at the other end when Marshall was bowling to Gower in a county championship match. From twenty-two yards away it was a wonderful contest, with Marshall's naturally competitive nature making him strain every sinew to get Gower out. Only from that position – leaning on one's bat and determined not to leave the non-striker's crease – can you appreciate the extra time to see the ball that sets batsmen like Gower apart from lesser mortals. Sometimes, having played Marshall defensively off the front foot, Gower would smile up the pitch, nod his head and say, 'Well bowled.' Then a graceful flash of the bat would send the next ball flying through point for four, at which Marshall would acknowledge the stroke. It was high-octane stuff with no quarter given, but carried out in an atmosphere of absolute mutual respect. I was almost sorry when Marshall ruthlessly brushed me aside at his first opportunity, because it had been a very special experience.

To be fair, Marshall and I always got on very well. He apologised whenever he hit me, which I took to be a compliment. On this occasion, a couple of hostile deliveries flew past my nose at high speed, and I could see Willey, the next man to bat, sitting and laughing on the pavilion balcony. Marshall dug another ball in short which fizzed nastily towards my ribs and passed down the leg side to the wicketkeeper. Someone on the field uttered a stifled appeal for caught behind – not much of one, I accept, but enough for a sporting 'walker' like me to do the decent thing and give myself out. After all, there must have been a chance that the ball had flicked my glove on the way past.

There was some surprise amongst the Hampshire fielders when I tucked my bat under my arm and set off for the pavilion. Sam Cook, the umpire, certainly was not expecting it, while Marshall, who had turned and started to walk back to the start of his run-up, could not believe his eyes as I overtook him.

'Where are you going, man?'

'I'm out, Malcolm. A little glove. Well bowled.'

The mood had changed somewhat on our balcony, and I had not made it to the small gate by the sightscreen when a furious Willey appeared, pulling on his helmet.

'I'll have you for this,' he hissed through clenched teeth.

After taking some nasty blows from Marshall, Willey settled the score in the next match, which was played in the peaceful setting of Chesterfield's Queen's Park. It is a beautiful cricket ground, surrounded by trees and with a duck pond at the far end, but it lost all its serenity and calm whenever Michael Holding was bowling for Derbyshire, when it quickly came to resemble a war zone. As it was a local derby there was a decent crowd gathered as I went out to bat, fully padded up from head to toe. The pavilion at Queen's Park is a wonderful building, with a large balcony running virtually the entire length of its first floor, on which the redundant members of the batting team sit in the open air and watch the game.

Again, it was one of those surreal journeys to the middle, and I was halfway there when it was rudely interrupted by a recognisable voice shouting from the balcony:

'Oi! You forgot something!'

I knew it was Willey, and decided to ignore him and stare determinedly at the ground, although the cheer from the crowd suggested that something was going on behind me. Thud! A large white and almost fully unravelled toilet roll landed at my feet: Willey had launched it like a streamer from the players' balcony to create surely the most humiliating entrance by a batsman in the history of cricket.

County cricket was a hard slog around the country, with matches directly following each other, often with a long car journey in between. Andy Roberts, the wonderful West Indian fast bowler, was my regular chauffeur when he played for Leicestershire. As a cricketer he was the silent, moody type, preferring a glare to abusing – known as sledging – the batsman, but in the car we would have animated discussions about bowling. Andy was used to pottering around the quiet, potholed roads of Antigua, and our wide, open roads quickly encouraged him to drive as fast as he bowled, but a good deal less accurately. When he retired, I was promoted to one of the lucky five drivers on the car list. This was one of the benefits of being among the senior players in the team, because it meant you got to take your car on away trips, which was not only more convenient, but meant you received additional expenses for the cost of the journey. I often had Chris Lewis, as talented a cricketer as I have ever seen, as my rather erratic navigator. A wonderful athlete with a physique to die for, he was capable of bowling genuinely fast, and was a sensational fielder. He was also a good enough batsman to score a century for England.

Lewis was shy, gentle, definitely a loner, and a most unusual dresser with a particular fondness for strange hats, including one with a racoon's tail that dangled down the back of his neck. He would devote hours to signing autographs for children, who he would strictly arrange into an orderly queue, yet he could also be exasperatingly disorganised, to the extent of turning up only half an hour before the scheduled start of a one-day international at The Oval in which he was due to play. He claimed to have had a puncture, but was dropped from the team.

I spent hours in the car with Chris, and reckoned to know him pretty well, so I was genuinely shocked when he was convicted of drug smuggling in 2009 and sentenced to thirteen years in prison. I cannot imagine the Chris Lewis I knew coping easily with that prospect, and it is a desperately sad episode to follow a cricket career that failed to fulfil its enormous potential.

With such a variety of characters in the dressing room, and the sheer joy of playing the game for a living, there cannot be many more enjoyable and satisfying careers than that of a professional cricketer. I think I was especially fortunate because – while acknowledging that this could sound like a Fred Trueman moment – I really believe that county cricket was at its strongest in the late 1970s and 1980s. Players of earlier generations will be horrified by that statement, and can make perfectly valid claims for their own eras if they like, but for me the clincher was the presence of so many talented overseas players in those years who returned summer after summer, and who really were proper full-time members of their county teams. There is so much coming and going these days, because of the increased international commitments, that it is impossible to remember who is playing for which county in any given week or competition. Most counties in my time had two world-class overseas professionals, and with England's cricketers also appearing between Tests, the quality of county cricket can surely never have been higher. Richard Hadlee and Clive Rice at Nottinghamshire, Imran Khan and Garth Le Roux at Sussex, Malcolm Marshall and Gordon Greenidge at Hampshire, Viv Richards and Joel Garner at Somerset – the list goes on and on of the partnerships of top cricketers who were deeply committed to their counties, their colleagues and their supporters.

Some of them were very approachable, too. I remember Hadlee, the calculating and robotically accurate New Zealand fast bowler, wandering up to me as I marked out my run-up before a championship match at Grace Road. He asked how the season was going, and I said it was OK, but that I had started to have a problem overstepping the crease, and bowling no-balls. I explained how I kept lengthening my run by an inch or two to compensate, but the problem just would not go away.

'That's exactly what you're doing wrong,' Hadlee replied. 'It sounds illogical, but you must always *shorten* your run-up by a foot. Your stride will be smaller, you won't stretch and you'll stop bowling no-balls. Works for me every time. Good luck.' And with that Hadlee – a member of the opposing team – walked off, having volunteered an absolutely priceless tip.

There were others who were not so kind. Most of the West Indian fast bowlers fell into this category, despite my shameless attempts to befriend them. These efforts included attending a Benefit event one evening for Wayne Daniel, who was a particular bully when charging in for Middlesex. I even made sure he saw me buying a raffle ticket, but he still tried to kill me next day. And then there was a very special category reserved for those overseas players who commanded such respect for their achievements and their sheer presence that one felt like doffing one's cap whenever they walked past.

In fact, there was only one man in this group: Vivian Richards, a batsman like no other in the way he ruthlessly dismembered bowling attacks, hitting the ball miles with apparent effortlessness. Others have come close to matching him in that department, but I have never seen such an intimidating figure as Richards at the crease. Mechanically chewing a piece of gum, he would swagger about, never the least bit hurriedly. He is massively built, more like a heavyweight boxer than a cricketer, with an enormous neck. Never helmeted, he always sweated profusely, and when focused on the serious business of batting, he smiled only very rarely.

My first conversation with Viv was brief, and rather hostile. As a young fast bowler and thus, in Viv's eyes, an upstart to be dismissively swatted away, I made a delivery rear from just short of a length which struck the great man's glove in front of his not inconsiderable nose. Disappointingly, the ball looped over the wicketkeeper's head and landed safely, but it was a moral victory, and I felt fully justified in releasing a loud cry of exasperation after an extended follow-through.

'You know what you are, man?' Viv shouted from only a couple of yards away, stabbing a finger at me, his eyes blazing with rage. 'You're a turkey. A f—ing turkey!'

This was remarkably perceptive, since Dad had been a poultry farmer, but I suspect Viv was not aware of that. Instead it is an example of how Viv loved a fight, and how an incident like that would get him going after, quite possibly, a sluggish start, the legacy of a night out in the bars of Taunton with his great friend Ian Botham. We got off lightly this time – he scored only 75.

Very few batsmen are good enough to take on fast bowlers verbally like that. The most common form of sledging is the other way round, with a fast bowler abusing or mocking a batsman with the aim of unsettling his concentration in the hope that he will make an error and get himself out. Sometimes it can get nasty and personal, in which case the umpire intervenes to calm tempers, but a lot of sledging is nothing more than humorous banter which can be very entertaining.

Viv was involved in my favourite example of sledging, which was both funny and harmless, but shows him at his intimidating best. It occurred in 1981, when a law was introduced limiting bowlers to just one bouncer an over. This was designed to put a brake on the dangerous fast bowling perfected so ruthlessly by the West Indians rather than to emasculate young English quicks. But my Leicestershire colleague Gordon Parsons was very aggressive, and since he routinely bowled at least four bouncers every over, the new regulation had a serious impact on his repertoire.

Tearing in down the hill against Somerset, Parsons struck early on this occasion when Phil Slocombe edged to slip. Typically, Gordon celebrated wildly, but the rest of us, and the bowlers in particular, were not quite so thrilled, because this breakthrough merely brought in the visitors' number 3.

We already knew that Viv was in a foul mood. He had been warming up that morning by hitting balls repeatedly against the fence, when Leicestershire's chief executive, Mike Turner, made a public announcement over the Tannoy.

'Will players please refrain from hitting balls into the advertising boards. And that includes you, Mr Richards.'

This was not a sensible tactic. Viv's upper lip curled, and he stomped back to the dressing room. When he came out to bat, it was the first we had seen of him since then; and what an entrance it was. He was at his arrogant, strutting best, thumping the top of his bat handle menacingly with the palm of his gloved hand with every step he took, and staring the bowler straight in the eye before taking guard.

I was standing at mid-off, and could savour every moment from close range. I knew exactly what Gordon would bowl to Richards first ball. In fact, everyone knew – even dear old Dot, one of our most loyal supporters, who was knitting away as usual in the deckchair by the little gate through which Viv had just marched. Viv looked very deliberately towards the deep-square-leg boundary, where a man was standing hopeful of a catch from the hook shot.

When the great man was ready, and not a moment before, he settled slowly over his bat. Gordon came charging in like a wild thing. Barely a second after he released the ball, the ground reverberated to what sounded like both barrels of a shotgun being simultaneously discharged. In fact it was Viv's bat making contact with the ball, which was now sailing high out of the ground. The next thing we heard was the shattering of the glass roof of a factory some distance along the adjoining street. It was a magnificent shot, and Dickie Bird relished the theatre of it all as he paused before turning and signalling the obvious to the scorebox. Then Dickie addressed Gordon, sufficiently loudly for Viv to hear.

'That's it, Gordy lad. That's your one bouncer for t'over.' At which point Viv rushed up the pitch, left arm raised, shouting, 'No, no, Dickie man. Tell him he can bowl as many as he wants!'

I note that Richards was eventually bowled by Agnew for 196. It was the last ball before lunch, and it struck him on his pad, then his thigh, and then his ankle before somehow trickling into his stumps just hard enough to knock one bail to the ground. They all count, I suppose, but Viv could barely drag himself away from the crease.

For a professional cricketer the summers were wonderful; the winters less so, unless one was on tour with England. The problem was that the players were employed only for six months, from April until September. Then your P45 would arrive in the post with the scheduled reporting date for the following year, and sometimes a note wishing everyone a happy Christmas. And that was that.

An average cricketing salary paid pretty well over a six-month period – about £12,000 – but not well enough to stretch over the whole year, so it was crucial to find work in the winters. But who would employ a cricketer who possessed no other skills or experience, and who would be leaving at the end of March anyway? It was an issue that must have dissuaded many talented players, particularly those with university degrees or other qualifications, from taking up the game professionally. I remember interviewing the former England captain, Tony Greig, about this subject, and he strongly advocated the return of the amateur cricketer. By insisting that all of its first-class cricketers are professional, England cannot be selecting from all of the best players in the country.

I drove a lorry for a couple of winters, delivering asbestos amongst other things around the country. The vehicle was so decrepit that I needed to stand up, pressing the accelerator pedal flat to the floor, to get up to speed. Rather like Johnners rebuilding his tank engine, it often seemed that there was more in the back of the lorry when I returned to the depot at the end of a day than when I had set off that morning. One of Leicestershire's benefactors kindly gave me a job in his window factory, and at least I managed to progress from the shop floor, where I was disastrous with a mallet, to the office. But none of this was really for me, and when I found myself with a young family, it started to become a worry.

Then, right on cue, came one of those life-changing moments. John Rawling, an old friend who was the sports producer at BBC Radio Leicester at the time, suggested that I give local radio a go for one winter, and see how it went. He warned me that I would be paid virtually nothing, which turned out to be true, and started me off producing short reports and colour pieces for the breakfast programme. One reason for local radio being such a brilliant starting point for wannabe broadcasters is that in no time you find yourself having to try your hand at everything. When youngsters ask me how to get into sports broadcasting, I always advise them to go and knock on the door of their local radio station. If no one hears you the first time, go and do it again.

Sure enough, it was not long before someone moved on to another post within the network, and I found myself preparing and presenting the early-morning sports desks with barely any experience whatsoever. But I loved the buzz of live broadcasting, and in the journalists at Radio Leicester I found like-minded people who worked hard and played hard in equal measure. The combination of working at Radio Leicester during the winter and playing for the county during the summer was absolutely ideal for me. It lasted for three happy years until I retired from professional cricket.

Part of the reason for the kick one gets out of live broadcasting is the knowledge that a cock-up is only just around the corner. With luck and skill, these minefields can be negotiated, but sometimes there is nothing one can do. One particularly disastrous opening to the Saturday-afternoon sports show, which I had only very recently been promoted to present, was described by the usually calm, polite and experienced Programme Organiser as 'The worst piece of radio I have ever heard.' That was a bit harsh, I thought: all I had done was failed to get on air for thirty seconds, and followed this with a sudden burst of music played at the wrong speed. Perhaps the fact that the song was Gerry Rafferty's 'Get it Right Next Time' did not help.

My worst howler would have a happy ending, at least. One of the duties of the early-morning sports presenter was to record the news circuit from London. This was a series of tapes and interview clips which was sent automatically every hour to all the local BBC radio stations, and which the newsreaders would use for their bulletins. My job was to record each one onto its own individual blue plastic cartridge, which was basically a continuous loop of tape, label it and hand the whole lot to the newsreader, who on this occasion was a tall and pretty blonde girl in her late teens called Emma Norris.

There were two potential pitfalls: the first was that you had to remember to erase each cartridge meticulously before recording the desired clip. This was vital, because otherwise the new recording would not work, and you would be left with the original, whatever it might have been. The second was that there were literally hundreds of identical blue cartridges lying about in the cluttered and untidy studio.

As it happened, England's cricketers were in Australia on Mike Gatting's Ashes-winning tour of 1986–87, and I had to record Peter West's live report on one of the Test matches from the Radio 4 *Today* programme, which I would then replay during my own bulletin. Unfortunately there was a breakdown in communications between the studio in London and Peter in Australia, so when I pressed the button with perfect timing, all I succeeded in recording was a harassed Radio 4 presenter calling out in increasing desperation, 'Hello, Peter. Peter, can you hear me? Peter?'

Disappointed, I went to broadcast my sports report, and returned to record the next news circuit from London for Emma, after which I duly handed her the cartridges.

Settling down to read the newspaper, I was surprised to hear a familiar voice drifting across the newsroom from one of the loudspeakers which relayed the station's output.

'Hello, Peter. Peter, can you hear me? Peter?' This was followed by Emma's standard BBC apology: 'I'm sorry. We don't seem to be able to bring you that report.'

Miss Norris was not her usual cheery self when she returned from the studio. Flinging the cartridge at me, she told me to make sure they had all been properly erased in future.

Shortly before the nine o'clock news, the Tannoy sparked into life with an urgent announcement from London. Another tape was on its way: 'Stand by to record in ten, nine, eight . . .'

Rushing into the studio, I grabbed a blue cartridge, shoved it into the slot and apparently recorded the item perfectly. It was an important soundbite, too: the Reverend Ian Paisley reacting angrily to a surprise visit to Northern Ireland by the Prime Minister.

With Emma already on her way to read the news, I triumphantly handed her what would now be her lead story. Moments later, the news jingle sounded. 'Radio Leicester news at nine o'clock, I'm Emma Norris. We have just heard that the Prime Minister, Margaret Thatcher, has made a surprise visit to Northern Ireland. This is the reaction of the Reverend Ian Paisley: "Hello, Peter. Peter, can you hear me? Peter?"'

That was the last time I was let loose on the early-morning circuit, but at least, in time, Emma managed to forgive me. We were married in 1995.

* * *

The realisation for the first time that there was life outside cricket was a great eye-opener. It had a profound impact on my game, too. Professional cricket is an uncertain career which can be ended at any time by injury or loss of form, and unless a county player is fortunate enough to enjoy a successful Benefit (a year of tax-free money-raising on his behalf), he will not earn nearly enough to set him up for the big wide world when his playing days are over. To know that all will be well at the end is enormously reassuring.

I took a hundred wickets for Leicestershire in the 1987 season, and the following year I came frustratingly close to the recall to the England team that I had set my heart on. David Gower was again the captain, but it was a disastrous Ashes campaign which, with just the final Test at The Oval to play, stood at 4–0 to Australia. Leicestershire was playing Surrey at Grace Road over the weekend before the Test, and England's squad had been announced, but time and again the telephone rang in our dressing room with bad news from a succession of fast bowlers reporting to David that they were injured, and could not play against Australia.

By the end of the day David looked a broken man, slumped in his seat and with no idea who to choose for England.

'What about Agnew?' suggested Peter Willey from his chair in the corner. 'He's bowling pretty well at the moment.'

David's face lit up. 'Of course!' he said. 'Jonathan, you're in. Go home, get your England stuff ready, and I'll call first thing tomorrow to confirm everything.'

Even though I was approximately the seventeenth choice, this was still fantastic news. I called Dad when I arrived home, told him to keep the Saturday of the Test match clear, and dug out my England cap and sweaters which had remained folded in a drawer ever since they were last used, briefly, in 1985. After three disappointing Test appearances, this was my second chance, and the opportunity to set the record straight that I had worked so hard for.

To be up early next morning to await the England captain's call was clearly a schoolboy error. David Gower's idea of 'first thing' is what most people would consider third thing, possibly even fourth. It seemed hours before the telephone finally rang.

'Got some bad news, I'm afraid,' David began. 'I couldn't persuade Ted Dexter or Mickey Stewart, so you're not in any more. They've gone for Alan Igglesden. Know anything about him?'

With that, David must have known his influence as England captain was over – and indeed Graham Gooch succeeded him after that Test. I felt utterly devastated, and knew I would never play for England again, which had been my main motivating force. So when the *Today* newspaper offered me the post of cricket correspondent the following summer, it was an easy decision to make. I might have been only thirty, which was no age to retire from professional cricket, and I could easily have played for another five years. But it was definitely time to move on.

THREE

Up to Speed

Brian Johnston was always endearingly candid about the good fortune he had enjoyed at key moments in his life. His Old Etonian connections, like 'Lobby' de Lotbiniere at the BBC, served him well, and while talent, charm and charisma helped to establish him as a national institution, there have been any number of similarly talented, charming and charismatic broadcasters for whom doors simply have not opened. But let us not fool ourselves. Everyone needs a slice of luck to get started, but it still requires energy, hard work, skill and commitment to make a success of things from there. Johnners always made what he did look incredibly easy, and broadcasting did come naturally to him, but it would be entirely wrong to assume that because it all looked like second nature, his brain was not working nineteen to the dozen.

As a cricketer, I do not think I necessarily had the rub of the green. I might well have played more times for England than I did; but then, I should have made a better fist of the opportunities I did have. Anyway, I am long since over that disappointment. However, from the moment I retired at the end of the 1990 season I unexpectedly benefited from being in the right place at the right time, and from a series of lucky breaks which propelled me at alarming speed onto *Test Match Special.*

The *Today* newspaper, now defunct, was a tabloid chiefly famous for its attempt to break the monopoly of Fleet Street and for its pioneering efforts to publish colour photographs, which it managed with mixed success. I wrote a county cricketer's diary during my last three seasons for Leicestershire, which one year was titled 'Round the Wicket with Jonathan Agnew'. As you may imagine, this resulted in tremendous ribaldry in the dressing room, and the column was renamed the following summer.

Over the years many former players have turned to writing about the game, but for a national tabloid newspaper to appoint a practising cricketer with minimal training and no experience as correspondent was an entirely new development. It was not universally popular among other journalists, who – rightly, as it has turned out – feared that my appointment would be the start of a trend which would make it very difficult for writers who had not played county cricket, at least, to keep their jobs. Today, the chief cricket correspondents of *The Times*, the *Daily Telegraph* and the *Guardian* are former internationals, and more past players write their own copy in newspapers than they used to.

It would be a great shame if the properly trained, cricket-loving journalist found that there was no longer room for him in the press box. Of course former cricketers provide an insight to the game that can only be gained through the experience of having been out in the middle. But ex-players are a rather cynical lot, and having treated the game as a job from a young age, our relationship with cricket is different to that of the fan. We can sometimes be a little jaded, and this is where the cricket-lover can shine, particularly in the coverage of one-day cricket, which has become tediously formulaic. The middle overs of a one-day international have now lost their momentum because of the introduction of 'power plays' early in the innings, in which the field restrictions encourage exciting batting. Maybe I have been unfortunate, but I seem to have watched a lot of games recently in which the team batting second loses too many early wickets, producing a dead match that drifts for up to forty overs before finally reaching its predictable conclusion. The last people to ask about the future of one-day cricket are the former players in television and radio commentary boxes. Few of us are enthused by that form of cricket any more, because we have seen too many dull, meaningless games. But it is an element of our job – all too often in recent years – to make one-sided one-day matches sound exciting. Part of a commentator's brief is to 'lift' the programme when the cricket is boring.

This is never easy, and nobody is better at it than Henry Blofeld. His love and enthusiasm for the game shine through every delivery he describes, with his right foot hammering away under the desk. Where would *Test Match Special* be without Brian Johnston, John Arlott, Tony Cozier and Christopher Martin-Jenkins, none of whom played first-class cricket? The colourful and knowledgeable accounts that we read in the newspapers over breakfast would have been immeasurably poorer without E.W. Swanton, Neville Cardus and John Woodcock, to name just three.

Clearly it is a sensitive subject, but it was not one I had really considered when I made my decision to leave Leicestershire and join *Today*. I did not feel any hostility directed at me when I set off for England's 1990–91 tour of Australia with my new colleagues from the national press, but it is fair to assume that not all of them would have been rooting for me. It was while I was flying from London to Perth that another of those fortuitous events occurred. Christopher Martin-Jenkins, who apart from a five-year break in the early 1980s had been the BBC cricket correspondent since Johnners retired in 1972, announced back in London that this tour would be his last for the BBC. He had decided to follow the path of his great mentor, E. W. Swanton, and join the *Daily Telegraph* the following summer. This made little or no impact on me at the time, because I did not know Chris very well, and besides, I was entirely focused on my new career at *Today*. After all, the newspaper had taken quite a gamble in taking me on, and, comfortably settled in my business-class seat, I felt very grateful for the opportunity of a new and exciting career in cricket journalism.

Working for a national tabloid was a challenge, and there was fierce competition amongst the pack of journalists I met on this first tour. Although the broadsheets have changed their approach in the last ten years, and their writers are now expected to report more of what happens off the field than they used to, there is still not the same pressure in that world as there is among the tabloid correspondents. Lurid headlines, which are written in the offices in London rather than by the journalist on the tour, are often very damaging indeed, and can seriously affect relations between the players and the media. It soon became clear to me that a tabloid journalist needs a thick skin to survive. The press conferences on that tour were not as controlled as they are today, and it was interesting to see how the same quote from a player or coach would be interpreted differently by the various correspondents. They were brilliant at gently nudging their interviewee in a certain direction by pre-planned questioning, and this often resulted in a response that had not been thought through properly, and gave us a story to write about. These days the England team's media relations officer thoroughly briefs his players before they appear in front of the press, and sits at their side throughout the press conference.

Today was very patient with me, and I suspect quite a lot of my early reports were largely rewritten in London. The evenings on tour were interesting, if often rather nerve-racking, because that was when you put your notebook away and did your best to have an enjoyable dinner with your fellow hacks, despite being in fierce competition with one another. Inevitably the talk would get round to what we had written that day, as if we were all gingerly testing each other out. As an apprentice newshound, it was always a relief to have it confirmed that I had accurately assessed what the story of the day was.

Peter Baxter, the BBC cricket producer, was covering the early part of the tour until CMJ was due to arrive at Christmas. Vastly experienced, Peter had been the producer of *Test Match Special* since 1973, and he loved touring. It would not be his duty actually to appoint CMJ's successor, but obviously he would have a major say in the matter. It is not essential that the producer and the correspondent are the best of friends, but they do need a close working relationship. With time ticking away before Peter returned home, clearly the issue of replacing Christopher was becoming a pressing matter for him.

I had first met Peter when I toured India with England in 1984–85. Three years later he had introduced a lunchtime feature called

'County Talk' to *Test Match Special* in which Vic Marks, Graeme Fowler and I would chat away to him about issues on the county circuit. It was good, light-hearted stuff, which was always entertaining, and it was the springboard for both Victor and Graeme to join *Test Match Special* as summarisers. It was also the reason Peter sounded me out while we walked through the pretty gardens between the WACA and our Perth hotel. Would I consider applying for cricket correspondent of the BBC? Ridiculous as it may seem now, I told Peter I was not interested because of the loyalty I felt to *Today*. I also knew that Peter was keen on the job himself, even if he knew deep down that he was unlikely to get it. The other candidates Peter was aware of included David Gower, Charles Colvile, Pat Murphy and Ralph Dellor. But he told me that I was his favourite, and made me promise to let him know if I had a change of heart.

As it turned out, this did not take long. I talked to some of the other journalists about the BBC job, and their view was that I should definitely apply for it. Then, with impeccable timing, *Today* pulled off the old tabloid trick of lifting a load of rubbish about a supposed tantrum in the nets by Phil Tufnell from the first edition of another newspaper and put it on their back page below an angry headline with my name on it. I felt outraged, because the initial report was thoroughly mischievous, so I contacted Peter immediately and told him to count me in.

The interview was conducted at Broadcasting House in London, the true home of BBC Radio. When I walked into the impressive foyer, which reeked of history, the welcome I received took me by surprise.

'Good morning, Mr Agnew. Are you here for your interview?' The receptionist was a tiny girl with a wonderful smile. 'Good luck, Mr Agnew,' she said as I was taken away to the awaiting lift.

I did not know it then, but that was my first meeting with Shilpa Patel, who has now worked on *Test Match Special* for fifteen years and has become one of my closest friends. Shilpa is the best fixer of interviews in the business, somehow persuading even the most reluctant celebrities to come on air and chat. She worked on Brian May, the lead guitarist of Queen, for days during a Test match at The Oval before he capitulated, whereupon he enjoyed himself so much that the following year he approached Shilpa and asked if he could come on again. The actor Hugh Grant is another who Shilpa bullied tirelessly throughout a Test match when he thought he had found sanctuary in a private box. He finally relented, and was a thoroughly entertaining guest during the last tea break at The Oval when England won the Ashes in 2005.

Another good example of Shilpa's tenacity is the manner in which she tracked down Daniel 'Harry Potter' Radcliffe at Lord's in 2007. It was the eve of Daniel's eighteenth birthday, and she knew he was at the ground, but did not know where. Shilpa spent hours scouring the crowd of 29,000 people through binoculars until she found him, hidden under a baseball cap in the top tier of the Compton Stand. Locating him was only the start; now she had to persuade him to be interviewed by me, so she disappeared into the stand to talk to him. So it was that Daniel Radcliffe became another in what is now a long line of innocent victims who have fallen for Shilpa's charms, and we had a lovely chat during lunch on his birthday in the Lord's Grandstand.

Shilpa also managed to persuade someone – I still do not know who it was – to give her the very menu that had been sent by the MCC to the Queen to choose from before her lunchtime visit to Lord's in 2009. A regal tick in black ink had been made alongside Her Majesty's selection from every course, even down to the wine. As you can imagine, Phil Tufnell and I had some fun with that on *Test Match Special*.

But what I think of as Shilpa's *tour de force* – thus far, at least – also took place during the Ashes Test at Lord's in 2009 when she got wind that the actor Russell Crowe was present as a guest of his cousin Jeff Crowe, the former New Zealand captain who was the match referee. She tracked him down to the MCC chief executive's box in the Grandstand – a favourite and highly successful celebrity hunting ground for her – and set off in hot pursuit. The plan was that I would go to him in the box for a quick interview using our wireless broadcasting equipment, so he would not have to run the public gauntlet by walking round the ground to the Media Centre. I gather that the response to her initial request did not come from him directly, and was merely two words. She returned to the commentary box crestfallen.

'What shall I do?' she said.

'Shilpa,' I replied, 'you know exactly what you are going to do. Get back over there!'

Twenty minutes later, Shilpa threw open the commentary-box door in triumph, and in walked Russell Crowe.

'We have been joined,' I informed our listeners, 'by the cousin of the match referee.'

For a man used to rousing and flattering introductions, Crowe seemed a little surprised by my deliberately subdued effort, but he then gave a deep, rumbling laugh and he was away. It is never easy conducting an interview while commentating at the same time, but Crowe was very perceptive in his observation that the Australians did not look like a unit that was likely to win the Ashes. Word of that reached their captain, Ricky Ponting, who vented his displeasure at Crowe's remarks the following day. Even by Shilpa's standards, getting Russell Crowe on *Test Match Special* was a coup, and we are very lucky to have her.

Shilpa is a great cricket enthusiast and a tremendous gossip, which is why she knew that I was to be interviewed for the vacant post of BBC cricket correspondent on that March morning in London. And she has definitely never called me Mr Agnew since.

The interview with Mike Lewis, the Head of Sport and Outside Broadcasts, was brief and informal. I strongly suspect that when he talked about my experience at BBC Radio Leicester he did so on the assumption that I had actually done some outside broadcasting, rather than merely studio presentation. I did not dissuade him of this, although I had never used a stopwatch in my life. After an anxious wait of about three weeks, Mike rang me to offer me the job.

I am sure he would not have done so without the newsgathering experience that my brief time at *Today* gave me, and had it not been for the fact that the England captain, Graham Gooch, gave me a big story at the end of that disastrous Ashes campaign when he told me that leading his team in Australia had often been like 'farting against thunder'. It produced wonderful headlines and copy for days, although I could not bring myself to write his actual quote in the paper. But others were braver than me, and it was great timing. I definitely owe Graham one for that, which was an example of how trusted former players can get a big story.

Six months after bowling my last ball for Leicestershire, I became the fourth BBC cricket correspondent since Brian Johnston was first appointed in 1963. The existence of the permanent position at the corporation had only come about because of yet another of Johnners' Old Etonian connections, this time in the form of Charles Max-Muller, who succeeded Seymour de Lotbiniere. Max-Muller had been campaigning for the creation of the role of cricket correspondent since the end of the 1958–59 MCC tour of Australia, which Johnners had covered for the BBC, but on an *ad hoc* arrangement under which he had to pay his own travel expenses. Because of a rapidly increasing workload, it was becoming clear that the BBC needed a regular presence on England tours. It took Max-Muller four years and another Ashes tour, which Brian covered in 1962–63, to win his argument, but he got there in the end. As Johnners was the man *in situ*, Max-Muller gave him the job.

Given the great tradition and responsibility that goes with the position, I am surprised that I was not more overawed to have been offered it than I probably should have been. I was introduced to my new colleagues in the sports room in Broadcasting House. This included an invitation to take part in the sports room cricket match that seemed to continue all day between the desks and machinery, regardless of the people sitting and trying to carefully edit tape or write reports. There was a dedicated studio attached to the sports room called '3H', and Julian Tutt interviewed me about my appointment. He asked how it felt to be following in the footsteps of Brian Johnston, Don Mosey and Christopher Martin-Jenkins, and having given the matter no real thought at all, I stuttered out some sort of inadequate and lightweight response. Tutt looked taken aback: it later emerged that he had been one of the disappointed candidates.

The focus of the first few weeks in the job was to learn the basics so I would be prepared and ready to go for the start of that summer's Test series against West Indies. This included disciplines like using a stopwatch to talk accurately to a specific length of time, and learning how to condense a match report to only 120 words – just what Mike Lewis had assumed I had been doing at Radio Leicester. Peter Baxter was my mentor, and it was soon clear to both of us that we would make a good team. In fact we would work closely together for the next seventeen years, and would each be best man at the other's wedding.

Peter took the decision that at first I would work on *Test Match Special* as an expert summariser rather than as a lead ball-by-ball commentator. This made a lot of sense. The previous cricket correspondents had been established broadcasters before they took the role, but I had never commentated on a match in my life. Peter already had it in his mind that I would be introduced to commentary during the Test against Sri Lanka at the end of the summer, but nobody knew if I would be any good at it or not. I suppose that had I not been up to scratch I would have returned to the summariser's role.

This method was also a gentle means of introducing me to the *TMS* listeners, who traditionally do not welcome change readily. The summariser's seat is a good place to learn the ropes, but it is especially important to pick up the leisurely pace of *Test Match Special.* It is always a temptation for newcomers to talk too much. In the case of commentators, that means gabbling far too fast, while inexperienced summarisers talk too much and so interrupt the gentle flow. Before you know it you are competing with each other. This is particularly a problem for those who have been used to working on Radio 5 Live during Test matches, as the style of that network encourages much more input from the expert than the reporter.

The only real frustration I experienced during my preparations was often being referred to on the radio as 'our cricket correspondent, Christopher Martin-Jenkins' by sports presenters who found the habit hard to break. It was always difficult to know quite what to say at the start of a report when one had been introduced as a completely different person, and I am sure that whoever takes the baton from me one day will suffer in exactly the same way.

The day before the first Test and my debut on *Test Match Special*, I set off for Leeds for what has since become the familiar routine of interviewing both captains and setting up the Test with preview material, voice pieces and so on for the breakfast programmes on the first morning of the game. It was incredibly exciting being at Headingley as Peter and the engineers prepared the commentary box for the following day, even if the condition of the box was something of an eye-opener.

The box at Headingley was perched high in the Rugby Stand, which divides the cricket ground from the rugby league stadium behind it. The only means of getting to it was to clamber between the wooden seats facing the rugby pitch. On reaching the summit, one was confronted to the right by a fragile and clearly unloved wooden door. It was completely accessible to the public, and I often wondered if the green 'BBC Test Match Special' sign that Peter carefully stuck to it with gaffer tape was in fact more of an invitation to enter than a deterrent.

Decrepit, dirty and with a threadbare carpet, this was not what I had expected of a radio commentary box. There were wires and headphones strewn all over the desk that ran along the front of the hopelessly cramped room, and a potentially lethal step down which you had to drop in order to take your position at the microphone. It was so cramped that the engineers shared their tiny space next to ours with a television cameraman who had to take the glass out of the window he was pointing his lens through. There was no heater to be seen – and probably no room for one anyway – so on a cold day it was freezing up there. Believe it or not, that box remained in precisely the same derelict condition until it was finally torn down after the 2009 season – eighteen years later. While we all hanker after the old Lord's commentary box in some respects, clambering in and out of that place at Headingley is certainly something none of us misses in the least.

I imagined that there might have been a *Test Match Special* get-together that first evening, not least to welcome the new boy to the ranks and to give me the chance to meet my new colleagues. But in those days the team did not stay in the same hotel – or even sometimes in the same town. Peter and I were stationed in Bramhope, while Brian Johnston, for example, always chose to stay at Arthington Hall near Otley, which was the ancestral home of one of his Old Etonian chums, Charles Sheepshanks. They were all creatures of habit, the *TMS* crew – none more so than Johnners – and tended to do the same thing at the same place year after year. But, as I was about to discover, there was an edge to the atmosphere during this particular Test which did little to foster harmonious relations in the commentary box.

Don Mosey was a regular commentator on *Test Match Special* after a career in newspapers, and had been BBC cricket correspondent for a year when Christopher Martin-Jenkins took a break in the 1980s. He was an opinionated Yorkshireman who had an almost obsessive aversion to what he perceived as a BBC bias that favoured public schoolboys over those, like him, who had attended grammar school. It was interesting, however, that despite Brian Johnston clearly having benefited more than most from his Eton connections, Mosey had nothing but admiration and affection for him. His autobiography, *The Alderman's Tale*, was not due for publication until the Edgbaston Test in nearly two months' time, but already it was widely known that he had written some stinging criticisms of a number of his *TMS* colleagues. No one yet knew the precise details, although Peter suspected – rightly, as it turned out – that he and Christopher were the most likely targets of Mosey's wrath. An atmosphere of tension and uncertainty hung over the commentary box throughout the match.

Finally the morning of my first Test as BBC cricket correspondent arrived. Peter helped me through some live early reports from the ground, which were then done on a rotation basis, with all the commentators taking turns at the early alarm call. After breakfast with the ladies of the splendid Ugly Mugs café across the road, which has since become part of my routine, it was time to return to Headingley. My next appointment was my first appearance on *Test Match Special.*

The first regular I bumped into inside the ground was a man who, temporarily at least, was no longer a member of the team. Henry Blofeld was at the height of his powers, and much in demand as a broadcaster. He spent much of the year commentating overseas, on Indian television in particular. Now he had been lured to Sky television for a fee far in excess of anything he might have expected from the BBC. Even so, the move to a direct competitor was something of a gamble, since it meant he could no longer work on *Test Match Special.* I remember Johnners having to clarify himself more than once when answering enquiries from listeners concerned about Henry's absence from the radio airwaves that summer. 'Blowers has gone to Sky,' he said mischievously, prompting many people to believe that Henry had gone to the great commentary box above.

There was no awkwardness when Henry and I chanced upon each other on the outfield, just below the commentary box. We did not know each other very well, and it also being his first day in a new job, he was a little twitchy and even more animated than usual. But he did stride up to me to wish me good luck, and offered me a priceless piece of advice: 'Whatever you do, be yourself,' he cautioned. 'Don't try and copy anybody.' With that, and probably a cheery 'my dear old thing', he was away.

It was about a quarter past nine when I climbed the stairs of the Rugby Stand, took a deep breath outside the battered old door and stepped cautiously inside. There was only one other person in the commentary box: an elderly man wearing a bright, canary-yellow jersey. He had his back to me, and was meticulously studying the contents of a number of cardboard boxes which had been carefully stacked in the far corner. He must have heard the door squeak as

I entered, because he immediately turned to face me, cradling a box containing what I could now see to be a chocolate cake under his left arm.

'Ah!' he chortled, beaming broadly and extending his right hand. 'You must be Aggers. Welcome to *Test Match Special*.' At last I had met Brian Johnston.

I had never been called 'Aggers' before. In the Leicestershire dressing room I had generally been known as 'Aggy', while 'Spiro', after the disgraced former US Vice President, remains a favourite of Ian Chappell and Ian Botham. Sadly, having been sworn enemies for years, it is safe to assume that that is one of the few things they share. But on 6 June 1991 I became the latest in a long line of Brian's friends and colleagues to have the Oxford '-ers' tacked onto his or her surname, and it has stuck ever since. Only a cherished few such as 'Godders' (Godfrey Evans) and 'Paulers' (Brian's wife, Pauline) enjoyed what was presumably the affectionate touch of having the suffix attached to their Christian names.

There was not much time for small talk as others started to arrive and fill the commentary box to bursting point. Bill Frindall, the scorer, came panting up the steps lugging bags of books, folders and general paraphernalia. Next was Trevor Bailey, one of the long-standing expert summarisers, who seemed terse but amicable. Fred Trueman stomped heavily inside, smoke billowing from his pipe, and chuntering grumpily about the stewards on the rugby ground car park. This was, I soon found out, a regular gripe of his. Finally Don Mosey, a heavy smoker, appeared at the door out of breath. I was a little wary as I shook his hand for the first time, but this was the first Test of a new summer, after all, so for the majority it was a reunion, and nothing damaging having yet appeared in print, the others welcomed him warmly enough. Although there was some tension in the air, for now at least the anticipation of an exciting summer of cricket and hours of broadcasting on *Test Match Special* was all that mattered.

Johnners was of course the main man, the presenter of the programme and the first name on the commentary rota. Pinned to the wall was the schedule, which was broken down into twenty-minute segments with the initials of the commentator for that period written alongside. Brian was 'BJ', and in fact was referred to as BJ in conversation as often as he was Johnners, especially by Peter and Don ('DM'). Because there had already been a 'JA' (John Arlott), it would have been dreadfully disrespectful to the great man if I had inherited his *TMS* rota reference, so to make absolutely clear the distinction between us, my full set of initials – 'JPA' – was always used wherever in the world Peter stuck up his rota. Nowadays Peter's successor, Adam Mountford, prefers the more informal practice of using our Christian names.

The rota is always studied carefully at the start of the day, because it is considered very bad form to miss the beginning of a slot. It also gives you more time to prepare if you have been allotted a particularly high number of appearances that day with Geoffrey Boycott; deep breaths and extra stamina required.

Of course I was nervous; terribly nervous. Just as bowling my first balls for Leicestershire and then for England had been surreal experiences in which I vividly remember my head swimming, and not feeling in control of what I was doing, the first day on *Test Match Special* passed in a blur. I do recall how much fun it was, and how remarkably relaxed the other broadcasters were, despite the fact that they were commentating to millions of people all over the world. Nobody sat me down and gave me any coaching or advice as such, which might seem surprising, but *Test Match Special* is very much a programme of individual styles. That day I had a stint with all of the commentators, and quickly realised that each has his own way of doing essentially the same job, making each of them very different to interact with as a summariser.

My previous experience of summarising had been at a handful of domestic quarter or semi finals after Leicestershire had been knocked out of one-day competitions, and those had been with reporters rather than commentators. Given that this was their big opportunity to impress, and might possibly even lead to a career in the big time at *Test Match Special*, they were understandably nervous.

They also leaned on their summarisers far too heavily, which encouraged the bad habit of speaking too much even if there was very little worthwhile to say. Commentators need to be descriptive, while experts must be drilled to talk only when they have something of value to add.

It was the top division on duty with Johnners at Leeds: Don, Christopher and Tony Cozier, the fabulous West Indian commentator. All of them were straightforward to work alongside, in that they stuck pretty much to the cricket. That meant, from a summariser's point of view, leaving the commentator to describe the run of play before offering considered thoughts and observations between overs. But Johnners was a real challenge, and I am not alone in having found my early encounters with him during my first match intimidating. Vic Marks, as outstanding and easy-going a summariser as there is, talks about the nervousness and apprehension he felt when sitting alongside Brian. Poor old Victor, a gentle soul, even felt overwhelmed by the entirely generous welcome and *bonhomie* that was extended to him on his first appearance on *Test Match Special.*

It was not just because of the pressure and the feeling of inadequacy we inevitably felt when broadcasting with a truly great performer, although that had a lot to do with it. After all, Johnners was someone Vic and I had both grown up with, and had achieved hero status years ago. But given that he was the man people wanted to listen to, how much should I speak? What would happen if I accidentally interrupted him, or worse still, spoke over him, which inexperienced summarisers often do? If he made a mistake, should I correct him? Most of all, until I found the confidence to play him at his own game, the biggest challenge of working with Brian was that the conversation could go darting off in virtually any direction, and onto any random topic, at any moment. He was utterly unpredictable. How do you respond to: 'Have you ever been shunted by a Pakistani, Aggers?' delivered between balls with a deliberate twinkle of the eye that no one else could see? (It turned out that one of his many correspondents had been involved in a car crash with an Asian gentleman.) Johnners' unpredictable digressions were all about timing, and were often made in the knowledge that there was no time for a reply even if you were quick enough to think of one. It was a wonderful lesson in how to broaden the commentary and involve the other members of the team; to tease them and poke a bit of fun at their expense, but also to be self-deprecating. Johnners often managed this by playing the forgetful old fuddy-duddy. By encouraging others in the team to enter into rapport with him, he enabled their real characters to come out and reveal themselves to the listeners. Not only did this bring a personal touch to the programme, it was also an element in giving Johnners the scope to create the nicknames for which *Test Match Special* became so well known.

The listeners believed that they knew each and every member of the team anyway, and the addition of a descriptive nickname added to that feeling of intimacy. 'The Bearded Wonder' could have been merely a straightforward description of Bill, the wonder scorer who could find the answer to even the most challenging and obscure cricket question. But it was cleverer than that, because it meant that a listener could conjure up a much more accurate image of what Bill, who sat to our left, actually looked like. He had a beard. It seems obvious, but unless you tell people, how are they to know? This was just one of the ways in which Johnners breathed life into the programme. He always referred to Fred Trueman as 'Sir Fredrick', and did so in a rather deferential manner, although this was also a gentle dig at Fred, who believed until his dying day that he should have been knighted, at the very least. And 'the Alderman' was a perfectly fitting description of a man who could both sound and behave pompously, although Johnners had first created it when he and Don Mosey had worked together on a quiz show, and part of Don's duties was to organise the post-programme entertainment in the Mayor of Lancaster's parlour. The nickname may have been created harmlessly and with an air of innocence, but it was in fact a brilliantly acerbic nudge at Mosey's self-importance.

This extra dimension that Brian brought to *Test Match Special* was an important part of what made it so much more than just another sports programme. Sitting beside him and being part of his soap opera, or when off-duty, watching him at work, I began to appreciate how he made the commentary flow. When to have a leg-pull; when to stick to the cricket; above all, how to bring in the personal touch which made every one of Brian's listeners feel he was talking only to them. This is something only a very few broadcasters have the knack of being able to do, and the response from listeners, in the form of cakes, and chocolate cakes in particular, demonstrated their genuine affection for Johnners – as well as guaranteeing the sender a grateful mention on the radio, of course. It was a lady called Aileen Cohen who baked the first *TMS* cake, after Brian had rather mischievously handed back to the studio announcer for the tea break at Lord's, bemoaning the fact that the cricketers were about to enjoy a nice cup of tea and a slice of cake, while in the commentary box there was none. This was entirely light-hearted, of course, but on hearing it, Aileen fired up her oven, baked a cake and appeared at the Grace Gates next day to present it to Brian. Some time after Brian's death, Aileen wrote to me and asked me to meet her between commentary stints at the same spot. There she stood, an elderly lady by then, clutching a tin with a freshly baked chocolate cake inside. What a tradition she began all those years ago!

Given that the arrival of a younger man might have been interpreted by my fellow summarisers Fred Trueman and Trevor Bailey as a threat, the attitude of both towards me could not have been kinder. Trevor had been christened 'the Boil' by Brian – not, this time, to highlight any aspect of his character or any unsightly physical disfigurement, but because while playing football for Cambridge University somewhere in Europe, he and Doug Insole, who also played cricket for England and became a leading administrator of the game, were introduced to the crowd over the public-address system as 'Boiley' and 'Eynsole'.

If there is a contrast between the styles and techniques of the commentators, then Bailey and Trueman could not have been more different as summarisers. Watching the relaxed way they went about their business after years of experience gave me tremendous confidence.

There really was not a shred of any nerves in that commentary box. The key to their success was that they did not speak unless they really had something of interest to offer; a discipline that has slipped over the years. Trevor never used two words when one would do – sometimes, I felt, to the point of being mischievous. He was not the man to have with you when, at the end of the day's play, Peter would hand you a stopwatch and a note that read: 'Out at 20 mins on the clock. Good luck.' This meant that you had twenty minutes until the next junction on the network, and would require a certain amount of assistance from the summariser to get you through to the point at which you could finally say goodbye for the day. A reasonable first question under those circumstances might be: 'Well, Trevor, what do you think of the day's play?' in the hope of an answer lasting at least two minutes. Instead, Trevor's response, delivered in his distinctively clipped and dismissive tone, might be: 'Yes. A good day.' And that was it. Thanks a lot.

At the second Test in Madras in February 1993, with the clock ticking towards the end of the programme, I asked Trevor to give his thoughts on the three Indian spinners who had been responsible for England's demise in the first Test of the series. Trevor had just arrived in India, and had not seen that game in Calcutta, so, to be helpful, I handed him Bill's beautifully crafted bowling figures so he could get the names right. Disastrously, however, Trevor did not have his glasses on, and was unable to read the names, although they were written very clearly: Venkatapthy Raju, Anil Kumble and Rajesh Chauhan. Despite looking a little flustered, Trevor was undeterred, and declared succinctly and magisterially: 'Ragi: ordinary. Kimble: good bowler. Shoosson: chucker.' Follow that.

Trevor's facial expressions often said more than his words. He would screw up his face, to the point at which his eyes were firmly shut, and thoughtfully suck in air through pursed lips. This was a sign of reflection and great satisfaction, and would be followed, after a pause and a nod of the head, with: 'Good player.' That was high praise indeed.

He surprised me once when we were discussing the subject of beamers – dangerous head-high full tosses that are considered to be thoroughly unsporting. 'I used to bowl beamers quite deliberately,' Trevor announced casually, and then recounted with some relish how he had broken the hand of Vic Munden, a Leicestershire batsman of his generation, with a fast ball aimed straight at his nose. Trevor was notorious, of course, for bowling wide down the leg side as a defensive measure, and his ability to cling to the crease for hours without scoring many runs – 68 from 427 balls at Brisbane in December 1958 being a notable case in point – earned him the nickname 'Barnacle' Bailey. His staccato speech made him an ideal foil for the burbling Johnston, and Trevor was always impressively fast to find the perfect sharp retort to one of Brian's sudden leaps into the unexpected.

I had been apprehensive about meeting Fred Trueman. His stature as one of the greatest of all fast bowlers was legendary, and he was equally well known on the county cricket circuit for his ability to deliver the sharpest of criticisms of the modern game in his weekly column in the *Sunday People*. He had given me a touch a few years before – deservedly, I am sure – and I had been left in no doubt that he did not rate my cricketing skills too highly. Now I would be passing my judgements alongside his on a level of cricket that I could not exactly claim to have conquered.

During a break for bad weather in the course of my first Test, I was given the chance to talk to Fred about fast bowling and how it had changed over the years. It was fascinating, and Fred became so energised by the conversation that he actually stood up and heaved himself up the step to the back of the box, took off his jacket and demonstrated his bowling action. It may not have made for great radio, but it was tremendous fun, and that discussion did wonders in easing my anxiety, and kick-started what became an excellent on-air rapport.

In fact, I very quickly grew to love Fred. I would puff him up by reminding him that of the 311 Test wickets we had taken between us, he had 307 of them, which stood for years as the all-time record. Figures and statistics were always very important to Fred. And, like all the very best sportsmen, he had absolutely no doubt about his ability. 'Hey, Aggers!' he once shouted across a crowded table in

Geoffrey Boycott's kitchen during a lunch party there. 'You're a bloody lucky so-and-so, you know?' I drew closer. 'You got to bowl to Viv Richards,' he continued, drawing howls of laughter from everyone in the vicinity.

'Go on then, Fred,' I replied. 'Make your point.'

'I'd have opened him up like a can of beans,' Fred announced. 'First ball: outswinger starting leg stump. He'd try and flick it through midwicket and I'd hit top of off. Simple.' It was delivered with a smile, but I was not fooled for a moment: he honestly believed it.

Fred and Brian were a great double act. Where else would you find two characters who were so different to one another in every respect? The Old Etonian Grenadier Guardsman, and the son of a Yorkshire coal miner. Johnners delighted in winding Fred up, which was never difficult, and was always quick to deflate his ego, albeit gently, when Fred was off his long run. 'I don't know what's going off out there,' was Fred's trademark cry of exasperation. 'I just don't know what's going off.' 'But you're supposed to tell us, Fred,' I recall Brian replying.

Fred was not always kindly, and it seemed to me that there were certain England cricketers he did not rate at all, regardless of how well they might have played. Derek Pringle definitely fell into this category. I am not sure if the true reason for Fred's impatience towards him was because of Derek's earring, which he famously flaunted when he was first selected for a Test at Lord's, his snazzy Porsche sports car or his Cambridge University background. In fact, it was probably down to all three. In 1992, when England were playing the first Test against Pakistan at Edgbaston, Pringle walked out to bat with England replying to Pakistan's first innings of 446 for 4 declared. Fred was on the air with Johnners, and I was sitting behind him, watching the game.

As Pringle approached the pitch, Fred announced: 'Not a bad player, this lad Pringle. Here's a great chance to show what he can do for his country. Good luck, son.' Then, turning to me and shielding his microphone with his hand to stop him being heard by the listening millions, he muttered, 'Who the bloody 'ell picked this prat?'

* * *

The basic structure of the programme when I joined *TMS* was very much the same as it is now. Each commentator would have a twenty-minute slot, while the summarisers worked for half an hour at a time. Bill sat to the commentator's left, so his score sheets were within easy reach. While the commentator and summariser each had a microphone extending from the desk on a long pole, Bill had a hand-held lip mike with a switch on the handle that had to be pressed for him to be heard on the air. This had been introduced by Peter that year, mainly to restrict the cacophony of snorts, grunts and other extraneous noises Bill would emit regularly, and sometimes alarmingly, throughout the day. Because Bill now had to attract the commentator's attention before broadcasting – usually by a series of prods and snorts – it also limited his contributions somewhat; a point, I suspect, that had not been lost during Peter's deliberations on the matter. This had not gone down at all well with Bill, who chuntered a great deal in his corner.

Bill was an extremely fastidious individual. Of course you have to be organised to keep score in the meticulous and orderly fashion he did, but the business of recording every ball on his scoresheets was only one very small part of Bill's role. In order to be able to give advance notice of a record partnership, or some other significant development, Bill needed a mountain of files, record books, and of course his laptop, the screen of which would constantly flicker between Cricinfo and Testmatchextra.com. There was always a roll of extra-strong mints in front of him, and three old-fashioned wind-up stopwatches attached in a row to a handmade backing board. The left- and right-hand watches displayed the amount of time each batsman had been in, and the middle one showed the total time the team had been batting. It was a clever arrangement, in that Bill was able to start all three watches at once, as he had to do each morning when the umpire called 'Play', or to stop them all when there was an interval or a break in play. A satisfied snort from my left would indicate that, each one having carefully been fully wound, the clocks were ticking away happily and we were set for another day. After Bill died, his widow Debbie kindly donated the three watches to *Test Match*

Special, and they are now in the care of our statistician Malcolm Ashton.

I soon learned that Bill would command his corner throughout a Test match, to the point that it became virtually an exclusion zone. Woe betide any commentator who accidentally strayed into his territory, and this extended to include the lunch and tea intervals, when Bill was not on duty or not even in the box. When I was hosting a busy on-air discussion in a desperately crowded box, my chair might inadvertently – and reasonably – slip into Bill's area while he was absent. His return would be accompanied by a succession of tremendous snorts, stamping feet and harrumphs, like a volatile male elephant in musth. If all of that failed to have the desired effect, my chair would receive a sharp shove in the back, whether or not I was actually broadcasting at the time.

Bill always had a very different attitude towards visitors, however. They would be warmly welcomed to his corner, and patiently shown the unique system he had devised, which brought such valuable illustration and information to his scoring. Given that it was the dream of most of our visitors to sit and watch Bill in action, this very much made their day. I remember Norman Tebbit, the Conservative peer, sitting at Bill's shoulder for hours one Saturday as every delivery of a day's play at Lord's was painstakingly recorded in the most intricate detail. I will refrain from delving too deeply into every feature of Bill's modification of the linear scoring method, because he has devoted an entire chapter to it in his excellent autobiography, *Bearders: My Life in Cricket*. Besides, even after eighteen years I could not make head nor tail of the squiggles, arrows, blibs and blobs in black ink that he could interpret with such accuracy that he could tell me, even days later, precisely where Kevin Pietersen struck his third boundary on the first morning, and then how many the same batsman had scored when he gave a difficult half-chance into the slip cordon sometime that afternoon. Bill was absolutely remarkable, to the extent that when he announced, always gleefully, that the scoreboard was wrong, we never doubted him for a moment, and stuck with Bill's score until the board was corrected. All of this while putting up with our silly pranks, researching queries from listeners and maintaining his detailed scoreboard for *The Times*, which he proudly posted at the close of play every evening.

Scoring has always struck me as a rather dull occupation – I would much rather be playing, after all. But it is a pastime that brings great pleasure to many thousands of people every weekend, from village greens to county cricket clubs. It is a wonderful way to be deeply involved with the game, and with a club, without having to be a good player. Professional cricketers seem to be divided into two groups when it comes to statistics: those who avidly keep a record of their facts and figures, often in their heads; and those who really could not care less. I certainly fell into the second group, with the exception of the latter part of the 1987 season, when I was homing in on taking a hundred wickets in a season. That was the only time I knew precisely how many wickets I had taken, and I celebrated the moment that I finally trapped my hundredth victim, Kent's Mark Benson, by falling over in mock exhaustion.

Being hopeless at maths and mental arithmetic has not helped to give me an interest in statistics, but working with Bill for all those years changed that, to an extent at least. Bill gave context to facts and figures, giving the most seemingly meaningless statistic some measure of interest and meaning. His greatest skill was to put fun into scoring, and he attracted a huge following because of it.

When we were off duty, there was a scramble for the vacant chairs along the back wall of the commentary box. This became more of a challenge after lunch, when Fred used to enjoy an afternoon nap. Johnners rarely left the box, making use of his time off air to catch up with his correspondence, of which there was a great deal. The one distraction he had, which seems almost as extraordinary now as it did then, was his daily catch-up with the Australian soap *Neighbours*. Whenever possible, Brian would settle back and watch the midday episode during the lunch interval at the Test match. This was easier in those days than now, because we did not generally have to fill the lunch and tea breaks during the week. Johnners would sit at the commentary desk, his gaze firmly fixed on the monitor, which was actually positioned there for us to watch action replays, rather than for his daily fix of *Neighbours*. Sometimes he was unable to watch the programme in the commentary box, so he invested in a tiny portable television, with a tremendously long, extendable aerial, which he could hold and watch in peace and quiet outside.

It may seem utterly incongruous that Johnners, the Grenadier Guard and national institution, was addicted to something as apparently trivial as *Neighbours*. Often that day's episode would be referred to later in commentary: 'I must tell you, Fred, I'm dreadfully worried about Mrs Mangel . . .'

Even more unlikely were the telephone conversations between Johnners and John Paul Getty II, the reclusive oil billionaire with whom he had struck up an improbable friendship. Getty was introduced to cricket by Mick Jagger – a friend from the 1960s social scene – and quickly fell in love with the game. He also shared Johnners' passion for *Neighbours*. The two of them would often compare notes at the end of another dramatic instalment from Ramsey Street, and this led to Getty asking Brian to manage his early cricket matches at his estate at Wormsley in Buckinghamshire.

These were extraordinary occasions, at which you did not know who you were going to bump into in the luncheon marquee: actors, politicians, models or singers. The first match was staged in 1992, and I played for Brian's team. There were no spectators as such, just invited guests including the Prime Minister, John Major, who spent much of the afternoon bowling at children against one of the canvas sides of the marquee, Colin Cowdrey, Peter May and just about everybody who had anything to do with cricket. Oh, and the Queen Mother popped in for tea. Wormsley is a beautiful ground, which Getty created with just a little help from Surrey's Harry Brind, who was the leading groundsman in the country at the time. It is surrounded entirely by woodland, approached by a very long drive and just a short stroll from the main house. Enormous red kites soar gracefully overhead to complete a setting which is wonderfully tranquil, but in which you regularly have to pinch yourself as a much-needed reality check.

Emma and I had an unforgettable lunch there shortly before Getty died in 2003. By then I had happily removed myself from the playing rota, and was firmly on the lunch-guest list only. With the teams back on the field after the interval, Emma and I settled down for a bottle of wine with Getty and the great Australian all-rounder Keith Miller, just the four of us. Miller was not a well man by then – he would die the following year – but he still had a glint in his eye, and was very pleased to find himself next to Emma. 'If you think you're going to ask me about cricket, son, forget it!' he said to me.

But I wanted to know what it was like playing in the years after the Second World War, and how the players' attitude to the game, even at international level, must have been affected by their wartime experiences. Miller, who had been a fighter pilot, told me of the time he returned to his base in Hampshire having been given a day's leave to play cricket in London. The Military Police were out in force when he got back, and the Fire Brigade were hosing down a pub that had been levelled by a German bomb. All the friends from Australia who he had signed up with had been sitting in that pub when the bomb struck. There were no survivors. Had it not been for cricket, Keith would have died in there with them. No wonder he, and others of that time, took such a relaxed but also dashing and cavalier approach to cricket after that.

'You two must go and see my library at the house,' Getty urged Emma and me, in a voice so soft we had to strain to listen. 'There's an interesting new addition.'

Up we went, and indeed the new addition was quite interesting. It was a first edition of Chaucer's *Canterbury Tales*, which he had bought for US$7.5 million and which was housed in a specially sealed and temperature-controlled glass case. How the other half live, as they say. Yet there was never a suggestion of snootiness, snobbery or vulgarity at Wormsley; Getty was not that kind of man. One evening he regaled me with stories about a period in his life of which he was not so proud, drug-taking in Morocco with various rock stars of the time. His second wife, Talitha, died from a heroin overdose in 1971. That is what drove him into depression, despair and reclusion. Cricket, and the nurse who was to become Lady Victoria Getty, finally opened his eyes and brought him back into the world again.

Getty's relationship with Johnners also played its part in that, and it was clear from the days at Wormsley that the two men had a great affection for one another. Brian's job was to meet and greet everybody, sit them all down for lunch and generally ensure that the day went with a swing. Since everyone was there to have a good time, this was not difficult. After Brian's death, the role was assumed by the *bon viveur* and Hampshire's last amateur captain, Colin Ingleby-Mackenzie. A larger-than-life character, and the President of MCC who finally oversaw the inclusion of women members to what had been an all-male establishment, Ingleby, as he was known, was also reputedly the last person to see Lord Lucan before he vanished from the face of the earth.

These were relaxed, highly enjoyable days out into a different world. As at work, Brian would do his best, dress-wise, without going over the top. He dressed like your grandfather might when he went to church: suitably smart, with a jacket, usually a cream shirt and a tie; but he could never be accused of being a natty dresser. It did not help that he was colour blind, which I noticed for the first time while sitting at the front of the Headingley box during my first Test with the *TMS* team. Glancing backwards, I was surprised to notice that Brian had a penchant for brightly coloured socks. Yellow was a particular favourite, showing brightly above his favourite brown and white co-respondent's shoes, which he always wore during a Test match. His colour blindness explained some of his startling announcements about what colour dress a woman in the crowd might be wearing, for example, when the rest of us could see that in fact it was no such colour at all.

His daughter Clare told me about his rare shopping trips: 'He used to come home gleeful after an expedition to M&S to buy sweaters, and would proudly show us two, both of which were either the same colour, or not the colour he thought they were. I always wondered if he could see his wonderful bright Caribbean shirts he adored so much, and as for wearing bright-coloured boxers under his white trousers, which were diaphanous; he probably never saw that either.'

Goodness knows what he would have made of the coloured clothes now worn in one-day cricket. The listeners would not have known who was batting or fielding, or even, possibly, which teams were playing.

On the Saturday of that first Leeds Test the actor David Tomlinson, of *Mary Poppins* and *Bedknobs and Broomsticks* fame, was Brian's guest taking 'A View from the Boundary'. I have now inherited that slot, and greatly cherish it for the challenge it provides in interviewing cricket-loving celebrities about their lives and their attraction to the great game. Some interviews turn out better than others, not least because the guests can be surprisingly nervous, and Brian would concede that this chat was not one of his better efforts. David certainly was not nervous, but this 'View' struggled through over-familiarity.

It always pays to have a quick chat with the guest before we go on air, to make them feel at ease and to check a fact or two – I insist on it wherever possible – but it can be a problem if you know him or her well, or have spent the previous evening with them. Making conversation over dinner, one can easily burn off all the questions that should have been saved for the interview. This leaves the pair of you feeling as if you are repeating yourselves come Saturday lunchtime, with the result that the interview is not nearly as lively and spontaneous as it should be.

That is what happened this time, albeit with unusual panache. On the Friday evening Tomlinson picked Peter Baxter and me up from our hotel in Bramhope in his Rolls-Royce, no less, and drove us to Arthington Hall, where Johnners and Pauline were staying. What followed was a thoroughly convivial evening, full of wonderful stories and leg-pulling, but it did become a preview of the main event the following lunchtime, which fell disappointingly flat.

Even a new boy could detect that all was not well behind the scenes during my first Test in the commentary box. On air, I am sure that

Test Match Special sounded exactly the same as it always did, and that listeners would have been none the wiser, but the tension surrounding Don Mosey's impending book was becoming uncomfortable. There was an extraordinary moment when Don approached me in the box and asked if he could have a quiet word with me outside, in the Rugby Stand. As we sat on one of the wooden benches with our backs to the cricket, I wondered what on earth this was all about.

Don lit a cigarette. 'I want you to know,' he said, absolutely seriously, 'that I do not hold the fact that you went to public school against you.' Stunned, I thanked him, noting that Don Mosey had a serious chip on his shoulder.

A little later I relayed this encounter to Johnners in the engineers' room. He found it hysterical.

'Have you heard, Backers?' he called out to Peter. 'The Alderman doesn't rate Uppingham School.'

Of course it was absurd, but this bluff Yorkshireman's grievance against public schoolboys was the focal point of his deeply personal and bitter attacks on Peter Baxter and Christopher Martin-Jenkins. He convinced himself that they had only got where they were because of their 'privileged' upbringings. The impeccable records of both men show how ridiculous that notion was.

Shortly before the Edgbaston Test, where the book was officially launched on the opening day, Johnners got his hands on an early copy and handed it to Peter. 'It gives me no pleasure whatsoever to give you this,' he said.

Of Christopher Martin-Jenkins, who had been preferred to himself as cricket correspondent when Brian retired from the position in 1992, Mosey wrote: 'I had heard of children being born with a silver spoon in the mouth, but for Chris to walk so easily into the cricket correspondent's post with relatively little experience smacked of being born with a diamond-encrusted golden spoon thrust well down the throat.'

Peter Baxter and Henry Blofeld were also the subject of personal insults based entirely upon their backgrounds. For Mosey to have thought that he could write about his colleagues in such a derogatory way, and for their relations not to suffer as a consequence, suggests either staggering naïvety or arrogance. In fact, he had got it into his head that he was going to be dropped from the programme at the end of the previous summer, and by the time Peter invited him to commentate on the 1991 series against the West Indies, the book deal and the publication date were already in place. It would have been better for everyone concerned had Don declined the invitation and retired.

The atmosphere at Edgbaston was terrible; so bad, in fact, that Johnners seriously considered jacking the whole thing in. On the first day, after a mountain of books had been delivered to the commentary box for Don to autograph, I thought it best to leave and sit outside. Johnners joined me. He told me of his sadness at the affair, and how badly he thought Don had behaved. The man who had worked so hard to make *Test Match Special* sound like a friendly and happy family could not bear to see what was happening behind the scenes. Mosey never worked on *Test Match Special* again after that summer, and although he was not involved directly in the decision to drop him, Brian believed it was inevitable.

Just when it seemed that things could not possibly get worse came the dinner to end all dinners, in which frustration and bitterness rose angrily to the surface and left everyone connected with *Test Match Special* seriously worried about its future. The in-fighting that night was so bad that it even made the back page of the *Daily Mirror*.

The get-together was the idea of Mike Lewis, the man who had appointed me as correspondent, and it was held at the end of the first day's play at Pebble Mill, which was only a stone's throw from Edgbaston. Essentially it was a *Test Match Special* dinner, with the commentators and summarisers all present. The special guest was Mickey Stewart, the England coach, and Lewis had also invited Pat Murphy, BBC Radio's reporter at the Test, who had taken my appointment as correspondent ahead of him particularly badly. Lewis was presumably attempting to extend an olive branch to Murphy, and to make him feel included in the BBC cricket unit.

So the atmosphere was terribly uncomfortable as we all sat down to dinner. To make matters even worse, the table was set out in a large square, with a big gap in the middle so you had to shout to make conversation with the person opposite. With everything that was going on in the background, one could only sympathise with Lewis, who was responsible for the seating plan that evening. He faced an impossible task. Disastrously, he placed Mickey Stewart within shouting range of Fred Trueman, who in no time was extremely argumentative, demanding to know why he was never consulted in the coaching of England's fast bowlers. He was also scathing in his criticism of Ted Dexter, the chairman of selectors at the time. A terrible row between the two quickly erupted, and it seemed to be veering dangerously out of control when Mickey shouted: 'This isn't the place for this, Fred. Let's go outside.'

Both men rose to their feet, and Mickey strode angrily to the door, which he flung open wide, only to discover that it opened onto a broom cupboard.

If there was any laughter from the rest of us, it was very much of the nervous variety. Lewis suddenly stood up and proposed a loyal toast. This had not been planned, but he hoped, reasonably enough, that it would diffuse the situation.

Up we all got, and raised our glasses, at which point I heard Johnners, standing to my left, mutter loudly: 'Oh no.'

There was Murphy, still sitting with his arms folded determinedly across his chest. As the disbelieving gathering stared down at him, he repeatedly maintained that he was exercising his democratic right as a republican. Anyone is entitled to their view, but Brian and others took it terribly badly feeling that as well as being embarrassing beyond belief, this was absolutely not the right time or the right company in which to make this kind of political statement. Johnners in particular regarded it as disloyalty to the monarch, not to mention brazenly disrespectful of Mike Lewis, our host and Murphy's boss. Even eighteen years later, at the launch of Peter Baxter's autobiography *Inside the Box*, Murphy's presence prompted Brian's son Barry to recall how angry and upset his father had been by the incident when he returned home following the Test.

Above Brian at the age of eleven in 1923, the year following the tragic death of his father.

Right Described at school as a 'very efficient' and unfailingly keen wicketkeeper, Brian never achieved his great ambitions of appearing behind the timbers at Lord's for Eton vs Harrow, or for Oxford in the Varsity match.

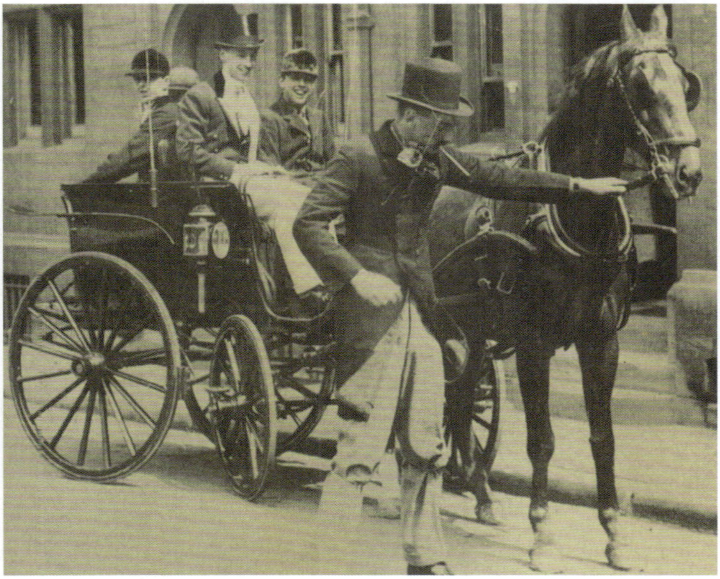

Left Brian as the groom and William Douglas-Home (second from left) arrive in style for a lecture in May 1934. The pair, and their horse 'Lily', became a familiar sight around the streets of Oxford.

Left Brian playing the fool at Oxford. William Douglas-Home would not have been far away.

Below Brian knew from an early age that he didn't want to pursue a career as a coffee merchant in the family firm, E. Johnston & Co. Nevertheless, after leaving Oxford he dutifully gave it a try. Here he is in the Hamburg office of the company's German agent, the former U-boat captain Herr Korner, in November 1935.

Left Some downtime in April 1945 during the Allied invasion of Germany, towards the end of which Brian was awarded the Military Cross. His citation included the words: 'His own dynamic personality, coupled with his untiring determination and cheerfulness under fire, have inspired those around him always to reach the highest standard of efficiency.'

Right Johnners was a regular source of entertainment in the Officers' Mess.

Brian, in his demob suit, introducing *Works Wonders* for BBC Radio. The programme, each episode of which was broadcast from a different factory, featured musical and variety performances by the employees.

Above Brian looking suitably apprehensive before spending a night in the Chamber of Horrors at Madame Tussaud's for the first programme of *Let's Go Somewhere*, broadcast live on 23 October 1948. Looming menacingly in the background are the murderers Frederick Seddon, Arthur Devereux and Herbert Bennett.

Right The way outside broadcasts used to be – Brian road tests a penny-farthing at Herne Hill in south London, with a sound engineer running alongside carrying the precious cable.

Above Preparing for a day commentating on a Test match for BBC Television with Peter West, E.W. 'Jim' Swanton and Roy Webber.

Left The consummate outside broadcasts commentator, perched precariously on a roof but intent on the job at hand, as always.

Brian in classic pose, with ballpoint pen dangling around his neck, at Old Trafford for the first Ashes Test during his final summer, in June 1993.

Above Geoffrey Boycott receiving the Man of the Match Award from Brian Johnston for his 52 made in 43 overs in the Fenner Trophy semi-final against Kent at Scarborough in 1974.

Right Brian, in dapper correspondent's shoes, interviewing his great friend Colin Cowdrey, then President of MCC, at Lord's during his 733rd and final *Down Your Way*, 20 May 1987.

It was certainly the only time I ever saw Brian come close to losing his temper, and speaking to friends of his down the years, it is clear that this was a very rare event indeed. The man who was renowned for his ability to see only the good in everything was starting to despair, and when Brian left Pebble Mill that night, Peter noticed how ashen he looked. 'I knew what he was thinking,' Peter told me. 'He was ready to throw in the towel. I made him promise to ring me before doing anything.'

Test Match Special was at a crossroads. After only four Tests, and having been led to believe that the genial *bonhomie* that radiated happily from the radio was a genuine reflection of the way everyone on the programme got on with one another, I was deeply disappointed. Everybody's morale, but especially Brian's, desperately needed a lift. Thankfully, within a fortnight we were all laughing again, and *Test Match Special* was making the headlines for the right reasons.

FOUR

The Leg Over

While the listeners loved the banter and humour in which Johnners indulged, it was not universally popular with his colleagues on *Test Match Special*, especially the old-school variety who had been brought up to regard cricket commentary as a serious business. For them, the cricket itself was of paramount importance, and should not be diluted by what they perceived as childish pranks. Alan Ross fell into this category, and John Arlott too, despite possessing a brilliant wit of his own. These days, might they call it 'dumbing down'? But under Brian's influence the programme's popularity soared as *TMS* reached out to an entirely new audience, with, for the first time, the whole family feeling that this was an entertainment for them, rather than just for the cricket-loving dad.

The relationship between Johnston and Arlott was not an entirely comfortable one. They were, after all, poles apart in just about every aspect of their lives, especially politics. Arlott twice stood unsuccessfully for Parliament as a Liberal candidate, and he and Johnners were on opposite sides on the question of whether England should continue to play sport against teams representing the oppressive and racist political regime of South Africa. When presented with an immigration form prior to entering South Africa on the 1948 MCC tour, Arlott wrote the word 'human' in the box which required him to declare his racial group. In the early 1980s Johnners addressed a large gathering of MCC members in London, arguing firmly that while he disagreed with South Africa's politics, he remained in favour of maintaining sporting contact, on the grounds that politics should not interfere with sport. One can only imagine what the atmosphere was like in the commentary box whenever the issue of South Africa raised its head.

I have also heard it said that Arlott felt Johnners rather trivialised Test cricket with his light-hearted style of commentary. Johnners, for his part, thoroughly disapproved of the amount of alcohol, claret mainly, that Arlott consumed in the course of the working day. But the two men were giants in their specialised field, and at the top of their trade. There must surely have been a competitive edge between them, and the programme would have been all the better for it. For me, and thousands of other listeners, the style of the master poet Arlott, who cleverly used long periods of silence to such dramatic effect, made a perfect contrast to the burbling, jocular and friendly tones of Johnners. That would certainly have been the case when bad weather interrupted play and opened up the opportunity for hours of chatter, which for many listeners is the best part of the programme, and is probably what *Test Match Special* is most famous for. It was made so by the magical conversations involving Johnners, Arlott, Fred Trueman and Trevor Bailey, who would hold listeners spellbound in their cars or in their gardens. There is no other programme on the radio that gives a broadcaster as much freedom as *TMS*.

Stoppages in play give one the opportunity to talk about almost anything, from trips down memory lane (particularly in Fred's case) to answering questions from listeners and generally keeping the output needle flicking in Broadcasting House as the hours while away. It is a shame that because of pressure from the network we tend to hand back to the studio earlier these days than used to be the case, because the advent of instant means of communication and reaction from listeners, like email and Twitter, means that filling the time is definitely easier now, as well as adding interest and variety to the conversation on-air. This audience participation – which Brian would have loved, incidentally – makes the programme feel more inclusive, too.

Since Brian was the absolute master at conducting a conversation with anybody about anything, he was in his element in these situations, and this is one area in which I learned a great deal from him. I remember, in my first Test as a commentator in 1991, making copious notes at the back of the box on subjects that I thought I could cover during my stint of leading the conversation if bad light or rain stopped play. It was a safety net, but I never needed it. Somehow the banter simply took its own course, driven by the professionalism of my colleagues who would slip seamlessly into storytelling mode, with one throwaway line leading us down the next unexpected route, and on to more stories. It is sensible, when in 'filling' mode, to abandon the twenty-minute rota, and if someone is on a roll in the lead commentator's chair, to let him carry on until he has finished. This can sometimes lead to marathons, but it has the benefit that a theme can be developed which runs its course smoothly and seamlessly, before the next commentator comes in and takes the conversation off in a new direction altogether.

Johnners' technique was to let people speak and, most important, actually to listen to what they were saying. That sounds obvious, but it is a failing of many broadcasters that on-air interviews become stilted and bitty. It often only requires a response such as 'Really?' to develop a conversation of the sort one might have over the garden fence with the next-door neighbour. It is more natural, in other words, and more likely to result in greater depth and interest, than sitting down with a list of notes and questions that are ticked off as you go through them in the order in which they are scribbled down.

Nevertheless, some of Brian's apparently off-the-cuff comments on *TMS* were, I am sure, thought up in advance. I can say that because I do it too. You might not know when the opportunity to use them will arise, but funny lines and possibilities do suddenly pop into one's mind when driving down the motorway, for example, and are carefully put to one side for later. An example of Brian employing this technique was when Glenn Turner, the fine New Zealand opening batsman, took a direct blow to the box and was felled for several minutes. When the pain finally subsided, Turner got to his feet and gestured that he would continue batting, at which point Brian said: 'Very plucky of him. Yes, definitely going to have a try. One ball left.' Had his summariser collapsed in laughter, or had there been any complaints from listeners, he could quite innocently and plausibly have passed his remark off as a simple statement of the number of deliveries remaining in the over – except that he was Johnners. Brian was constantly on the lookout for any whiff of a *double entendre*, which he would then highlight with great relish on the off chance that anyone might have missed it – which, of course, most of us had. An example of the level we are talking about here came when I received in the post, from a clearly bored correspondent, a 'Moustached XI', in batting order. When I got to Clive Lloyd at number 5, I happened to toss in, as an aside, that Lloyd had 'a particularly big one', referring, of course, to his moustache. The gleeful trumpeting, snorts and gales of laughter from the back of the commentary box that greeted this entirely innocent remark quite threw me and Fred Trueman – who was on air with me – off our strides.

Perhaps the most famous, and most obviously contrived, example of using names and cricketing terms to create a prep-school giggle while keeping an entirely straight face is 'The bowler's Holding, the batsman's Willey.' Classic Johnston, yet there is no record of it ever actually having been said on air. There is no tape, and nobody working on *Test Match Special* at the time can remember it ever having been broadcast. It is undoubtedly something that Brian might have said, and certainly something he would have *loved* to have said. But he didn't, at least not while commentating, anyway.

One technique that Brian employed during extended breaks in play was to go through the scorecard thoroughly, comprehensively and regularly. This serves to bring new listeners up to date with what has happened before the interruption, but it also, from the broadcaster's point of view, takes up valuable time and gives you time to think about what you are going to say next. This, I find, is especially useful during the 'View from the Boundary' spot in Saturday lunch intervals. Only rarely have we met the celebrity cricket-lovers we interview, and therefore we have no idea how they will stand up to a live thirty-minute conversation. It is good practice to give a lunch score and a reminder of who the guest is at some point during the interview, and I do so when I am wondering what to ask next.

It was Brian's insistence on reading the scorecard that led to our classic broadcast.

Friday, 9 August 1991 dawned as the second day of any Test match at The Oval might do, but ended with *Test Match Special* in chaos, and me wondering if, after only four months in my new role, I had badly overstepped the mark. It was also the day that Brian Johnston and I stumbled headlong into the creation of a broadcasting partnership that, at the moment at any rate, seems destined to mean that our names will forever be linked with each other's.

It had been a closely fought and entertaining series, with West Indies winning at Trent Bridge and Edgbaston after England's victory in the opening Test at Headingley and a draw at Lord's. With England 2–1 down, and needing a win in this, the final Test, to avoid the usual series defeat against the West Indies of that time, the selectors found themselves under mounting pressure. England's batting had looked fragile in the previous two games – no one more so than Graeme Hick, who had come into the team at the beginning of the series as the Messiah, having scored fifty-seven first-class centuries before qualifying to play for England, but who was now dropped after a torrid experience against Malcolm Marshall, Curtly Ambrose, Patrick Patterson and Courtney Walsh. It was an awesome attack – the last of the great West Indian fast bowling quartets that had dominated world cricket for fifteen years. Jack Russell, England's popular and accomplished wicketkeeper, gave way to Alec Stewart, who was a stronger batsman, but with the stage so perfectly set for an act of heroism, there was only one name on the lips of the man in the street, and on the back pages of the national newspapers: Ian Botham.

Botham had not played a Test for two years. Unsure of the circumstances behind his prolonged absence, I approached him in a hotel bar recently for an explanation. 'Er,' he started. 'It wasn't *that* ban, was it?' (Meaning the brief suspension he received in 1986 for smoking cannabis.) I assured him that it was not, because I graphically remembered him returning after that misdemeanour with outrageously bleached hair in a match against New Zealand, and taking a wicket with his second ball to equal Dennis Lillee's all-time record of 355 Test wickets. Ten balls later he took another, to create history. Only Ian could have such an apparently hazy memory of such a momentous personal achievement, and it sums up his approach to these things. Ian lives each day for that day only, often spectacularly to the full, before moving on – a little more sedately nowadays – to the next.

I have never been more than a fringe member of Botham's social circle, which is probably the safest place to be. I always enjoy bumping into him in a hotel bar and sharing a glass or two of wine, but to do it regularly would require boundless stamina. His colleagues in the Sky TV commentary box employ a rota system that limits the punishing after-effects of regular nights out with Ian, although these days his eyes slowly close and the lights go out much earlier than they used to do. Flying home from Johannesburg at the end of the 2009–10 tour of South Africa, I found myself sitting a couple of rows in front of Ian. He had clearly started his celebrations early, so I prepared myself for a long night. Not so. As soon as the seatbelt sign went off, I glanced anxiously behind me to see him already fast asleep. He remained like that almost until we began our descent into London ten hours later.

Ian was an immensely strong man, whose body somehow absorbed and shrugged off the excesses of the previous night more easily than anyone I have ever known. Indeed, we finally got to the reason for his absence in 1990 and 1991 during a second bottle of Chardonnay. He was out of international cricket for two years virtually to the day following a serious back operation from which, he says, he never fully recovered. His magnificent bowling action became laboured, and he put on weight – but he was still Ian Botham, and his massive self-belief remained undiminished. He was undeniably the man for a crisis. Consequently, his name was all over the news in the lead-up to that final Test in 1991, including, inevitably, reminders of cannabis-smoking, drunken nights out and an allegation from a former beauty queen – denied by Ian – that the pair once broke a bed in the course of a passionate encounter in Barbados.

The Oval was full to capacity when England resumed their first innings on the second morning. Ian Botham was the next man in, and Robin Smith and Alec Stewart added 32 runs before Stewart was out for 31. The entire crowd rose to its feet to celebrate Botham's return to Test cricket, and there was a tremendous sense of excitement and anticipation as he made a typically gladiatorial entrance, swinging his arms in preparation, we all hoped, for some swashbuckling hitting. In fact, the match situation required some circumspection. Botham and Smith carefully added 73, with Smith reaching his century before his friend and Hampshire team-mate, the great Malcolm Marshall, trapped him LBW. Botham's cautious innings, either side of lunch, was rather out of character, but he was up against one of the finest and most hostile pace attacks produced even by the West Indies. He had hit only three fours in the 81 balls he had received when towards the end of the afternoon session, with his score on 31, he faced the towering Curtly Ambrose, who was bowling from the Vauxhall End. Ambrose hurled down a bouncer, the ball flying towards Botham's head, and instinctively he tried to hook it. But the ball was too fast, and struck him on the body. Worse still, he lost his balance as he performed a rather ungainly pirouette. Realising that the momentum of the failed stroke was taking his body straight into his wicket, all he could do was try to step over the stumps as, with his back to the bowler, he attempted to avert impending disaster. As he did so, his right thigh flicked off the leg bail. To be dismissed hit wicket is unusual, and Botham walked off cursing his bad luck, while up in the *Test Match Special* commentary box Christopher Martin-Jenkins meticulously described his dramatic downfall.

Although England went on to make a first innings total of 419, from which they would go on to win the match, Botham's departure from the spotlight had created something of an anti-climax. It was time for a cup of tea.

The media area has changed at The Oval now. Back in 1991 we were all housed at the pavilion end. The *TMS* commentary position was on the third floor, looking down from a tremendous height. The press box was to our left, on the level below, and it was there that one could grab some refreshment and have a chat with friends who were writing for the newspapers. One of these, John Etheridge, who still works for the *Sun*, was also helping himself to a cuppa, and we started to chat about Botham's dismissal. Others joined us.

'I know what our headline will be,' John said playfully. 'Ian Botham cocks it up by not getting his leg over!' We all had a good laugh and then went our separate ways, me back to the commentary box, with John's comment planted fatefully in my mind.

Shortly after my return, the umpires took the players off the field because of bad light. Johnners was in the commentator's seat, and since the position next to him had been vacated, Peter Baxter pulled out the chair and ushered me in with a flourish of his right hand. Moments later, he placed a piece of paper between us on which he had written, in capital letters, the single word 'FILL'. That is *Test Match Special* speak for 'Keep talking for as long as you possibly can.'

And that is why what happened next was centred on the reading of the scorecard. During this potentially lengthy break in play, Johnners was bringing everyone up to date, but like an experienced batsman doing some gardening of the pitch just before the lunch interval, he was taking up some valuable time as well. That was very evident by his inviting me to give my view on every wicket and minor detail, with him adding some thoughts of his own as well. It was good old-fashioned filling, the Johnners way.

It started innocently enough, although I recall there was a bit of an edge to it. I was excited and more than a little nervous, because this was the first time I had been in this situation with Brian. Memories of the farm flooded back, and I knew Dad would be anxiously listening with an element of disbelief that I was in this position. Brian was in rather a mischievous mood. I was, after all, the young pup, and I think he felt this was his chance to find out what I was made of.

Clutching Bill Frindall's meticulous scorecard in his left hand, and with his reading glasses perched on the end of his nose, Brian started to recount the day's events. I was sitting to his left, while to my immediate left Tony Cozier was tapping out his daily report for his newspaper in Barbados. All of our microphones, including Tony's, were live. It did not take long for us to run into trouble.

Brian was so laid-back on the air, and created such a relaxed and informal atmosphere, that it was easy to forget that you were in fact broadcasting to millions of people. It felt like a one-to-one chat with your kindly old grandfather. And there was something about his facial expressions that always made me laugh. Brian had enormous drooping eyebrows and, of course, a famously big nose. He would often lift one eyebrow quizzically at you: not in a stern manner, but more probing for something to smile at, or searching for an opportunity to share a joke. This was always the case when he rumbled the possibility of a *double entendre* or when the subject was slightly risqué. He was daring you to laugh first, at which point he would delight in feigning absolute innocence, knowing in fact that he had stitched you up. It was with that raised eyebrow that he looked at me and suggested that Ian Botham's inner thigh had removed the bail.

'Yes,' I replied. 'He just didn't quite get his leg over.'

I do not know to this day what made me utter those words, other than that by the way he looked at me, Brian had challenged me to come up with something. I had no intention of repeating John Etheridge's line, but out it came. The impact was devastating.

A hesitation of a second and a half can seem like a lifetime on radio, and is certainly long enough for an astute listener to detect that there is a problem. That was approximately the time that it took Brian to recover. I remember him turning to me with a look of absolute horror on his face. He immediately flushed bright red, and within that brief moment, the calmest and most relaxed broadcaster became uncharacteristically flustered as he floundered about, trying to find the words with which to carry on. Already suppressing a desperate attack of the giggles, he turned away from me, and determinedly buried his nose in the scorecard. He would not have been helped by another distraction which can clearly be heard in that second-and-a-half hiatus: the unmistakable sound of clattering china. Bill Frindall had been quietly enjoying the rare opportunity to get out of his chair, stretch his legs at the back of the commentary box and savour a cup of tea. He had just raised the cup to his lips when I made my fateful remark. Crash! Bill slammed his cup down into the saucer in disbelief. Given that he was another one who would never miss an excuse for a mischievous chuckle, Bill was pretty confident that this could develop, and quickly slipped back into his seat to Brian's right to make sure he did not miss anything.

Brian was clearly struggling, but it seemed quite harmless to start with.

'Anyhow,' he said, desperately trying to suppress a chuckle, 'he did very well indeed, batting 131 minutes, and hit three fours, and then we had Lewis playing extremely well for his 47 not out . . .'

I stared straight ahead, avoiding eye contact at all costs, while Brian tried to use the scorecard as a means of getting back on track; but he could hear me giggling as quietly as I could.

'Aggers, do stop it!' he said firmly, but the chuckle that immediately followed showed just how close he was to breaking down. Frindall also started to laugh.

'He was joined by DeFreitas,' Johnners said, soldiering on determinedly, 'who was in for forty minutes; a useful little partnership there. They put on 35 in forty minutes before he was caught by Dujon off Walsh . . .'

He so nearly made it, and under the circumstances it was a heroic effort. But while composing his thoughts to describe David Lawrence's brief cameo that followed, he was scuppered by Frindall, whose wickedly-timed snort reawakened the image of Botham failing to get his leg over. It also let Brian know that everyone was laughing all around him. It was Frindall's snigger that sealed Brian's fate, and took us into the forty-five seconds in which *Test Match Special* all but fell off the air.

'Lawrence, uh, always entertaining, batted for thir . . . thirty-five minutes. Hit a four over the wicketkeeper's h . . . Aggers, for goodness sake stop it . . . he hit a f . . .'

This was the point at which I realised we were in real trouble. Johnners had collapsed helplessly beside me, and I knew that if I tried to speak it would sound ridiculous. There was another long pause, which was broken by Peter rushing from the back of the box and hissing through clenched teeth: 'Will somebody say something!'

I do not blame Peter for his failure to find the situation amusing, because at the time, live in the commentary box, it sounded very different to the way it sounds when played back and listened to through speakers or headphones. With 20,000 people at The Oval that day, and with our window open, it was not possible to hear the squeaks and wheezes that make the Leg Over so funny. To Peter, who was not wearing headphones at the time, it seemed that there was nothing but silence, which is why he was moved to urge someone to say something. Anything.

He would have been better off had he directed his plea to Tony Cozier, who was still sitting beside me. Beavering away on his typewriter, Tony was concentrating and straight-faced, so he could have come to our rescue at any moment. Indeed, it seemed very surprising that, consummate broadcaster and commentator that he is, he declined to do so. When he was challenged about this later, it transpired that this was his revenge for Brian having typically set him up in the commentary box in Port of Spain, almost twenty-five years before.

Tony had entered the box during a break for rain to hear Johnners say, apparently on air, 'Well, there are the up-to-date statistics of the MCC team, their exact batting and bowling figures, and their ages and birth dates. Now I will ask Tony Cozier to give the same details for the West Indies team. Tony . . .'

It goes without saying that Tony was horrified and, for once, quite speechless as he frantically gestured to Brian that he did not have all that information to hand. He tried to change the subject by telling the listeners about the conditions on the ground, but Johnners would have none of it, and insisted on Tony providing the information as requested. Finally Brian handed back to the studio, only then, of course, to tell a humiliated Tony that they had not been on air.

It was a classic Johnners prank, but now it came back to haunt him. Tony has since written that in his opinion his finest ever piece of commentary was not saying anything at all on that occasion at

The Oval in 1991. On reflection, it was entirely the right thing for him to have done, but it left us high and dry.

Brian was incapable of responding to Peter's urgent plea, so I thought I should at least attempt to offer something thoughtful about Lawrence's innings.

'Yes, Lawrence,' I began confidently, 'played extremely well . . .' And that was it. I also broke down, and now neither of us could say a word.

'He hit . . .' Johnners squeaked. 'He hit a four over the wicketkeeper's head, and he was out for 9 . . .' Some sniffing is now audible, because he was dabbing away his tears and wiping his nose with a large handkerchief which he held in front of his face while trying desperately to pull himself together. 'And Tufnell came in and batted for twelve minutes, then he was caught by Haynes off Patterson for 2. And there were 54 extras, and England were all out for 419. I've stopped laughing now.'

He stuffed his hankie back into his trouser pocket. It was all over, and he regained control. After some deep breaths, my composure also returned, and we managed to see *Test Match Special* quietly off the air a few minutes later.

Incidentally, Brian's last sentence, 'I've stopped laughing now,' was used as the final words in his obituary on the BBC Nine O'Clock News on the day he died. Some people thought it was in poor taste. I believed it was absolutely appropriate, and very moving.

It was probably just as well that play was abandoned for the day shortly afterwards. The atmosphere in the box was rather tense, to put it mildly, and the four or five people who had witnessed the incident at first hand were unsure what to say and how to react. We did not consider for a single moment listening back to it, even though the engineers, one floor below us, had recorded every word. Usually after a funny incident their room is the first port of call, but not this time. Brian and Peter Baxter both left the commentary box far from happy with what had just taken place; Brian was concerned that he had been unprofessional, and even that he had made a fool of himself, while Peter had entirely failed to see the funny side.

In no time, it seemed, everyone else had left too, and I was the only person still in the box. I remember how uncomfortable and alone I felt that evening as I sat writing my close-of-play reports: to have caused the main man to leave for the night shaking his head in genuine disappointment did not seem the best of career moves – and this was only my first summer in the job. I was quite sure that it had been very funny, but I was concerned about the reaction it had produced. There was nobody around to talk to about what had happened – none of my mates in the press box had heard it – and I did not dare phone my father in case it had been excruciatingly embarrassing. It would be excessive to say that I feared for my job, but I spent a very uncomfortable night, and I was not looking forward to facing everyone the following morning.

An early appointment with the *Today* programme on Radio 4 required me to be in my position at The Oval early next day, and this was the first indication I had that all might be well. Instead of quizzing me about the state of the game and asking me to look ahead to the prospects for the day in his usual probing style, Garry Richardson began our slot with a tape of the Leg Over. This was the first time I had heard it. When it ended, the whole *Today* studio was in fits, as indeed was I – more in relief than anything else.

My confidence grew as more and more people popped their heads around the commentary-box door; it seemed that every radio station in the country had played the Leg Over on their breakfast programmes, to great national amusement. The post arrived, and although most of the envelopes were addressed to Johnners, as usual, those for me were all from delighted listeners, some of them with stories of having been stuck in traffic jams at the time, and looking about to see the other drivers sitting around them all in hysterics. One correspondent described how he had been up a ladder, hanging wallpaper in his spare bedroom, and had to hang on for dear life as he roared with laughter at the chaos emanating from his radio. News reached me from Broadcasting House that the sports room's studio 3H had become the centre of operations for people wanting hastily dubbed cassette copies. One such customer, the very serious-sounding

Radio 4 newsreader Brian Perkins, had been seen leaning heavily against the studio wall clutching his sides, with tears streaming down his cheeks as his copy was being made.

I was still worried that Peter, who arrived shortly after my *Today* performance, would need to be convinced that what was, after all, a cock-up – on his programme – could be regarded as anything less than a disaster. Brian's reaction would be key to winning Peter over, and the moment he walked through the door I could sense that the mood of the previous evening had lifted. Gleefully he announced that the comedian Ronnie Corbett had been in touch, describing how his wife, who was driving at the time, had been forced to pull onto the hard shoulder until she had recovered. 'I suppose,' Brian said a little dramatically, 'I had better hear it for myself.'

'Come on, Johnners,' I said confidently, and took him down a level to the engineers' room directly beneath the commentary box. I suppose I should not have been surprised at what we saw when I opened the door: there were piles of blank cassettes stacked on the floor ready to go, and the lads were franking off copies as fast as they could make them.

The engineers' quarters on outside broadcasts are always cramped, and full of very complicated-looking equipment bursting with knobs and switches, and there are wires and cables everywhere. Johnners and I had to stoop as Andy Leslie, the chief engineer, rewound the tape and pressed 'Play'. I watched Brian intently, desperate to see what his reaction would be, and did not have to wait long before the tears started streaming down his face in what was almost an action replay of the day before. 'Oh, Aggers!' he wheezed when it was all over, 'I must have a copy!' By the time we had returned to the commentary box, the photographers had arrived and Johnners and I did our best to recreate the scene, Johnners by squawking, 'Aggers, for goodness sake, stop it!' over and over again until they were satisfied. By now it was very clear that the old boy was relishing it. This was confirmed when he interviewed Peter O'Toole, the 'View from the Boundary' guest at lunchtime, and started off by saying, 'You might have heard that Aggers and I disgraced ourselves yesterday . . .' and then embarking on a discussion about the perils of actors corpsing on stage.

The BBC itself remained very quiet on the matter. I wonder what might have happened today, almost twenty years on and in an altogether different broadcasting atmosphere. True, this was nowhere near as serious as the Jonathan Ross and Russell Brand incident, but the BBC often seems to find it difficult to laugh at itself these days. Perhaps it was fortunate that the incident took place on the weekend, because if any of the bosses had initially been upset, it was the talk of the town by Monday, and any thought of disciplinary action or reprimands would have been ridiculous. The icing on the cake was when Radio 4's *Pick of the Week* was inundated by requests for the Leg Over to be played again, and there was even a suggestion of it being nominated for a Sony Award. Peter, although thoroughly won over by now, was not entirely convinced by that. 'How can you enter a mistake for an award?' I remember him wondering, thoroughly bemused.

There can be few people on the cricketing planet who have not heard the Leg Over by now. However, if by some chance it has passed you by – or if you just feel inclined to enjoy the ninety seconds of mayhem again – type 'Leg Over incident' into Google, and you will be taken straight to it.

I would have Eleanor Oldroyd, the BBC Radio 5 Live sports presenter, to thank for putting me in a position similar to Brian's at The Oval when, during a live chat in the studio before the Lord's Test the following summer, she offered: 'Some good news for England is that Ian Botham's groin is back to full strength!' As soon as she said it, Elly shot a hand in front of her mouth in horror, giggled, and her face went bright crimson. My failed attempt to plough on despite desperately wanting the welcome relief of bursting out laughing is also easily found on the internet by tapping in 'Ian Botham's groin': another chaotic piece of broadcasting due to the fatal combination of Sir Beefy and sexual innuendo.

The Leg Over was a career-maker for me. In just a minute and a half, my profile was raised to an entirely unprecedented level. It also helped me to become accepted as a member of *Test Match Special*. Although there was a fifty-year age gap between us, it was to create a perception of Brian and me as something of a double act, and it encouraged the rash of practical jokes we would play on each other in the years that followed.

Brian had been very kind and approachable during the previous four Tests that summer, but I think he was still weighing up the value of my contribution to the programme. That was not helped, I suspect, by my introduction to *Test Match Special* as a so-called expert summariser, rather than a ball-by-ball commentator. Compared to the outstanding former players turned broadcasters who have filled that role both before and since, I was pretty lightweight. But now Brian had identified a sense of humour similar to his own, and he knew that we could have some fun together.

However, he did not feel able to work with me on air again until well into the next summer, when England played Pakistan. 'I know if we look at each other, it'll be hopeless,' he explained to Peter Baxter. When we were finally reunited for an end-of-play summary, which even then was against Peter's better judgment, Brian only agreed to do so if he sat in the very left-hand corner of the wide Lord's box and I sat in the right-hand corner, with our backs to each other. It was ridiculous, and it failed anyway, not just because of the inevitable frisson of childish excitement that gripped us both – and the real sense of danger felt by Peter – but because Brian outrageously described Javed Miandad as having played a typically innovative stroke by 'opening his legs like a croquet hoop and tickling the ball between them'. I could not believe my ears, and shot Brian a frantic glance, which he met, bright red in the face, and we both collapsed. But rather than wheezing and squeaking and struggling on as he had in the Leg Over the previous year, Brian remained absolutely silent for what seemed like an eternity. So long, in fact, that my Auntie Peggy, listening up the road in Hampstead, assumed that the batteries in her radio had died, and set about dismantling it in order to replace them.

Brian clearly felt that the lesson of the Leg Over was that when struck by an attack of the giggles, the best option is to give in, and not to attempt to speak. For my part, I was pathetically incapable of saying anything. The silence was eventually broken by the sound of stamping feet and the commentary-box door being slammed shut as Peter stormed out in a rage. Although Johnners and I had a good laugh about it afterwards, each blaming the other for what had happened, we crept away like naughty schoolboys that evening, him to his home nearby in Boundary Road and me to the hotel adjacent to Lord's, where already much of the conversation around the bar was about the latest Johnners and Aggers incident.

The Leg Over has been enjoyed by millions of people, but for me it remains a personal and treasured memory of Brian. It was something we shared, just the two of us, and it will always keep us inextricably linked. I have no idea how many times I have now heard it. Thousands, certainly. Tens of thousands? It feels like it sometimes. Of course there are occasions when I find it funnier than others, depending on my mood. It can be quite difficult under the spotlight, on a stage in front of hundreds of people, when it is the fifth time I have heard it that week. It is also regularly used as a means of introducing me on radio programmes, particularly, as I have discovered, in Australia, where I set aside a day early on every Ashes tour to appear on as many local ABC stations as can be accommodated – and there are sixty of them. Sitting in my hotel room, I wait for the telephone to ring almost as soon as the previous interview has ended, and I can be pretty sure that when I lift the receiver, it will be at the point of: 'Aggers, for goodness sake, stop it . . .' The clip will end, and a cheery voice with an Australian accent will welcome me to the show with: 'I bet you haven't heard that for a while, Aggers!' 'Er, well, actually . . .'

The Leg Over is so popular in Australia that it has been used in a commercial for a well-known chocolate bar, and in England it has been played during at least one cricket-lover's funeral. The only accolade I feel slightly uncomfortable with is the title 'Best Sporting Commentary Ever', which it was awarded as the result of a vote on BBC Radio 5 Live. It was very kind, of course, but the Leg Over is not really an award-winning piece of commentary. Ian Robertson's brilliant description of Jonny Wilkinson's drop goal to win the 2003 Rugby World Cup for England is wonderful commentary. Just about everything uttered by John Arlott is classic commentary. I would even like to think that some of my stuff over the years might be considered half-decent radio commentary. But the Leg Over? It was a cock-up, pure and simple. As Ian Botham observed afterwards, however, it was 'bloody hilarious'.

FIVE

'What are You Two up to Now?'

Even when he had reached eighty, Brian Johnston's energy and appetite for fun remained undiminished. At a time of life when, frankly, one is surely entitled to have a grumble about anything that takes your fancy, the only thing that provoked even mild irritation in Johnners was defensive bowling outside the leg stump; and this infuriated him. If he was commentating at the time he would be very outspoken about this negative tactic, which, as cricket's most enthusiastic fan, he just could not understand, let alone want to explain or justify to the listeners. When he came off air he would remove his headphones, shake his head and sit heavily in a chair at the back of the box. 'This is simply ghastly, Aggers,' I remember him muttering on one such occasion. 'What are they doing to the game?' I had to agree with him; although my years as a professional cricketer gave me some sympathy with defensive tactics, my move to the commentary box opened my eyes to the absolutely essential requirement that cricketers must also entertain.

Commentating under those circumstances is not fun at all, and the commentary can feel as if it is terribly dull, even if in fact it is not. Players have to be aware of the wider audience that is watching or listening, and the image of the game that they are presenting while at the same time trying to win a cricket match. It is the old dilemma of finding the right blend of providing elegant and entertaining cricket while also preserving the need to win, and if that is not possible, preventing defeat.

Johnners was always the leading source of humour on *Test Match*

Special, and the most likely to play a practical joke. However, in me and David Lloyd – my first victim in first-class cricket, and by now an excellent and established *TMS* summariser – there were two others in the team who relished the same childish humour and shared a penchant for wind-ups. I am sure that under different circumstances we would have been more reticent and cautious, in case we brought *Test Match Special* into disrepute. But when the programme's front man was actively encouraging gentle tomfoolery, and was also such an obvious target for it, Bumble and I felt that we were able to run riot.

Essential to a good wind-up on the radio is the victim not sensing that anything is out of the ordinary. This is easier said than done, because Johnners was a seriously experienced broadcaster, and the best-laid plans can go awry if others are in on it, when obvious sniggering can give the game away. For that reason, we never included Bill Frindall in any of our schemes: he could not be trusted to keep a straight face for long enough. Bill was also the one who least approved of deliberate wind-ups, preferring us to be concentrating on the cricket instead. Although his relationship with Henry Blofeld was not always harmonious, Bill did assume the role of vetting the assorted faxes and letters that were handed to Blowers while he was on air, and he delighted in rumbling any spoofs planted by us if he could.

After decades of live broadcasting, Johnners was able to detect anything that did not sound or feel right, more through instinct than anything else. And, as he would prove to me, he remained the master at setting up and pulling off a practical joke.

The first proper wind-up of Johnners was the work of David Lloyd, and occurred during the Edgbaston Test of 1992, which was my second season on *Test Match Special*. I had now graduated to commentator rather than summariser. This was significant, because for the first time *TMS* was being broadcast on Radio 3 FM rather than on our usual medium-wave frequency, which had been sold off by the government. Our sound engineers, who had never had the opportunity of dealing with anything other than dull old mono on medium wave, were having great fun with the stereo possibilities that FM gave them. This included making Bill's voice come out of the left speaker, the summariser's from the right, and the commentator's from somewhere in the middle. Mexican waves were a highlight, somehow giving the illusion of sweeping from one speaker to the other. Although we were far from popular with the classical music buffs who had to go without their favourite programmes during cricket matches, *Test Match Special* has never sounded better.

In order to ease our way onto Radio 3 FM, and to offer some sort of olive branch to the disgruntled music lovers, it was decided that we should ask a well-known classical musician to appear on the first 'View from the Boundary' of the summer. This was not an easy task for Louise, our researcher at the time, and the search was expanded to include anyone remotely involved with classical music who also loved cricket. Johnners was becoming increasingly uncomfortable about the idea: music hall was more his thing, after all, and he knew little about classical music. He was all too aware that the pressure was on to find somebody from that background at all costs, and he was worried that this might be a very awkward interview indeed.

After some time, the perfect guest was found: a conductor called James Judd. Although he is considered to be one of the pre-eminent interpreters of British orchestral music, and is certainly a cricket fan, neither James nor his reputation was known to any of us. Johnners was now definitely worried and was urgently in need of some background information on Mr Judd.

It is remarkable what the BBC cuttings library can provide when you need it; before the advent of the internet, this was the fount of all knowledge about our 'View from the Boundary' guests as far as we were concerned. It is vital to do as much research as possible before the interviews, which are half an hour long, with no opportunity of handing back to a studio if things are not going well, and Johnners was soon busily poring over the photocopies of various newspaper interviews Judd had given over the years. Early on the Saturday morning, traditionally the day of the interview, Johnners was putting the finishing touches to his notes when a fax from the BBC Research Unit suddenly appeared in the commentary box from somewhere. Listed under the heading 'James Judd: Additional Information' were all sorts of intriguing facts and fascinating titbits about our man, none of which had been included in the main brief from the cuttings library. I immediately recognised Bumble's handwriting.

But Johnners could hardly believe his luck, and scrawled everything down as fast as he could. The first unusual piece of information was that James's nickname was 'Ratty', because he was a keen ferret fancier. He was the guest conductor of the Reykjavik Philharmonic and was sponsored by Weetabix. He was a devoted supporter of Aldershot Football Club, and his greatest claim to fame was writing the title song for the film *Every Which Way But Loose*, starring Clint Eastwood and an orangutan called Clyde.

Johnners was completely taken in by it all, and was beside himself with excitement. But this was an important interview as far as BBC politics were concerned, so while it was hilarious watching him carrying on about 'Ratty' Judd, we were all aware that he needed to know the truth. He returned rather crestfallen after Peter Baxter had broken the bad news to him in the corridor shortly before Judd's arrival, but he still loved the wind-up, to the extent of greeting the startled conductor with a cry of 'Hello, Ratty!' when he arrived at the door of the commentary box. Naturally, everything was explained to Judd, and a few days after a very entertaining interview we each received a copy of his latest compact disc, of Elgar's 1st Symphony. Inside each case was the handwritten inscription 'With thanks for a wonderful day at *Test Match Special*. Kind regards, Ratty.'

I took this idea one stage further with Jeremy Coney in New Zealand. It was an unusual arrangement, in that Jeremy and Bryan Waddle, my colleagues on New Zealand's *Radio Sport* programme, interviewed a celebrity or former cricketer during the tea break, live on New Zealand television. Jeremy had leaned on me throughout the trip for inside information about the English guests he interviewed, and the final interview of the trip was to be with John Snow, the former

England fast bowler. As usual, Jeremy sought me out and tapped me up for any titbits he could use. I gave him the usual background about John: he is a vicar's son, keen on poetry, a self-confessed rebel – and has raised thousands of pounds for charity by free-fall parachute jumping from 10,000 feet. 'But,' I cautioned, 'he's very coy about his charity work, and doesn't like to talk about it, so don't mention it until you're on air.'

Jeremy scurried off delighted, and as he and Bryan introduced Snow at the start of the tea break, we all crammed into the television commentary box to watch. Sure enough, about five minutes in, Jeremy changed the subject. 'I know,' he said gently, 'that you're very shy about your charity work, but that you've raised a lot of money over the years. Perhaps you can tell the viewers how you've done that.'

'I'm sorry,' replied a surprised Snow, 'I'm not with you.'

'You know. All those free-fall parachute jumps from 10,000 feet,' prompted Jeremy.

'I reckon you've been wound up by Aggers,' chuckled Snow as the camera switched to show a stony-faced Coney.

Flushed with success, I repeated the free-fall parachute prank on Graeme Fowler, another of our summarisers, who was preparing to interview the World Cup-winning footballer Nobby Stiles. So delighted was Fowler by this additional information, which had arrived by a most authentic-looking fax, that he was unable to contain himself, and let it slip out on air before the interview. No one was more surprised than Nobby, who was listening to the radio on his way to Old Trafford at the time, and almost drove off the road.

Timing is always important. On one occasion Johnners was busy describing the presentation ceremony at the end of a Test at Edgbaston, and could not find the sheet of paper that the sponsors, Cornhill Insurance, always gave us with the running order and the names of the dignitaries who were lining up on the podium. That was because I had doctored it. The name of the general manager of Cornhill Insurance, Cecil Burrows, had been carefully obscured with Tippex, a photocopy taken and a new name typed in the now empty space alongside his title. With Johnners frantically looking for the piece of paper, and, crucially, with no time for him to read it through first, I thrust it into his hand.

'So everyone is now ready for the presentation ceremony,' Johnners said with relief. 'Down there on the podium we have A.C. Smith, the Secretary of the Test and County Cricket Board, the man-of-the-match adjudicator, Fred Trueman, and' – he proceeded to read without a flicker – 'the General Manager of Cornhill Insurance, Hugh Jarce.'

With the rest of us in stitches, and the Australian commentator Neville Oliver absolutely doubled up in hysterics, Johnners continued breezily with the presentations, blissfully unaware of what he had said.

In the early 1990s the commentary box seemed to be full of litter. Letters, faxes, notes and discarded newspapers lay all over the place. It was a paper culture, with every instruction from Peter Baxter being neatly jotted down on a Post-it if he had time, or hurriedly scribbled on the first sheet of paper he could find if it was urgent. There was paper everywhere, and Peter had to tidy it all away every evening. The commentators were all well drilled at reading out whatever was put in front of them. With spoof messages doing the rounds on a regular basis, Johnners and, when he returned to the fold, Blowers, started to handle letters, faxes and instructions as gingerly as if they were unexploded grenades. It was often impossible to detect a hoax, because even then, in the very early days of laptops, I could sit innocently in the box behind them and create a perfect letter-heading with fancy fonts, under which anything at all could be written. I could then fax it straight from the laptop to the printer about a yard away. All I had to do was keep a straight face and pretend I was typing an article or something. It was cutting-edge technology for those days, and completely beyond the understanding of the majority of my colleagues on *Test Match Special*, who would happily admit to being technological dinosaurs, and who consequently found themselves regularly outsmarted.

The wind-ups could be very simple, and purely for our own amusement. One fax to Henry Blofeld arrived at Old Trafford, supposedly sent by Roger, a bored office worker in the Kellogg's building which stands outside the ground, at the Warwick Road end. 'Please read this out, Blowers,' it said, 'and I will wave to you from my window.' 'Well absolutely, my dear old thing,' said Henry, and duly obliged. Then, peering vaguely into the distance towards Manchester, he said: 'Oh, look, I can see Roger waving back!' The listeners would have been entirely unaware that Roger did not exist, let alone was waving happily at Henry, but it gave us all a good chuckle.

One of my favourite spoofs again involved Blowers, who initially at least really did read out anything that was placed in front of him without checking it first. Peter became increasingly worried about this, and tried to prevent it from happening, so the trick was to wait until he was called away from the box on the telephone, or for some other reason, and then strike.

On one such occasion another fax arrived, this time with a perfectly crafted letterhead from Stephenson's Carpets Ltd, Sheffield.

> *Dear Mr Blofeld,*
>
> *We are all listening to Test Match Special at work and think you are the best commentator in the world.* [This was to guarantee it would be read out.] *If you give us a mention, we will send you a free carpet.* [Equally effective.]
>
> *Best wishes from us all at Stephenson's Carpets.*

Blowers was delighted, and gave everyone at Stephenson's Carpets the most generous and effusive of greetings from us all at *TMS*, before settling back in his chair to continue commentating, at the same time happily anticipating good news about a replacement for his sitting-room carpet.

It did not take long before the fax machine whirred into life again, and I pressed another sheet of paper into Henry's hand. This one was from Jones's Carpets Ltd, also in Sheffield.

Dear Mr Blofeld,

We are appalled at the entirely gratuitous advert you gave to our keenest local competitor on your programme this morning. If you do not redress the balance and broadcast that we, in fact, produce the best carpets in Sheffield, I shall report you to the Director General of the BBC.

Yours sincerely, Robert Jones, Jones's Carpets Ltd

There was a long pause after Henry read this out. He was mortified, and in his panic he got himself in a terrible tangle, floundering around desperately as he tried to rectify the situation. Behind him we were all in stitches. He never did receive his carpet. Funny, that.

Sometimes, even if Johnners rumbled a plot, he would go along with it anyway. Perhaps the cricket was rather dull and things needed livening up a little, or he just wanted to involve the audience in some commentary-box high jinks. 'Here's a letter from The Laurels,' he started once, with a tremendous flourish, 'Cherry Tree Avenue, Diss in Norfolk. It's a very interesting question about the LBW law. In comes Such, and he bowls, and it's pushed away to mid-off for no run. Anyway' – delivered entirely innocently – 'thank you very much indeed for your letter, Mr Biggun . . .' (much background hilarity).

Peter Baxter's role in all of this was very interesting. Clearly, as the producer of the programme, he was ultimately responsible for what was broadcast on *Test Match Special*, but in reality that takes some doing. The producer has no control whatsoever over what is said by the commentators, or indeed, by anybody who has a live microphone in front of their mouths. He might not be in the commentary box for some of the time, let alone keeping tabs on what is going on and being said. Often it is the responsibility of the commentator to take control of the situation, as happened when I was joined for the first time by the former great Australian fast bowler Jeff Thomson. Thommo's terrifying reputation with a ball in his hand was matched only by that of his prowess as a habitual swearer, so it was with a measure of anxiety that I introduced him to our Radio 4 audience.

Within five minutes he had slipped out two 'bastards' and a 'bugger'. By his standards he was probably showing admirable restraint, but this could not continue, and I had a terrible sweat on, dreading him opening his mouth for fear of what might come out next. Thankfully we were due a Shipping Forecast, so I handed the British audience back to the studio, remembering that we were still on air throughout Australia. It is not easy to admonish a colleague for swearing while broadcasting at the same time, especially when that person does not regard the words in question as remotely objectionable, and routinely uses them in almost every sentence.

Carefully, I tried to get the message across in my commentary to Australia by reminding Thommo that his countryfolk are perhaps a little more relaxed about the use of strong language on the radio than we old traditionalists in the Mother Country, and when *Test Match Special* returned, a chastened Thommo proceeded to behave impeccably.

Peter trusted us not to do anything that might damage the programme, and that element is essential to the production of *Test Match Special*, which is so fluid that it is unlike anything else on radio. There is no script and no preparation for what drama might unfold during the day; what happens on air is determined by events on the field. The commentators must have the freedom to express themselves without feeling that they are being in any way constrained or monitored, and in effect we produce the output as we go along. Peter did grow to recognise the tell-tale signs that something was being planned. Bumble and I might be caught whispering in a corner, or huddled over my laptop. Peter would raise his eyes and groan, 'Oh, no. What are you two up to now?'

He was worried that Blowers, in particular, might read literally anything out on air, and indeed he did once come within a whisker of blurting out a word that, in broadcasting terms, is a career-finisher when we were sent an alternative Shipping Forecast which included subtle changes to the names of the regions. It was created by Andrew Crawford, one of our continuity announcers on Radio 4, who must have been bored in the studio at the time, and who wrote the version with his cunningly altered names underneath the original. He faxed his offering across to us at The Oval, and somehow it ended up in Henry's hands.

I deliberately covered up the new names with my finger until Blowers was about to read them, which he did with increasing enthusiasm as he realised what was going on. Crawford cleverly lured him in with a couple of harmless ones such as 'North Utsire' becoming 'North of Shilpa' – named after Shilpa Patel, our assistant producer. Blowers laughed when I revealed that 'South Utsire' had become 'South of Shilpa', and on he went, with my finger firmly concealing each alteration, until he reached Rockall. Somehow a sixth sense prompted Peter to leap spectacularly across the box and snatch the piece of paper just in time. '*Fu . . . oh my dear old thing!*'

Peter was always happy as long as things were reasonably controlled, and he enjoyed a classic wind-up as much as anybody. He maintains that he was entirely innocent in another Johnston/Agnew *faux pas* which occurred at Old Trafford in 1992, although he played a crucial part in it.

Peter was coming under a lot of pressure to put Johnners and me on air together again. But now that I was a commentator rather than a summariser, there were far fewer opportunities, because the structure of the programme means that two commentators rarely broadcast simultaneously. The Leg Over was still fresh in listeners' memories, and a constant stream of letters demonstrated how much they wanted to reunite the double act, in the hope, no doubt, of further broadcasting disasters. Although, thanks to Brian's remark about Javed Miandad, we had failed to get through the end-of-play summary in the first Test at Lord's earlier in the summer, he and I were keen to show that we really could work together after all. We approached Peter and told him that we were ready to give it a go, and that this time we would not let him down. After some consideration he decided that we could team up for the 'Listeners' Letters' spot during one tea break. Surely, he must have thought, nothing can go wrong answering a few harmless letters for fifteen minutes.

It went so well for fourteen of those fifteen minutes. Johnners behaved himself impeccably, and only very rarely did we make eye contact, for fear of making the other laugh. When I saw that the umpires were on their way down the pavilion steps to start the final session of the day, I suggested that we answer one final letter. This was the moment at which either a crucial weakness in the system of deciding which letter was chosen to be read out on air was exposed, or Peter mischievously selected a particular one. Whichever it was, the result was the same, in that the commentator had to read the letters out on air without having had a chance to scan through them first. As I suggested to Brian that we should squeeze one more in, Peter – in all innocence, he insists – handed me the letter he had chosen, and I started to read it out.

'Gentlemen,' it began, 'can you explain why in the game of cricket an appeals procedure is necessary or justifiable?' The letter went on to make the point that excessive, histrionic appealing by fielding teams was leading to bad behaviour on the pitch and that if an umpire just gave batsmen out, without the necessity for an appeal, it would quieten things down a bit. Actually, it was not a bad point.

As I reached the end of the letter, I glanced down at the correspondent's name and did a double take; there was absolutely no way I could read it out without collapsing in gales of laughter. I could feel a giggle brewing, and said, 'It's from Berkshire,' before chuckling loudly.

Johnners could detect that I had a problem. Rather than taking the safety-first approach and letting it go, he said: 'Give it here.' This was fatal, because all the listeners now knew that he had the letter in his hands, and would have to read out the name of the sender. I handed it over to him, fearing the worst.

Immediately, Brian looked at the name at the bottom of the page. His reaction was identical to that of a year ago when I suggested that Ian Botham had been unable to get his leg over. He seemed stunned for about a second and a half, in which his face turned puce and he blinked furiously as his eyes began to water. He took a deep breath. 'It's not from the Prime Minister, William Pitt,' he declared determinedly. 'This is from William H. Titt, and he says . . .' That was it.

Johnners buried his face in his hands, and together we sat there, rocking in mirth, until Trevor moved in with a mild rebuke.

'The umpires are coming out,' he said sternly. All you can hear then is Johnners laughing as, helpless, he had to be helped to a chair behind us.

When order was restored, Brian felt rather bad about the incident, and decided that he ought to write to Mr Titt and apologise for having laughed at his name. This he duly did, although he never received a reply. We can only hope that Mr Titt did not hear it.

Not all of our mistakes are the result of carefully hatched plans; many are entirely innocent, an inevitable result of live and unscripted broadcasting. I was on air with Johnners on one occasion at Edgbaston when he produced a letter from the small selection he would sift from his vast pile of correspondence and take to the microphone to read out on the air.

'Here's a letter all the way from Baghdad, Aggers,' he announced. 'Comes from a Mr Richter, who says he loves listening to *Test Match Special* on the BBC World Service as it keeps him in touch with home. Well, Mr Richter, many thanks for dropping us a line. It must be absolutely lovely in Baghdad at this time of year; nice and hot, with all the flowers coming out and so on . . .' Something did not feel right to me, and while Johnners kept rambling on about the joys of Baghdad, the name Richter definitely rang an alarm bell.

Everything became clear the following day when, to his great embarrassment, Brian received a letter from an organisation called the Friends of Ian Richter, which explained that this unfortunate man – a British chemical engineer – had served five years of a life sentence which had been handed down to him on an entirely trumped-up charge of paying illegal commissions to a former Mayor of Baghdad. A tiny short-wave radio was the only concession he had been allowed in all of that time, and that was how, locked up in his tiny cell, he was able to listen to *Test Match Special*. What an emotional and bewildering experience that must have been for him: to be transported home for a few short hours by such a quintessentially English radio programme, and yet in reality to be deprived of his freedom for so long. Brian hastily apologised to Mr Richter, who was released later that year by the Iraqi government in exchange for the unblocking of funds which had been frozen in London following Iraq's invasion of Kuwait. The following summer he was one of Brian's guests on 'A View from the Boundary', in which he described in moving detail his experiences in prison, including listening to *Test Match Special* in those dire circumstances. He confirmed that he had heard Brian read his letter out on the air, and the apology that followed.

If anything sums up Brian's seemingly tireless appetite for fun and games, it is the summer of 1993, his final cricket season. He died the following January, but in his eighty-second year he showed that he could be as playful as ever, and that his love of a practical joke was undiminished.

Test Match Special was being shunted around the airwaves. Radio 3 medium wave, our traditional spot, was now home to a commercial pop station, and after a controversial season on Radio 3 FM, which caused uproar amongst lovers of classical music, we were on the move again. The commercial station Classic FM was to be launched in the very near future, and as a test transmission was broadcasting birdsong on its frequency during the summer of 1992. This was the subject of many newspaper stories and general comment, and Johnners even mentioned on *TMS* once that he had been listening to the birdsong, much to the fury of the BBC management, who were worried about the impact Classic FM would have on Radio 3. Brian's *faux pas* hardly helped *TMS*'s cause, and the following year we found ourselves on the newly created BBC Radio 5.

These were the early days of Radio 5, before it had acquired the 'Live' element of its title following a relaunch. Its original brief was rather confusing, in that it included children's programmes. I once had to interrupt one such programme, *Wiggly Park*, which was gently narrated by Andrew Sachs every morning and featured stories about some animals who lived on a threatened plot of land. Thanks to some terrible timing, England lost the final of the 1992 World Cup in Melbourne right in the middle of an episode of *Wiggly Park*, and I had to break into the programme to report the cricket news, knowing that if I had any audience at all, its average age would have been no more than six.

Radio 5 also carried educational material alongside its sport output, and while the station was a far cry from the twenty-four-hour rolling news giant that it is today, it was definitely aimed at a younger audience than we had previously been used to on *Test Match Special*. For the first time, *TMS* acquired a signature tune at the beginning of the programme. BBC television was broadcasting live cricket at the time, and 'Soul Limbo', the catchy theme tune by Booker T and the MGs, definitely belonged to them. It was only some years after BBC lost the rights to the television coverage that I suggested to Peter Baxter that we should adopt 'Soul Limbo' on *Test Match Special*. Peter needed a little persuasion, but it is now very much part of the furniture, and 'Soul Limbo's' association with cricket is recognised the world over.

The theme tune chosen by BBC Radio 5 for their launch of *Test Match Special* in 1993, however, was neither catchy nor remotely associated with cricket. Loud and jangling, I suppose it would pass muster on a football or a general sports programme, but it was far too brash for something as genteel as *Test Match Special*. Worse still, after the initial crashing and banging introduction, there was an eight-second window in which the music was dipped to allow a 'tease'; this was usually a reminder of the state of the game, and involved speaking very quickly, disc-jockey style, without pausing for breath. After eight seconds you stopped talking, the music picked up again and continued on its raucous way until you started the broadcast. Thinking back, whoever thought this was the way to start *TMS* every morning must have been bonkers.

It was obvious to Peter, who certainly was not in favour of this new development, that the only person in our team remotely young enough to get away with the tease was me. It would have sounded crazy had Johnners or even Christopher Martin-Jenkins popped up on the radio attempting a Chris Moyles-style voice-over to this pop music, so every morning I had to be in position early to practise the introduction, including the tease, before doing the real thing live.

Johnners always thought this was hilarious, and my early attempts were made to the accompaniment of his ridiculous hunting horn '*whoop whoops*' in the background. I soldiered on, ignoring his attempts to put me off, but it got to the stage where I was becoming increasingly self-conscious about the whole thing. This was particularly the case when it came to writing the words to fit precisely into the eight-second gap. Johnners always took huge delight in taking the mickey about my choice of phrase, or the punchy sentence I thought appropriate for the dreadfully corny music. Even though I tried several different ways to get him out of the box when I was about to perform, he made sure he never missed a single opening of the programme.

The only day we did not have to start with the dreaded music was Sunday, not on any religious grounds, but because rather than going on air at 10.30 as we did every other day, the preceding programme finished bang on eleven o'clock. Had we played the music, we would have missed at least the first delivery of the day, and possibly a wicket, so we started 'dry', saying: 'Good morning, everyone, and welcome to Edgbaston . . .' just as we always used to do. Johnners had not yet twigged that there was no theme music on Sundays.

I hatched my plot at Headingley, where the fourth Test of the series against Australia was being played. By this time I felt badly in need of exacting some revenge for Johnners' merciless leg-pulling. It needed Peter's cooperation, as most of the wind-ups did, and when I explained my ruse to him he was delighted. The outline of the plan was to tell Brian at 10.15 on Sunday that I had been held up in traffic on the M1, having nipped home to Leicestershire for the night, and that he would have to stand in for me. He would have only fifteen minutes to write his tease, practise it, and then get *Test Match Special* on the air. Our engineers were also in on the act, because they had to record the signature tune from the studio in London on the Saturday afternoon to replay it when Johnners was in the hot seat the following morning. Peter's job was to give Brian as rough a time as possible over the timing of the tease and his choice of words – while appearing to be giving him every possible assistance, of course

– and then to con him that he was going live and doing it for real. That done, I would appear at the door of the commentary box.

I arrived at Headingley in plenty of time on the Sunday morning, but kept myself well out of sight until Peter broke the bad news to Brian and the plan swung into action. The engineers' room at Leeds was separated from the commentary box by two doors and a walkway, so I sat with them and listened as everything clicked into place.

England's situation in the game was hopeless, which made Brian's phrase in the eight-second window even more ridiculous than it sounded.

'Still 458 runs behind, and thirteen wickets in hand: can England force a draw?'

Peter was directing operations through Brian's headphones, and made him go over and over it again.

'That was a second too long,' he chided.

'A what?' shrieked Johnners, aware that the clock was ticking quickly to the moment he believed *Test Match Special* was due to go on air.

On the tape of the incident there are some tremendous snorts and chuckles from Frindall, who had no idea what was going on, and there is one take in which Johnners collapses in a classic corpse. Then he had to go live; or so he thought.

'I'm a one-take man,' he announced.

For Brian's original words to fit an eight-second burst they had been subbed down, but they would still have to delivered at a furious speed: 'Still 458 runs behind with two days to go, can England force a draw?' He hit the mark more or less perfectly, but it had made him sweat. When I made my grand entrance, throwing the door to the commentary box wide and applauding, Johnners realised he had been well and truly fooled, and roared with laughter.

To have put one over such an experienced broadcaster as Johnners, it needed to be a good hit, but typically I got far too cocky, and went around Headingley telling everybody I could find. This included our near neighbours in the BBC television commentary box. Time and again I regaled Richie Benaud and Tony Lewis with the story of how

Johnners had been conned, and while they both found it very entertaining, I was far too pleased with myself to notice that privately they were all agreed that I badly needed bringing down to earth.

I gather that the BBC TV floor manager, Steve Pierson, played a big part in what happened next. His job was to organise each day's live shoots by liaising with the director about the lighting, camera positions and where the presenter and his guests would either stand or sit. When the cricket was actually being played, Steve had some down time, and being as mischievous as anybody, he was able to put a plan together. Meanwhile, I had spent the time before the start of the next match at Edgbaston assembling a short feature on women's cricket for *Grandstand* on BBC 1. It was shown on the Saturday before the Test started, and proved quite popular. So although visits from Keith McKenzie, the overall director of BBC TV's cricket coverage, were unusual, I was not terribly surprised the following Saturday morning when he dropped in to the box and asked me to do an interview for *Grandstand* during the lunch interval that day. The subject would be the lack of English fast bowlers – an all-too familiar topic. I spent much of the morning researching and preparing for my big opportunity. This was, after all, a great chance for me to show the television bosses what I could do, and who knew where it might lead?

The location for my shoot was the usual BBC TV outside position on the roof of the Edgbaston pavilion. Exposed to the elements, it is not a glamorous spot, but it was where Tony Lewis and Peter West before him had presented the BBC television coverage for years. The crew, including cameramen, a sound man, an assistant or two and Steve Pierson, had already gathered when I made the hazardous climb up a network of ladders to the temporary site amongst some scaffolding. I was to have two guests with me: Jack Bannister, who was a regular television commentator in those days, and Fred Trueman, who arrived out of breath and smoking a massive cigar. There was smoke blowing all over the place.

This was to be recorded 'as live' for *Grandstand*, which meant it was to all intents and purposes live, the idea being that the viewers would have no idea that it was pre-recorded. That meant it had to be done in one take, and had to be perfect, because there was no time to edit out mistakes. Everyone was bustling about in preparation. Steve put an earpiece in my left ear; when I later saw the tape, I realised it was a huge, cork-like object which protruded at least an inch out of my ear at a wild angle, and looked ridiculous. Keith McKenzie's voice crackled into my ear. It was the first time I had worked with him, and he sounded very strict indeed.

'He's shining up!' I heard him bark. 'Get some powder on his face!'

Steve stepped forward with a make-up kit, and liberally plastered my face with foundation powder.

'With all that make-up on, I'll kiss 'im,' I heard Fred mutter to Jack before another thick cloud of cigar smoke blew straight into my face.

Keith counted me in, and after a short introduction to camera I posed the first question to Fred: 'Why aren't there any fast bowlers any more.'

'I don't know,' Fred replied. 'If I knew the answer I wouldn't be here talking to you, would I?'

I turned to Jack, who paused for what seemed like an eternity.

'I agree with Fred,' he said finally.

And on it went for an absolutely agonising ten minutes, with McKenzie yelling so loudly into my ear at times that I could not hear what anyone was saying. Fred, his hair blowing wildly in the wind and puffing his cigar, talked about salmon fishing and then damp-proof courses, while Jack said absolutely nothing at all. 'This is dreadful!' shouted Keith in my earpiece.

It was about halfway through that I suspected something was wrong and that I had been set up, but there was no way I could take the risk and stop the recording. Apart from Jack and Fred, everything else was as it should be. It all sounded so realistic in my ear, and the monitor in front of me was showing several different camera shots. Fred's cigar went out and, on screen, he produced his lighter and fired it up again. Jack, being an old pro, was listening through his earpiece to Keith shouting at me, and deliberately stopped one of his rambling answers when he knew I could only hear Keith, and had no idea what Jack had been talking about. The agonising pause, as I flounder vaguely about, looks dreadful on the tape. Finally, to my huge relief, the one-minute count to the end of the interview began in my ear and I was able to thank my guests and, feeling completely worn out, say goodbye.

As soon as I felt it was safe to do so, I started to demand who had set me up. Jack began laughing, but there was silence in my earpiece.

'Set-up?' said Fred. 'That wasn't a set-up.' (There is some suspicion that Fred, who had been a late replacement for Bob Willis, did not actually know what he was involved in, and may in fact have been taking it seriously throughout.)

Eventually I heard a familiar voice in my ear: 'I think the veteran long-nosed commentator has got his revenge.'

'You bastard, Johnston!' was all I could shout in response.

Many of the staff working on the BBC television outside broadcast that day had given up their lunch break to enable Johnners to pull off one of the great set-ups. I am not sure they would have done so for anybody else.

Now it was Brian's opportunity to bask in glory. Humiliated, I clambered back down the ladders and into what I hoped would be the haven of our commentary box, only to discover that everyone had been watching it in there. Richie Benaud, chuckling away next door, described it in typically Australian terms as 'a ripper', and Johnners received a hero's reception when he returned from the car park, where he had been sitting in the director's lorry alongside Keith McKenzie. I had to congratulate him on a brilliant wind-up.

That evening, as I left the ground and walked through the players' car park, Graham Gooch hailed me. 'Blimey, Aggers,' he said, 'what was going on at lunch with you on the telly?'

It turned out that the whole ghastly episode had also been beamed straight into the England and Australian dressing rooms. It took me weeks to live it down.

SIX

Not Cricket

With his conversational style and natural ability to communicate, Brian Johnston was instrumental in broadening *Test Match Special*'s appeal when he joined the programme full-time in 1970. His recent sacking from the television commentary box had caused much rancour, and some personal embarrassment too, because he remained BBC cricket correspondent until he retired from the position on his sixtieth birthday in 1972. He was succeeded in that role by Christopher Martin-Jenkins, but since Johnners remained as the presenter of *TMS* – the front man, if you like – for the next twenty-one years, and had been involved with cricket for so long, his views on the game continued to carry great weight.

On *Test Match Special* all usually appears to be well with the world whatever the scoreboard might say to the contrary, and through cheerful banter and gentle leg-pulling we commentators do our best to convey the pleasures of watching and talking about cricket. Therefore it can come as quite a shock for listeners suddenly to hear the correspondent adopt a serious or outspoken position on a pressing cricketing issue. Some do not like it at all, and make their feelings strongly known by letter or, these days, email. But while *Test Match Special* prides itself on its *bonhomie* and good companionship, sometimes subjects do arise that are more important even than the quality of Mrs Arbuthnot's lemon drizzle cake.

The role of correspondent has changed over the years, and now involves many additional demands. There are more radio stations, including the rolling news of Radio 5 Live, and there is also the twenty-four-hour BBC News Channel on television to service, as well as writing for the BBC website. I have a broadcasting circuit in my home, which means I can simply plug my headphones into a magic box and instantly appear on virtually any radio station in the world. It is all a far cry even from my early days in the job, when I would have to drive to the nearest local BBC Radio station and book a studio, and it certainly makes it more palatable to appear on early-morning breakfast radio. This is usually dealt with while I am still in my dressing gown and slippers, which might make one or two people think next time they hear me on the *Today* programme. The downside, of course, is that I am always on call, and am sometimes expected to broadcast almost instantly. This can often result in my sounding rather rushed when first put on air.

A good example of this was when the news broke of Andrew Flintoff's latest knee injury, which he sustained while playing in South Africa shortly before the Ashes summer of 2009. I was enjoying a quiet lunch in the pub next door when my mobile phone rang. It was the BBC sports room in London, telling me that I was to be on air in ten minutes to give my reaction. I ran home and charged upstairs to my office. Having plugged in my equipment, I had about three minutes in which to compose my thoughts. To my horror, I suffered a spectacular senior moment when I realised that I could not remember which knee Flintoff had previously been troubled with. To be fair, the situation was complicated by the fact that he also had regular problems with his left ankle, but I needed to know if he had suffered a new injury to a different knee, or a recurrence of an old injury, which would probably be more serious and might even jeopardise his prospects of appearing in the Ashes. I was saved by Twitter, which just happened to be running on my office computer.

For those not in the know, Twitter is a relatively new means of interactive communication which is incredibly fast, by which your followers receive your brief messages – limited to 140 characters – on their computers or mobile telephones, and can respond to them. At the time I had a loyal band of approximately 25,000 followers, and I hammered out a quick missive:

'Help! About to go on air. Which is Flintoff's dodgy knee?'

In no time my computer screen was filled with hundreds of replies, almost all of which stated that it was his right knee. It was, I suppose, the Twitter equivalent of 'Ask the Audience' in *Who Wants to be a Millionaire?* I had no alternative but to go with the majority. Of course, they turned out to be correct.

While the demands have changed over the years, the role and responsibilities of the BBC cricket correspondent are largely the same as when the job was first created for Brian in 1963. Very basically, these include reporting and commentating on England's matches both home and away, covering some county cricket (which, with the packed international calendar these days is all but impossible), and being available to report news developments, deaths and so on. In all of these things the BBC correspondent has to be impartial. While that is open to interpretation, I take it to mean that, from a cricketing perspective, you have to be fair to both teams, and always to give both points of view. It is worth noting, however, that sports correspondents operate to a different set of rules from our colleagues in news, in that we are encouraged to give an opinion on matters affecting our particular sport. After all, it would be impossible to comment on a team selection, for example, if we were not able to pass judgement on inclusions and exclusions. It is valid for me to suggest, for example, that Jones is lucky to keep his place in the team while Smith is very unfortunate to be overlooked once again, and I can certainly speculate about the positions of the captain or the coach, particularly if the team is performing badly. A BBC journalist reporting on the political scene has no such freedom, and must maintain a more rigorous neutrality.

Everyone who has held the position of cricket correspondent has done the job differently, but it interested me how personally involved Brian appeared to become while dealing with two of the biggest issues to affect cricket when he had the role. I am certain that I would not be allowed to show my colours now in the way he appeared to do as correspondent when the issue of South Africa's continued participation in Test cricket came to a head in the late 1960s. Ten years later, Brian found that he had considerably more support from his peers than he had over South Africa when he condemned the Kerry Packer affair, which seriously threatened to split world cricket.

I was much too young to understand South African politics, and the debate that raged in Britain when the crisis over Basil D'Oliveira's selection for the winter tour in 1968 focused the minds of many in this country on apartheid. My first clue about Brian's position on the matter came from Peter Baxter. It was the summer of 1994, only a few months after Brian had died in January, and the South African cricket team was touring England for the first time since 1965. Peter asked me who I would like to interview in 'A View from the Boundary', and without a moment's hesitation I told him it should be Peter Hain.

Now a senior Labour politician, Hain was raised in South Africa. His parents were anti-apartheid activists, for which they were made 'banned persons' and jailed. Persistently harassed by the police, the family left South Africa and settled in England in 1966. In no time, Hain was one of the leading figures in the British anti-apartheid movement, becoming chairman of the Stop the Tour campaign, which focused on the South African rugby tour in 1969, and was instrumental in bringing about the cancellation of the cricket tour in 1970.

I had interviewed him on a number of occasions both before and after the South Africans returned to world cricket in 1991, and knew he had a fascinating story to tell. For instance, in order to disrupt the proposed Lord's Test of 1970 his movement had rented a flat overlooking the ground, and amongst other things, planned to dive-bomb the players with radio-controlled planes. It seemed to me that he was absolutely the right man to invite to Lord's to watch the multi-racial South African team that he had campaigned for so vigorously.

I think Peter was rather surprised by my choice, but he quickly saw the merit in it. 'I'll tell you what, though,' he said. 'There's no way we could have had Hain in the *TMS* box had Johnners still been alive.' He explained that, like many others who wanted to maintain sporting contact with South Africa, in the belief that gentle persuasion rather than confrontation would be the most effective method of bringing about the dismantling of its abhorrent political system, Brian could not forgive Hain for the very active role he played in the cancellation of the 1970 tour.

I was recently told a remarkable story by one of cricket's great survivors, South Africa's former captain and leading administrator, Dr Ali Bacher, which underlines how strongly Brian believed that Test cricket should continue to be played between the two countries. With no cricket scheduled for England in the winter of 1969–70 (can you believe that these days?), Bacher told me that Brian was invited to commentate on the series in South Africa, who were playing host to Australia. Brian was to be the 'neutral' commentator on the South African Broadcasting Corporation, and the BBC gave him permission to go.

At the same time, the South African rugby team, the Springboks, were touring the United Kingdom amid great political tension. After repeated pitch invasions in the early matches, most of the games had to be played behind barbed wire, and there were mass protests which often descended into violence. It was the first time such scenes had been seen on British television, and this had the effect of increasing the general public's awareness of apartheid and the growing opposition to it.

In South Africa, meanwhile, the cricketers were watching anxiously, because they were due to tour England in the summer. The rugby tour had been a disaster both on the field, where the Springboks won only one of their four Test matches, and off it because of the refusal of the captain, Dawie de Villiers, to be drawn into commenting on the politics of his country. He was regularly bombarded with what became an increasingly familiar question: 'How can normal sport be played in an abnormal society?' He was unwilling to give an answer in public.

In March 1970, while the fourth and final Test between South Africa and Australia was being played in Port Elizabeth, Brian received an extraordinary invitation. It was just a matter of a few weeks before

South Africa were due to depart for their tour of England, and Ali Bacher was a very worried man. He had seen how badly de Villiers had fared with the British press, and he knew that, as captain, he would be the man in the firing line when his team got to England. So he asked Brian and the *Daily Telegraph* correspondent Michael Melford, who was also keeping himself busy during a blank winter by reporting on the series, to meet him and his vice captain, Eddie Barlow, in a hotel room one evening after play had finished for the day. The plan was for the two English correspondents to prepare them for the reception they could expect from the media that summer.

It conjures up an astonishing image – these were highly unusual times, after all – but Brian and Melford created a mock press conference in the hotel room. In turn, they fired an array of hostile and politically charged questions at Bacher and Barlow of the type that de Villiers had failed to cope with on the rugby tour. 'Johnners was helping us,' Bacher told me. 'He really wanted our tour that summer to take place.'

Interestingly, Brian wrote about that 1969–70 series between South Africa and Australia in some detail in his autobiography, including his delight at watching what he regarded as the finest batting partnership he had ever seen, when Barry Richards scored 140 and Graeme Pollock 274 in the second Test in Durban, but he does not mention that evening he spent with the South African captain and vice captain in Port Elizabeth. That does strike me as strange unless, possibly, he thought in hindsight that he ought not to have been there. It is worth noting, however, that he makes his views on South Africa very clear: 'I am one of those people who do not think that politics should interfere with sport . . . but I definitely do not support apartheid and the way it inflicts unnecessary indignities and restrictions on black and coloured people.'

In 1982, in a heated open debate between members of the MCC at Central Hall in Westminster, Brian argued passionately that the England team should be allowed to tour South Africa. This was a controversial stance, bearing in mind the existence of the Gleneagles Agreement, which had been unanimously approved by the Commonwealth countries in 1977, to discourage sporting contact with South Africa. The proposed tour did not take place.

When Peter Hain arrived at Lord's for his interview with me three years after South Africa had been welcomed back into the cricketing fraternity, the various reactions to his presence in the box from members of the *Test Match Special* team were fascinating, and certainly made Peter Baxter's cautionary words to me ring very true. I introduced him to Trevor Bailey, who without a word turned his back on him, and refused to acknowledge his presence, let alone speak to him, during the whole of his visit. It was pretty obvious that Trevor had been of the same view as Brian, and even twenty-five years later he could not bring himself to forgive the man they dubbed 'Hain the Pain'.

I thought Trevor got it wrong that day, not least because there is no doubt that depriving South Africa of the sporting contact it craved was a crucial element in the eventual bringing down of the apartheid system. It is not a policy that would suit every situation: a sporting boycott of its neighbour Zimbabwe, for instance, would not have the slightest impact on the oppressive regime there, because sport is not an important part in the everyday life of ordinary Zimbabweans. But Hain, with his strong South African connections, knew where to hit and hurt the influential white minority in his former country. The strategy, and the ugly scenes on rugby fields during the 1969–70 Springbok tour, offended many people. Ultimately, though, it worked to the benefit of millions of underprivileged South Africans, and it seemed rather sad to me that it should not be accepted and appreciated for its success, even by those who had opposed the boycott at the time. Trevor's response did, however, give me a glimpse into how deeply divided opinion had been about how best to deal with the South African situation at the time. Neither he nor Brian supported apartheid in any way, shape or form, but they believed that by keeping the channels of communication open by playing sport, a resolution might be found more easily than through disruptive and sometimes violent confrontation in and around British sports grounds.

Trevor's reaction was in stark contrast to that of another of our expert summarisers that day. Barry Richards had every right to feel bitterness and enmity towards Hain, because his international career was ruined by the sporting boycott that was imposed on South Africa, at first informally through the threat of protest, and then by the Gleneagles Agreement. One of the greatest batsmen the game has ever seen, Richards was probably the biggest loser when South Africa was condemned to the cricketing wilderness. He made his debut in the first of the four Tests against Australia that Johnners watched in 1970, scored 508 runs at an average of 72 in the series before the curtain was brought down on his career. By his own admission, Richards was frustrated: he described himself to me as 'an angry young man', and it took a long time for him to accept his lot. To add to the irony of the situation at Lord's, Richards was one of Hain's cricketing heroes. Following Trevor's very obvious rebuttal, Hain was understandably tentative when he offered Barry his hand as I introduced them.

'We've never met,' said Peter.

'No, we haven't,' replied Barry. Then, referring to Peter's prolific anti-apartheid campaign, he added, 'But I must have received hundreds of letters from you over the years.'

The ice was broken, and probably the most unlikely pair of spectators at Lord's that day stood in the commentary box and talked about South African cricket until it was time for Peter to give his lunchtime interview. It was precisely the outcome I had hoped for, and one very good reason why I had felt that Hain was the right person to be there. Later, Hain told me that during the course of their conversation Richards told him that while he had been very angry at the time, he now recognised that the boycott of South African sport had been the best course of action. My respect for Barry Richards soared that day.

It was a significant Test for another reason, too, as I discovered for the first time the difficulty of combining a chatty *Test Match Special* persona with the serious role of a correspondent dealing with a major news story. This was the match most remembered now, I suppose, for the 'Dirt in the Pocket' incident. Mike Atherton, England's young captain, was captured on television apparently rubbing soil from his trouser pocket on the ball. Some of us believed that this was intended to assist his bowlers in finding some reverse swing in hot and difficult conditions, and was against the laws of cricket. It was one of those sagas that blow up from nowhere, and in those days, long before the England and Wales Cricket Board took a firm grip on its handling of the media, it developed at an alarming rate. At one point Atherton was pushed into a crowded and broiling hot press conference at Lord's to explain himself, with none of us present – Atherton included – being aware that the event was being broadcast live on television.

It was a complicated story to explain to listeners. Reverse swing and ball-tampering was a particularly hot potato at the time, and the British media had been very keen to prove that Pakistan's fast bowlers Waqar Younis and Wasim Akram were masters of tampering with the ball, probably by scratching it. The climate of suspicion partly influenced me when I said on air that Atherton had been caught and, being captain, should resign. I was determined to show impartiality, and I do not regret expressing that opinion. Perhaps naïvely, I had not expected the reaction it provoked from some sections of the media, and from a not insignificant number of listeners to *Test Match Special.* They much preferred Aggers the practical joker to Jonathan Agnew, the cricket correspondent who was suggesting that England's popular and fresh-faced young captain had been caught breaking the laws and should fall on his sword.

I then made the mistake of becoming personally attached to the story. In one broadcast, in which I was trying to justify my opinion, I referred to my friendship with Atherton. My intention was to demonstrate that I was not waging some sort of personal campaign against him. But not only was the word 'friendship' inaccurate – we had a very good working relationship at the time, but nothing more – my personal relationship with Atherton was irrelevant. It provoked more fury from some listeners, who now took the view that I was stabbing a friend in the back.

Members of the press fell out with each other spectacularly as battle lines were drawn over the affair, and some of those scars remain in the press box today. It was a lesson to me that you should never express any personal feelings when covering a news story. At the same time, it was the moment *Test Match Special* listeners realised that their cricket correspondent has more to do than commentate and write silly spoof letters from Ivor Biggun. After an understandably tricky period in the aftermath, Mike and I are fine now, and I have great admiration for the way he has forged a very successful career as chief cricket correspondent for *The Times*. I do sometimes wonder how he might have covered the story had he been in our camp in 1994, but it is a subject we have never talked about. A young and inexperienced captain and a not quite so young, but equally inexperienced correspondent both learned lessons from Dirt in the Pocket.

Perhaps the best way to understand the impact of Kerry Packer's Circus, as it became known, in the late 1970s is to imagine a breakaway Indian Twenty20 League buying up the best cricketers in the world to play on a rival television network at the same time as Test cricket is being staged, and those players being banned from representing their countries in any form of the game. That, incidentally, is something that could actually happen, and is one of the main concerns facing cricket's administrators. One crucial difference between that possible course of events and Packer's World Series Cricket (WSC) in 1977 is the amount of money international cricketers earn these days. Packer was able to use the players' dissatisfaction to his advantage, and his supporters would claim, with some justice, that all professional cricketers, whether signed up by him or not, saw their earnings improve significantly as a result of the rebellion he brought about. A pirate league today would require immense financial backing to entice all the best cricketers away from Test cricket as Packer was able to do.

The right to televise cricket in Australia was at the heart of the Packer affair. The Australian Cricket Board had only ever dealt with the ABC, the Australian equivalent of the BBC, before Packer, who owned the commercial Channel 9, made an offer in 1976 of AU$1.5 million for TV rights. This was eight times the value of the previous contract, yet Packer was rebuffed in favour of the ABC, which offered just $210,000 over three years. Convinced that he was up against an 'old boy' network, Packer decided to set up his own cricket tournaments, and broadcast them exclusively on Channel 9. He signed up an Australian and a West Indies team, both of which consisted almost entirely of the first-choice players for their countries, and a Rest of the World team including six England players, as well as players from Pakistan and New Zealand, and also South Africans who, given that they were barred from international cricket, could hardly be blamed for seizing the opportunity WSC gave them. They played a series of unofficial Tests called 'Super Tests', as well as one-day matches, which were played for the first time under floodlights. Richie Benaud, who Packer shrewdly signed as a consultant, drew up the rules for each competition.

I was in Melbourne playing club cricket during the second year of WSC, and watched a one-day match at VFL Park, an Australian rules football stadium on the edge of the city. Clive Lloyd, the captain of the West Indies team, remembered me from my first-class debut against Lancashire a few months before, and invited me into their dressing room, where he introduced me to Michael Holding, Viv Richards and Andy Roberts, none of whom looked terribly chuffed to be wearing their coral-pink WSC outfits.

Live, the cricket did not seem up to much. The floodlighting was poor, the playing area was the wrong shape, the players were rightly suspicious of the temporary drop-in pitch, and there were very few spectators present. But I can vouch for just how exciting, brash and aggressive it appeared on television. The introduction of floodlights meant that for the first time cricket could be shown at peak viewing time, and the many innovations such as white balls, coloured clothes and fielding restrictions generated great entertainment. Pitch microphones brought every sledge straight into your living room, and there is little doubt that, despite the camp West Indian uniform, WSC traded on being macho and brutal. Traditionalists would not have admitted to liking it much, but it was thrilling for a youngster just starting out in the game.

However, World Series Cricket was clearly a very serious threat to the fabric and the structure of the international game. In England, whose captain, the South African-born Tony Greig, had emerged as being one of Packer's principal recruiting agents, there was understandable outrage and condemnation. Greig was stripped of the captaincy, but continued to play for England against the 1977 Australian tourists, of whom thirteen of the seventeen-man squad had signed up for the first series of World Series Cricket the following winter. That news had broken almost as soon as the Australians arrived for the start of their tour.

At the end of the Ashes series, which England won 3–0, it was announced by the English administration, the Test and County Cricket Board (TCCB) and the International Cricket Conference (ICC, now the International Cricket Council) that any cricketer who played World Series Cricket faced a ban from both international and county cricket. Three Packer players, Greig, John Snow and the South African Mike Proctor, who was employed by Gloucestershire CCC, took the authorities to the High Court, and against all expectations the rebels won their case. However, the counties reached agreement amongst themselves that the six English players who had signed for Packer – Alan Knott, Derek Underwood and Bob Woolmer from Kent, Warwickshire's Denis Amiss, and Snow and Greig from Sussex – would not be resigned for the 1978 season, it being their right to decide who they employed or not.

What a story all of this must have been to report on. Christopher Martin-Jenkins was the BBC cricket correspondent at the time, but Brian Johnston regularly voiced his outrage at World Series Cricket from his position in the *Test Match Special* commentary box. He was absolutely outraged when, in July 1978, Kent announced that it would employ its three WSC cricketers for the following season after all. This was a major change of heart, and broke the agreement between the counties. Johnners showed his fury at what he considered to be this betrayal by resigning his membership of Kent CCC on the spot and returning his club tie. He argued in an article in the October issue of *The Cricketer* magazine that Kent had been wrong to put its own interests ahead of those of England.

The Professional Cricketers' Association, which represents all international and county cricketers in England and Wales, had an important role to play, and under the presidency of John Arlott held some very lively meetings at Edgbaston cricket ground. A flavour of the atmosphere during the crisis, and of the strength of feeling against the World Series Cricketers even from their own colleagues, can be gained from two of the proposals that were tabled and recorded by Jack Bannister, the secretary of the PCA at the time.

> *Members of the Cricketers' Association will only play Test cricket with or against players not contracted to professional cricket outside the jurisdiction of the ICC and the TCCB.*
>
> *Proposed by Mike Hendrick. Seconded by Ian Botham.*

> *Members of the Cricketers' Association will not play first-class cricket or one-day cricket against any touring side which includes players contracted to professional cricket outside the jurisdiction of the ICC and the TCCB.*
>
> *Proposed by Bob Taylor. Seconded by Mike Gatting.*

I attended a meeting in 1979, when negotiations between the various parties were nearing a critical phase. This was the only time I ever encountered Arlott. He sat at a long table on a specially erected stage in one of Edgbaston's conference halls, and spoke very deliberately – and sometimes humorously – into the microphone with his distinctive throaty voice. Every word he uttered commanded the utmost respect from the packed room. Only nineteen years old, and attending my first players' meeting, it was a great experience for me to glimpse some of England's leading cricketers in the flesh for the first time. But what most struck me was the level of anger aimed at Tony Greig. Many of those present felt he should never have been captain of England in the first place, because of his strong South

African connections, and after having been given the position aspired to by every professional in the room, they felt he had badly let down English cricket. The honour of representing England was the ultimate ambition of everyone gathered at Edgbaston, and I for one have always hated seeing sportsmen misusing the privilege of playing for their country, or in any way taking it for granted or treating it lightly. The vilification of Greig was balanced, though, by his not unreasonable argument that cricketers as a whole needed to be paid more, especially honest county pros, many of whom earned less than the national average wage. World Series Cricket, we all hoped, would be a wake-up call to the game's administrators.

Kent's decision, which had riled Johnners so, proved to be the start of a painful process towards reconciliation between the two sides. England toured Australia later that year, with both teams deprived of their WSC cricketers, who were involved in their series in the same country at the same time. Packer gave a demonstration of his political clout by persuading the Premier of New South Wales, Neville Wran, to overturn the ban on WSC using grounds that were affiliated to the ACB, which gave him access to the prized Sydney Cricket Ground. A crowd of nearly 45,000 turned up to watch a match between Australia and the West Indies there, while a few days later the *bona fide* Australian team – essentially a second XI – were thumped by England in the first Ashes Test in Brisbane.

Johnners commentated on the radio during that series, and always took the opportunity firmly to bat for the traditionalists when it came to any conversation involving the Packer crisis. So passionate were the arguments on either side, particularly during that tour, when Test cricket and World Series Cricket were vying directly against each other, that even long-established friendships were threatened. This included Brian's relationship with Richie Benaud, with whom he had been the greatest of friends for years. In fact, when the crisis first blew up, Brian told Benaud never to raise the subject in his presence. Years later, Richie told me a wonderful tale from that tour involving Johnners, World Series Cricket and a lost tie, and while researching this book I sent him an email asking him for brief details of the story. I should have known that Richie – always the most fastidious and organised of men – would send me a beautifully detailed reply.

Dear Aggers

It took me a while to find the whole story, but I think this is as close as we will get.

When Brian used to come to Australia each year he was pleased when asked by various people, 'What is that tie?' It was always a club tie, and it was the only one he carried, and it was a bright blue background with cricket motifs, not as many as on the Johnners tie which exists today. He lost the tie in Australia in 1978–79 and complained about the loss at great length, mainly on the basis that at least you would expect things to be safe 'Down Under'.

After hearing a dozen or so complaints along those lines, John MacKinnon [an old friend of Brian's from the Sydney social set] *thought he would help, so he took his blue World Series Cricket tie off his tie rack, wrapped it carefully in a large envelope and sent it via a courier – Test player John Hampshire, who was returning to England having played a season with Tasmania in the Sheffield Shield. The note in the envelope said that MacKinners had found the missing tie, and emphasised the importance of Johnners acknowledging receipt since so much trouble had been taken in locating the thing. So Johnners duly wrote saying:*

1. *It wasn't in fact the missing tie but*
2. *This tie was very nice indeed and*
3. *He would happily wear it at his next visit to Lord's.*

When he wore it at the meeting no one paid much attention except John Woodcock [the *Times* cricket correspondent], *who recognised the logo and blasted BJ for wearing anything as gross as that, particularly at Lord's. Brian was very, very annoyed.*

MacKinnon was about to arrive in London, and was staying with the Johnstons, as he often did when they were living at Hamilton Terrace, not far from Lord's. When he arrived early in the evening the usual 'Care for a glass of wine?' was missing. Johnners said frostily,

'Bedroom on the third floor.' When MacKinners climbed the three flights of stairs with his luggage, there in front of the bedroom door was a round ball of cloth. Observing it more closely, MacKinnon saw it was a tie, knotted tightly a dozen times to form a clump, and soggy because it had been soaked in water.

When he went down the stairs he walked into the living room, smiled and said to Johnners: 'Brilliant.' Brian smiled broadly and said, 'Thank you very much; care for a glass of wine . . .?'

Richie

England won the Ashes series 5–1, which was far too much for the Australian public to bear. That, as well as financial necessity and common sense, helped drive the ACB into proper negotiations with WSC. Finally peace broke out the following summer, with Packer's Channel 9 successfully negotiating a ten-year broadcasting deal and the rebel players returning to the fold.

So entrenched were the views of those closely involved with the crisis at the time that men like Johnners and Jim Swanton always steadfastly refused to acknowledge any benefits that derived from World Series Cricket, although undoubtedly there were a number. Night cricket, fielding restrictions, a whole new approach to television coverage and more money for the players are all Packer's legacy, even if his means to bring them about were divisive and caused great bitterness.

Kerry Packer himself described his intervention as 'half-philanthropic', which is an expression that certainly could not be used to describe Allen Stanford, a Texan financier whose controversial recent association with cricket was likened by some to that of Packer.

It was with horror that in June 2008 I reported on the announcement of England's deal with Stanford. Less than a year later, he was arrested by the FBI and charged with fraud 'on a massive scale'. But it was not Stanford's alleged financial impropriety, which he denies, that angered me when his helicopter landed at Lord's that day, because we did not know about it. Instead, what was appalling was the concept of playing a cricket match for twenty million dollars – £12.27 million at the time – winner takes all. This seemed to me an absolute obscenity, trampling grotesquely over every tradition and principle that set cricket apart from other sports. It bewildered me that the administrators at the England and Wales Cricket Board who negotiated this hideous proposal with Stanford failed to appreciate and understand that. I wonder what they think now of the photographs that show them all gathered around the vast perspex case which supposedly housed the $20 million on offer. In their determination to demonstrate that they did not need to be in the same camp as the Indians, who had launched their exciting Twenty20 Premier League, they made a dreadful misjudgement.

England's cricketers might have been excited by the possibility of becoming millionaires overnight, but when they arrived in Antigua for the Stanford week at the end of the 2008 season, they quickly woke up to the fact that they were in a ghastly no-win situation. Stanford wandered in and out of their dressing room when he felt like it, and paraded around his pretty private ground, which lies barely a six hit from Antigua airport, with his own television cameraman in tow. During one of the early floodlit matches, play stopped as his grinning face appeared on the giant screen, which beamed the picture to the crowd like a drive-in movie. Sitting on his lap was England wicketkeeper Matt Prior's pregnant wife, and Stanford had his arm around two other young women who were attached to England cricketers. Out on the field, the players turned and watched the screen in disbelief. They were starting to realise what can happen when you sell your soul – or in their case, it is sold on your behalf.

Then there was the question of the match against the 'Stanford Superstars', a West Indian team led by Chris Gayle, with the prize of $20 million to the winner. How would England respond in the field if they won? The players held a four-hour meeting in their hotel to discuss the issue, because they now realised how greedy and tacky it would appear on television at home if they celebrated extravagantly. In the end they need not have bothered, because, disillusioned, distracted and angry, England were thrashed by ten wickets in a cringingly awful match. Stanford and the ECB got the finale they deserved, and later on Radio 5 Live I received calls from listeners that definitely made that phone-in unique: the majority of England supporters who spoke to me that night had genuinely wanted England to lose.

Johnners and many others might have hated what Packer stood for, but having held cricket to ransom, some good did emerge from World Series Cricket in the end. The only remotely positive outcome from the Stanford débâcle was the stern reminder it gave of what cricket stands for. It is a great shame that our administrators were in need of it.

The BBC is very sensitive to criticism, and guards its reputation for neutrality and accuracy very rigorously, so decisions that are made apparently well over our heads in the news department can have an impact even on the way we report cricket. One outcome of the Hutton Inquiry, which was set up in 2003 to investigate allegations of the 'sexing up' of the 'Dodgy Dossier' before the invasion of Iraq has been that before a story can be broadcast by the BBC it needs to be verified by two independent sources. On the one hand this sounds like a sensible check and balance, but on the other it makes breaking news – which is a journalist's basic instinct – virtually impossible. In May 2007 Sir Ian Blair, the Commissioner of the Metropolitan Police, told me that it would shortly be announced that the investigation by his force into the mysterious death during the World Cup the previous month of the Pakistan coach and former England cricketer Bob Woolmer, would categorically rule out foul play, and find that he died from natural causes. The Jamaican Police Force had originally stated that Woolmer had been murdered sometime during the night following Pakistan's unexpected defeat to Ireland, causing all manner of speculation in the media about who might have been responsible. The suspects ranged from underworld bookmakers to a disgruntled fan. Even the Pakistan players found themselves embroiled in the febrile atmosphere of suspicion and rumour-mongering, with

Mark Shields, Jamaica's Deputy Police Commissioner, declaring provocatively: 'It's too early to clear anyone, including the Pakistan team.' Sir Ian's tip-off, therefore, was very big news. But he gave it to me on the strict condition that it was off the record. Since it would be impossible for me to find the necessary two independent sources to give me the information *on* the record in order to comply with the BBC's strict guidelines, I could not run the story. Frustratingly, it appeared as an exclusive on the front page of the *Daily Mail* two weeks later.

Even the incident in which Jonathan Ross and Russell Brand left lewd messages on the actor Andrew Sachs's answer phone has had an impact on the way we work. Previously, Geoffrey Boycott and I would record a podcast for the BBC website every evening after play had finished for the day. But now, unless we contrive to broadcast it live as part of *Test Match Special* – which rather defeats the object, as potential listeners to the podcast might therefore have already heard it – it can only be recorded if the producer is present in the commentary box with us. He has to listen to every word, and then sign it off before it can go up on the website. Given that there are a million and one things for the producer to do at the end of play, this is terribly frustrating, besides giving the impression that two experienced broadcasters cannot be trusted to discuss a day at the cricket without being monitored.

News and opinion drive sports broadcasts as much as the scoreline, and for all the word games, pranks and *double entendres* that helped to get Johnners through a day of commentary, he cared passionately about the game. He hated negative tactics – he simply could not understand the point of making cricket boring and unattractive. This may in part have been a legacy of playing in his younger days for the sort of amateur clubs that Fred Trueman would dismiss as 'jazz hats', which seem to believe that the brighter the stripes on the players' caps and blazers, the better. Certainly none are more striking than those of one of Brian's favourite teams, the nomadic and definitely upper-crust I Zingari, whose colours are black, red and gold. There would have been no trace of hard-nosed professionalism in any game of cricket that Johnners played in his life, so he had great difficulty appreciating the steely approach that is often crucial to success in Test cricket. It is difficult to imagine that much sledging goes on in matches involving I Zingari even today, and certainly there would never have been any when Brian turned out for them. Although he loved the battle between fast bowler and batsman, he disliked aggression and nastiness on the field. For Brian, cricket had to be fun, and played in the right spirit, with batsmen being applauded politely to the crease and then walking if they edged the ball and were caught. The umpire's decision was final, and never to be challenged. Naturally it was disappointing to lose, but it was not the end of the world.

It was Brian's deep sense of the way the game should be played that roused him to produce one of the most stirring pieces of broadcasting I have ever heard. Combining his outrage at what was taking place on the field in front of him with his brilliant powers of description, Brian dispelled any thoughts that he was no more than a gentle and kindly old man. He was passionate, angry and compelling.

The reason for Brian's indignation was an incident involving the captain of the 1992 Pakistan touring team, Javed Miandad, and one of his young fast bowlers, Aaqib Javed. Their behaviour at Old Trafford on the fourth day of the third Test in that series rivalled that of the England captain Mike Gatting in the infamous row with the Pakistani umpire Shakoor Rana five years before, which all but severed cricketing relations between the two countries. This was the first England–Pakistan Test series since then, and it was already ill-tempered, with England suspecting ball-tampering by the great Pakistan pace bowlers Waqar Younis and Wasim Akram, who were making the ball reverse swing to an extent never seen before. For their part, the Pakistan team had feared that they would be hijacked by biased umpiring (this was in the days before the introduction of neutral umpires) and persecuted by a hostile British media.

It did not help when the Test and County Cricket Board decided to drop John Holder from the umpires' panel for the series. Holder was trusted by the Pakistanis, while the man who replaced him, Roy

Palmer, is the brother of Ken Palmer, whose umpiring Pakistan had officially complained about on their previous visit to England. Roy Palmer was a long-standing and popular official on the county circuit, and his integrity, in my experience, was beyond scrutiny. But Pakistan viewed his appointment at Old Trafford as inflammatory. It was also his first Test.

So there was a lot going on in the background as Johnners settled down for his final commentary stint of the day at the Stretford end of Old Trafford. Pakistan had scored 505 for 9 declared in their first innings, and when England slipped to 256 for 7, still needing 50 runs to avoid the follow-on, Pakistan were hopeful of winning the Test. But they were denied by Chris Lewis, Ian Salisbury and Tim Munton, all of whom batted bravely, and by the time the number 11, Devon Malcolm, strode out to bat the game was heading for a tame draw. Pakistan had given their all, but were now tired and exasperated. They wanted to get off the field.

Malcolm at his best was a fiery fast bowler, but only when he took to the charity circuit after his retirement was he, like me, anything but an absolute rabbit with the bat. When he arrived at the crease he was met by a volley of bouncers from nineteen-year-old Aaqib, who was volatile at the best of times, and now appeared to be wound up by his captain, Miandad, who was fielding at first slip. Malcolm did not handle this aggressive bowling very well, and eventually Roy Palmer, having already had a quiet word with the bowler, officially warned him for intimidatory bowling. Aaqib remonstrated with Palmer, and bowled another bouncer, which was called no-ball. However, the delivery was not called for being intimidatory: replays showed that Aaqib had delivered the ball from a substantial margin over the popping crease. In other words, he had shortened the length of the pitch, and thus increased his chances of hitting Malcolm. Other than the deliberate bowling of a beamer, running through the crease, as it is known, is just about the worst example of sportsmanship in cricket; especially when the target is a number 11.

It was definitely getting nasty out in the middle, and after Aaqib fired off yet another short ball to finish the over, Roy Palmer shook his head and made to give him his sweater, which was tucked into the belt of his white umpire's coat. Unfortunately, it needed an extra tug to release it, and with the bristling Aaqib waiting close by, the sweater made firm contact with his midriff as Palmer thrust it in his direction. Aaqib lost his temper, claiming that the umpire had shown disrespect by throwing the sweater at him, and Javed came running up from slip to join in what was becoming a furious row.

Johnners was describing the scene on *Test Match Special* on Radio 3, and just as an angry Pakistan fan invaded the pitch, pursued by members of the security staff, Radio 5 joined the commentary for a news update of forty seconds. This is supposed to be a general recap of the day's events and is difficult enough even for someone accustomed to broadcasting in soundbites, which all of us are who appear regularly on Radio 5 Live. For an eighty-year-old man with precious little experience of condensing his reports into such a short burst, to do so seamlessly while commentating on a rapidly developing and highly charged incident at the same time would have been quite a challenge. It was even more difficult because for at least a minute beforehand, Brian would have heard Radio 5's output in his headphones – usually consisting of a series of football score flashes – before the presenter handed over to him. That is always very off-putting.

So the timing of Radio 5's arrival could not have been worse, with Brian commentating on *Test Match Special* while listening out for his cue from Radio 5. But he put on a quite magnificent performance. He set out exactly what was happening in front of him, including the invading supporter who was bearing down on the umpire: 'Look out, Roy Palmer. Behind you!' I remember him saying with real urgency, which added great drama to the scene for those who could not see it for themselves. 'This is absolutely disgraceful,' he continued, before giving Radio 5 listeners a brief résumé of the match situation and finishing bang on forty seconds on the stopwatch. It could not have been done any better, and demonstrated tremendous broadcasting discipline and skill when it really mattered. With the clock ticking away, he had only one chance to get it right. He might have given the impression of being a chortling old buffer, armed with a handful of chocolate cake, but whether in jocular mood or passionately serious, it was further evidence Johnners was the consummate natural broadcaster.

In the 1980s I began to combine playing for Leicestershire in the summer with broadcasting for Radio Leicester during the off-season. I hope my taste in clothes has improved a bit since then.

My first Test as a member of the *TMS* team, Headingley, June 1991. The smiles for the camera masked the tension in the commentary box caused by the imminent publication of Don Mosey's acrimonious book. Left to right: Bill Frindall, Christopher Martin-Jenkins, Don Mosey, Fred Trueman, Tony Cozier, Johnners, Trevor Bailey, JA, Vic Marks, Peter Baxter, Mike Selvey.

Fred Trueman holding court in characteristically trenchant style over dinner at the Swan Hotel, Bucklow Hill, in 1991. Left to right: David Lloyd, Mike Hendrick, Johnners, my mullet, Fred, CM-J.

Trying to relive the classic moment of the day before: 'Aggers, for goodness sake, stop it!', Johnners squeaked, as we posed after the Leg Over at The Oval in August 1991.

The incident itself. Ian Botham doesn't quite get his leg over.

Right The great cake tradition. Johnners gratefully accepts a listener's offering.

Below The Queen presented the *TMS* team, here represented by Peter Baxter, Henry Blofeld and CM-J, with a cake when she visited Lord's in the summer of 2001. 'Did you make bake it yourself, Ma'am?' I asked cheekily. 'Not personally, but specially,' she replied.

Left Our latest celebrity cake-maker: pop singer and Test-cricket lover Lily Allen with her boyfriend Sam Cooper and a raspberry sponge at Lord's in 2010. The reaction to my interview with Lily at The Oval the previous summer took us both by surprise.

Opposite Smiles all round from a selection of those who have appeared in the 'View from the Boundary' slot: Clockwise from top left: Eric Clapton, David Cameron, Russell Crowe, Sanjeev Bhaskar and Sam Mendes, Robin Gibb, Rolf Harris, Daniel Radcliffe (on his eighteenth birthday), Sir Tom Courtenay.

Brian with his family on his 75th birthday in June 1987. Back row (left to right): David Oldridge (son-in-law), Barry, Ian. Middle row: Andrew, Gilly (daughter-in-law) with Harry, Brian, Pauline, Clare, Joanna. Front row: Rupert, Nicholas.

Peter Baxter presents Johnners with a bronze bust to commemorate his eightieth birthday, at Broadcasting House in October 1992. Also in the picture are Trevor Bailey, JA and, far right, Mike Lewis, head of BBC Radio Sport, who appointed me cricket correspondent the previous year.

When the BBC was denied entry to the ground for the first Test against Sri Lanka at Galle in February 2001 because of a dispute over broadcasting rights, I took to the ramparts of the nearby Dutch Fort and commentated in the shade of my driver Simmons's umbrella.

A rare honour. Ringing the bell for the start of the fourth day's play of the first Test between England and Bangladesh at Lord's in May 2010. Shilpa Patel and Michael Vaughan find the whole thing most amusing.

Brian in his study at Boundary Road. Did he really keep a protective box amongst the china figurines on his table (bottom right), or was this a deliberately placed piece of Johnners mischief?

SEVEN

Noises Off

If the episode on the pavilion roof at Edgbaston with Jack Bannister and Fred Trueman taught me that it was unwise to take on the master of the practical joke, it was only one of a series of lessons and tips that I was busily picking up while working with Brian as a young and raw commentator. In fact he influenced me to such an extent that his eldest son, Barry, tells me he often detects similarities in our broadcasting styles when he listens to *Test Match Special* today. For me there can be no greater compliment than that, although I certainly never set out to model myself on Brian – indeed, as Henry Blofeld warned me before my first Test match, to have done so would have been catastrophic. Without actually sitting me down and giving me lessons, Brian taught me how to commentate and how to communicate, the two essential qualities that form the foundation of *Test Match Special* and which I believe set it apart from other sports programmes.

Peter Baxter's decision to introduce me to *TMS* as a summariser before I turned to commentary helped me enormously. I had the opportunity to work alongside Johnners initially, and to get a feel for his relaxed, warm and chatty relationship with the summariser. His conversations, which could touch on virtually any subject, were usually humorous and light, rarely the least bit serious. When my turn came to sit in his seat, this invaluable experience gave me the confidence to commentate with no nerves and with absolute freedom. Above all, the message has to be that cricket is fun, and that the commentary box is a friendly place. This style felt entirely natural to me, as did the lesson I had learned from Johnners that there was no need to feel restricted to talking purely about the cricket. (Mind you, when Henry Blofeld returned to *Test Match Special* in 1994, following his brief flirtation with television, we were reminded of the true meaning of a lack of constraint in cricket commentary. Never can there have been more sightings of buses and pigeons.) Brian's example liberated me, and I do not think I could commentate in any other way. Christopher Martin-Jenkins, by contrast, focuses more deeply on the game itself, with analytical precision and clear, unfussy description. A keen student of the game, Chris also provides historical perspective to our coverage, another element that contributes to a successfully balanced programme which appeals to the varied tastes of our listeners.

The first lesson Brian taught me related to preparation. My short stint on the *Today* newspaper had opened my eyes to the records and notes that my colleagues in the written media maintain, some with admirable fastidiousness. Sheets of graph paper cleverly Sellotaped together somehow open miraculously to form a massive chart, showing every innings and every bowling analysis of all the England players of the last ten years. It is painstaking work, and having been a cricketer who never paid much attention to his own figures, let alone anybody else's, I really could not be bothered to keep any records apart from the very basics. When I became BBC cricket correspondent I was concerned that without the safety net of other journalists sitting around me in the press box, who I could occasionally ask a statistical question or two, I would have to be much more rigorous in my preparation before every Test match. I also thought it would make me sound more knowledgeable on air if I broadcast lots of facts and figures. But in fact that is the role of the scorer, and his interjections and observations bring him into the programme, as well as saving me a lot of hard work. Everyone's a winner!

Early every season Brian would always go to the county ground at New Road, Worcester. This was not merely because, aesthetically, it is one of the most appealing grounds on the circuit, or even because these days you might find the Governor of the Bank of England, Mervyn King, catching a well-deserved forty winks in a deckchair beneath a tree on the boundary edge. Brian always went to watch what traditionally used to be the opening first-class match of the international season, featuring the touring team of that particular summer against the home county. Close to the players, and in an informal and relaxed atmosphere, it was the ideal venue for mugging up on the visiting cricketers you might not have seen before, and who you would shortly have to recognise from distance in the commentary box.

I would be reporting on the match for the sports desks on BBC Radio, and I always looked forward to the day that Brian came to join us. Armed with a scorecard and a sheet of paper on which to write notes, he would sit on the bench outside the press box and carefully watch the cricket. Between reports, I sat beside him, and quickly learned some of the tricks he had picked up after forty-five years in the trade.

'Always look for the way they walk, Aggers,' he would say. 'Everybody's walk is different.'

And that is so true. There are quick, bustling walkers like Alec Stewart, and slow, plodding walkers like Ashley Giles. Some players, like Angus Fraser, lope around in a lugubrious manner, while others roll their shoulders as they walk (Matthew Hoggard does both). There are vigorous arm-swingers, and others – Chris Gayle – who often walk with their hands in their pockets. Unless there is something obvious, such as sporting a sun hat when everyone else on the field is wearing a cap, the way a fielder walks is the easiest way to identify him. Also, if I have something of a fixation with cricketers' hair – and I am often told that I do – it is because Johnners always made notes about hair styles, which make identification from ninety yards away easier. He also took notice of who fielded where, because at this level of cricket fielders tend to be in specialist positions. If an Australian was standing at first slip at Worcester, he would probably be standing there in the first Test three weeks later. All this was good, basic groundwork which ensured that when Brian was on duty to describe the opening over of a new series, he had a pretty good idea who most of the visiting side's fielders were. It was sensible as well as professional, because there is nothing more terrifying than not recognising anybody out there: in one case, a colleague of mine who shall remain nameless did not know who was actually bowling as he delivered the first ball of a Test series.

The only time I know of that Brian was unable to see a touring team in action before the Test was in 1991, when the Sri Lankans came to England for a one-off game at Lord's after the West Indies had gone home. In fact, this would be my first Test as a commentator. Instead, Johnners accepted an invitation from the Sri Lankan High Commissioner to attend a drinks function with the team a few days before the match. The players formed up to greet the guests, including Brian, who went along the line making mental notes about the physical appearance of each one as he was introduced to him. Tall. Short. Big ears – the usual sort of thing. At the very end of the line, a young cricketer thrust out his right hand and introduced himself as K.I.W. Wijegunawardene. 'But,' he added hastily to reassure a startled Johnners, 'in Australia the commentators just call me Alphabet.'

'Well, I shall call you Weegers,' declared Johnners. And so he did, for the whole Test match.

Once he had completed his homework, that was it. Johnners would sit in the commentator's chair armed with nothing more than his scorecard, on which he would have scribbled a thought or two that might have struck him as he sat and waited his turn, and one or two letters from listeners. These were used as fillers if there was an interruption in play, or if there was a point that he wanted to raise during his twenty-minute stint. He had nothing in terms of reference books or statistics. At first I was amazed, but after a day or two, his reasons became apparent. This was Brian's way of getting Bill Frindall involved, and therefore expanding the cast list of *Test Match Special*, to develop his firmly held belief that the programme should sound as if we were nothing more than a few friends spending a day at the cricket. After all, if the commentator is going to sit and spout out all the facts and stats, there is no way the character of the scorer can be developed. And *TMS* is all about the different characters of those involved.

This relaxed and conversational approach to commentating, in which the listener is being chatted to – rather than spoken at, or worse still, lectured – encourages an informal atmosphere in which it is quite acceptable for the commentator not to appear to be an expert. He can ask questions, either of the scorer or of the summariser sitting beside him. He can stand corrected. He can make mistakes. And in doing so he comes across as a normal human being. Getting something wrong might seem to be the cardinal sin of commentating – and you certainly don't want to do it *too* often – but Johnners showed me that it is possible to get away with a mistake on air by acknowledging it easily and honestly and then breezily moving on without sounding flustered or unduly bothered about it. It requires a lot of confidence to do, and you have to be at the top of your game, but I think our listeners respect that approach. It is a different mindset to football, where the commentators arrive armed with reams of statistics, facts and figures which are pumped out routinely during the match. They do not have a statistician sitting with a microphone beside them, presumably because football is a faster game. There is also a noticeable competitive edge between the commentators themselves in football that does not exist in cricket, which can lead to a simple mistake becoming something close to humiliation. Cricket is played at a gentler pace, and the commentary needs to breathe. It cannot do so in a blizzard of prepared, and often rather dull, statistics.

In one glorious early-morning exchange, Johnners demonstrated his professional side as well as dropping a large hint that, now he was eighty, his days of the breakfast-time report from the ground were well and truly over. This early shift is very much the short straw of the broadcasting day, and used to be shared around the team more than it is today. Essentially, it requires you to be in position in the commentary box from about a quarter to eight in the morning in order to have a chat with Radio 5 Live and Radio 4's *Today* programme about the prospects for the day ahead. On this occasion the interviewer on Radio 4 was a keen and thrusting Garry Richardson, who first had a quick chat with Brian on the telephone in order to brief him before their slot.

'Morning, Brian. This is Garry Richardson.'

'Mmm?' replied Brian diffidently, his nose buried in the *Daily Telegraph*.

'Well, I'd like to talk with you about the weather, the pitch conditions and how you think the day will develop, all in two and a half minutes – if that's all right with you.'

'Mmm?'

'OK. Thanks. Talk to you on air in a couple of minutes.'

Having picked up his stopwatch and put on the headphones, Brian continued to read his newspaper as he waited for his live cue. When Garry welcomed him to *Today* with a breezy 'Good morning,' Brian started the watch, and spoke non-stop for exactly two and a half minutes. He barely drew breath while he comprehensively discussed all of Garry's chosen topics.

'Er, thanks, Brian,' Garry stuttered when the old boy finally stopped talking. 'I thought I might get at least one question in. Now, football . . .'

It was a triumph for the wily Johnston, who was never asked to do the early shift again.

Peter Baxter's gentle approach to production was another very important factor in establishing what has become the overall feel of *Test Match Special.* He was fortunate in that he was dealing predominately with experienced commentators who he could trust, and this made it easier for him to be hands-off and let them get on with what they did best. After getting the programme on air, Peter would potter about at the back of the commentary box, adjusting rotas and organising the forthcoming winter coverage, but with one ear firmly on what we were saying on the air, just in case. This created a welcoming and informal atmosphere that always put inexperienced broadcasters and guests at their ease, and also encouraged ribaldry and leg-pulling. Peter could have his moments, but I never saw him angered by anything that was actually said on air. Henry sailed close to the wind a couple of times with attempts at humour that, on reflection, he might rather not have broadcast, but on rare occasions like that Peter was very calm and clear in dealing with any complaints. Technical problems were a different matter, and while they are the bugbear of any producer, it was usually best to steer a wide berth when Peter was tackling a faulty line himself, or trying to communicate at a time of crisis with an engineer who could not speak English. (It was often quite amusing, though.)

These were very happy days which passed by all too quickly. Johnners was a prolific user of the telephone, and he would often ring me at home between Tests to discuss some cricketing issue or other. This might involve England's selection for the next game, or just a word of encouragement, and to make sure I was enjoying myself. He would also always call shortly before I left home for a long tour. Having served his time overseas as correspondent, Brian knew only too well the trauma attached to leaving a young family at home for up to four months at a time. The conversation would invariably end with one of his ridiculous '*whoop whoops!*'

After Don Mosey retired at the end of 1991, the atmosphere in the commentary box immediately relaxed, and everyone genuinely got on very well with each other. It was not often that the whole group socialised together in the evenings during Test matches, because for some it might be a home game, while others had favourite hotels in which they stayed year after year. The Swan at Bucklow Hill was often a meeting place during the Old Trafford Test, because it was a particular favourite of Brian's and the senior *TMS* brigade, while I preferred a hotel in Hale, a short distance away, which was where my friends in the media pack stayed. But sometimes we did all meet up for dinner, and with Fred Trueman and Johnners in full flow, the conversation was always about cricket and wonderfully entertaining, with Fred's pipe belching smoke across the table as Brian quietly wound him up.

Johnners: Now then, Fred, can you name England's five fastest bowlers since the war?

Fred: Well, there's me for a start . . .

Johnners (interrupting): Of course. My mistake, Fred. Make it the top six.

The evenings were always better for David Lloyd being there too, because he was – and still is – a brilliant mimic of Fred, and delighted in pulling his leg. As long as Fred remained cheerful, all was well, but there were times when he 'went off on one', often a rather ill-tempered rant about the standard of modern cricket. These arguments were usually started (entirely deliberately) by Bumble casually dropping into conversation something along the lines of how tired England's fast bowlers were these days. We would wait for the inevitable explosion. Fred's outbursts were often quite amusing to start with, but when he started hammering away at the number of overs he and Brian Statham used to rack up before the end of June, it was time to make one's excuses and head off to bed.

The highlight of the social calendar during the summer was the Johnstons' garden party, which always coincided with Brian's birthday and the Lord's Test. By the time I joined *Test Match Special* their home was in Boundary Road in St John's Wood, a short walk from Lord's. Sadly, because of the inexorable passage of time, the guest list was thinning out a bit when I arrived, but I have happy memories of swinging gently under the floral canopy on the sun lounger with Jim Swanton. The first, and probably second, impression of Jim was of a pompous, crusty old so-and-so. But he was the doyen of cricket writers, and a kindly man who helped many young commentators and journalists, including Christopher Martin-Jenkins and Scyld Berry, to get a foot on the ladder when they were starting out. Richie Benaud was always there, of course, with his wife Daphne, who used to work for Swanton, and Ted Dexter, with whom I love to talk cricket. Dexter was often ridiculed during his time as chairman of selectors for being vague and out of touch, but much of this was put on for effect: he is certainly no fool, and is a very keen thinker on the game. A dashing right-hand batsman, a wannabe politician who once stood in a general election against the former Prime Minister Jim Callaghan, and a pilot who flew a light aircraft to Australia at the start of an England tour, he is one of those players from the past who I would love to have seen bat. The guests were a mixed bunch who all shared a love of cricket and a love of Brian: comedian Leslie Crowther, television presenter Judith Chalmers, whose husband Neil Durden-Smith used to commentate on *Test Match Special*, and Robert Hudson, one of the pioneers of cricket coverage on the radio. Brian's daughter Joanna, who was born with Downs Syndrome and of whom he was most protective, would be there too, handing out drinks and excitedly showing off her latest paintings, several of which have been exhibited.

It was not until during my early years on *Test Match Special* that the true scope of the programme became clear to me. *TMS* is much more than just the radio commentary on a cricket match: it is more like a soap opera. Largely due to Brian's special knack of communication, every one of the millions of listeners who were tuned in felt individually involved and part of the programme. It was by tapping into this feeling of inclusiveness that Brian was able to promote blind cricket, a cause especially close to his heart and one that still has a special bond with *Test Match Special* today. You only have to watch a game of blind cricket to be absolutely amazed by what these determined cricketers can achieve – they often play an exhibition match during a lunch interval of a Test at Lord's. Brian was directly involved as President of Metro Blind Sport, a sports and social club for the visually impaired in London. But the main reason for his interest in blind cricket was the responsibility he felt to our blind and visually impaired listeners. It may seem obvious, but a radio cricket commentator has to describe the play in a way that paints a picture for someone who cannot see. Blind listeners depend on us entirely, and glossing over a delivery mid-conversation with the summariser really is not good enough. One such listener, Melvin Collins, put this relationship perfectly into words during Brian's memorial service in Westminster Abbey:

> *He was a friend to those who never knew him, eyes to those who cannot see, warmth to those who were alone and depressed.*
>
> *God bless you, 'Johnners' for being a friend to me, for being my eyes during Test matches and for bringing joy when life was on top of me.*

It was always Brian's golden rule of commentary: imagine you are commentating to a blind person. I once received a letter from a blind listener who gently pulled me up for a brief and incomplete description I had given of a straight drive for four. He made the point that if, as I had described it, the stroke was hit along the ground, and straight down the ground, the ball would have hit the stumps at the bowler's end. So, which side of the wicket did it pass? He was right, of course: I had described the stroke, but for the blind listener the picture froze as the ball was struck down the pitch, rather than continuing on its way to the boundary rope, just to the on side of straight. That final detail would have rounded off the commentary more satisfactorily not merely for blind listeners, but for anyone who was not at the ground. Thinking of the blind listener makes your commentary much more detailed for everybody.

Brian's interest in blind cricket started in the early 1970s, when he was commentating full time on *Test Match Special.* By meeting blind supporters at Test matches, and receiving letters from them in the commentary box, he became aware not merely of how many blind listeners tune in to *Test Match Special*, but of how much they love cricket and the programme, despite not being able to see. In many cases, having been blind from birth or an early age, they have never seen a game of cricket in their lives, yet despite that they are able to derive understanding and much enjoyment of it from the commentary. This led to Brian's unstinting support of the Primary Club, a charity which was set up in 1955 to provide sports facilities for the blind and partially sighted, but which only really came to prominence when Brian started talking about it on *Test Match Special.*

In its first nine years, the Primary Club mustered total donations of £45. When Johnners was in his pomp on *TMS*, it was raising close to £200,000 a year. Eligibility could not be simpler: anyone who has been dismissed first ball in any form of the game, from a Test match to a game of French cricket in the back garden is invited to apply. Has there ever been a cricketer who has never had a golden duck?

Peter Baxter gave me an example of just how committed Brian was to the Primary Club and blind cricket. The Appeals Unit at the BBC, which controls the promotion of charitable appeals throughout the corporation, once contacted Peter and informed him that under new rules, all mentions of the Primary Club on *Test Match Special* had to stop. Peter telephoned Brian, who naturally was horrified by the news, and told him to hang on: he would call the Director-General of the BBC, who at the time was Michael Checkland. Twenty minutes later, Peter's phone rang.

'Don't worry, Backers,' Brian announced triumphantly. 'I've sorted it.'

It became one of *Test Match Special*'s many traditions that the Saturday of every Test is dedicated to the Primary Club, and we are expected to wear our club ties. Details of membership are always broadcast, and we often rope in any new summariser or commentator who has not yet joined. Jeremy Coney, the former New Zealand captain and an outstanding broadcaster, stubbornly maintained that he had never been out first ball, and could not be persuaded to part with any of his cash. As the emails poured in from resourceful listeners citing several occasions on which Coney had in fact recorded golden ducks in his long career, he reluctantly signed up.

After Brian's death, his wife Pauline presented me with his Primary Club tie, complete with gravy stain, and she continues to oversee the Brian Johnston Memorial Trust, which, among other things, still supports blind cricket. The Trust supplies the England blind cricket team with its kit, which bears the logo of the Johnners Trust, a caricature of his face. He would be very proud.

The Champagne Moment is another element that Brian introduced to *Test Match Special*, and that continues to be a welcome distraction in the commentary box. This is an award given in recognition of a special moment during a match, such as a brilliant catch or a batsman reaching his century with a six. It began in 1988, when the manager of the Savoy Grill, who was clearly a cricket enthusiast, spotted Johnners dining there one night. The following year was the Savoy's centenary, and he approached Brian with the suggestion that the occasion might be marked with something connected to the Ashes series of 1989. After some discussion, the idea of celebrating a specific incident was born, with the winner receiving a bottle of Savoy house champagne.

The first winner was Merv Hughes, whose brilliantly disguised slower delivery which bamboozled and bowled Chris Broad set the tone of the award perfectly. But after that summer – and with the centenary well and truly celebrated, despite England's catastrophic 4–0 thrashing – the Savoy decided not to continue with the Champagne Moment. Happily, Veuve Clicquot decided that *Test Match Special*'s Champagne Moment would be an ideal means of increasing awareness of its brand. Veuve Clicquot has provided a magnum of champagne to every winner since then, despatching bottles to Australia, New Zealand, South Africa and throughout the Caribbean for us to deliver personally: a photograph of Shane Warne brandishing his magnum with a brilliant view of Sydney harbour behind him is one of my favourites.

I did not, however, dare to deliver the prize to Inzamam-ul-Haq for his dismissal at Headingley in 2006, in which he hilariously resembled a ballet-dancing elephant performing a pirouette as he tried to avoid falling on his stumps. He ended up sitting on his bottom next to a demolished wicket, but at least I resisted the temptation to repeat any comment about not getting his leg over. It took Inzy some time to appreciate the funny side, and so chastened and theatrically crestfallen was he that later in the day I described his sluggish movements in the field as resembling those of 'a large animal that has been shot in the buttock with a tranquiliser dart'.

The Champagne Moment has become very popular with the players, and it was my pleasant duty one summer at Lord's to present the wonderful Indian batsman Sachin Tendulkar with the award from the previous Test. As arranged, I met the photographer Patrick Eagar in front of the Pavilion to await Tendulkar as he walked back from the nets at the Nursery end before the start of play. Sachin duly wandered across the ground towards us carrying his bats and pads, so Pat and I organised ourselves for the quick presentation and a photograph with the Pavilion as a backdrop. Just as Sachin reached us, Roger Knight, the Chief Executive of MCC at the time, appeared and told us that on no account were we to take a photo so close to the Pavilion, as it would offend the members. With time ticking away until India was due to take the field, I looked helplessly at Sachin.

'Don't worry, Jonathan,' he said softly. 'We'll go to the other end and do it there.'

So Sachin Tendulkar, the most in-demand cricketer in the world, put his kit down on the grass and led us back across the pitch towards the Nursery end, where, with the Grandstand as backdrop, he happily posed for his photograph with the champagne. Then we all walked back again. Class.

The voting process for the Champagne Moment is not exactly high-tech: the nominations – which often include some very frivolous suggestions of incidents in the commentary box during the game – are jotted down on a piece of paper by the producer, and passed around the commentary team. Some nominations are so in-house that they are unsuitable for broadcast, which means keeping the list away from Henry Blofeld when he is on air, otherwise he would almost certainly blunder into reading them out by mistake. In turn, we scribble our initials beside the one we have chosen, and the one with the most scribbles wins. The decision is unanimous surprisingly often, but if there is a dispute we consider what we think Johnners would have preferred, and go with that. Indeed, the suggestion from one of our listeners after Johnners died that the Champagne Moment should be renamed the Brian Johnston Champagne Moment was adopted immediately. It captures perfectly the spirit in which Johnners enjoyed his cricket, and the spirit of *Test Match Special*.

Hopefully, by continuing to award the Champagne Moment, we will help those ideals to live on for years to come.

A tradition that I have now inherited from Brian is conducting the interviews for 'A View from the Boundary', which usually take place during lunch on the Saturday of every Test, although because people are so busy these days we have become more flexible. The interviews last for about half an hour, so while they are usually very entertaining, they can be quite a challenge, especially as the guests are often surprisingly nervous. In my experience that is particularly the case with actors, although not by any means all of them. Whenever possible the interviews are conducted live, which the guests prefer anyway, because it means they get to have a day at the cricket sitting in the *Test Match Special* box. That makes it a perfect arrangement, because we can entice celebrities onto the programme by offering them a day that most cricket-lovers would give their eye teeth for.

There have been notable exceptions to that rule, among whom was His Royal Highness Prince Philip the Duke of Edinburgh. Johnners was something of a favourite with the Duke, and he was also regularly invited to have lunch with the Queen Mother, so it was not difficult to persuade the Duke, who had twice been the President of MCC, to be interviewed by Brian in 1987, which was the club's bicentenary. The interview was recorded in Prince Philip's study at Buckingham Palace, and by all accounts went very well, with him happily talking about his love of cricket. A part-time off-spinner, he once proudly captured the wicket of Tom Graveney in a charity match at Arundel, although I suspect Graveney probably did his duty for Queen and country that day.

Thirteen years later, in 2000, I found myself in the same room in Buckingham Palace waiting to interview Prince Philip. This was the fiftieth anniversary of the Lord's Taverners, the well-known charity founded by some actors in the Lord's Tavern in 1950 which raises money to help disabled and disadvantaged children play sport, and cricket in particular. Prince Philip had been their Patron – or twelfth man, as he was known – since the very start, and it had been arranged by the BBC that I should interview him as part of a programme to celebrate the work of the Taverners for Radio 5 Live. We had been allocated half an hour of the Prince's time, and had been told to submit our ten questions in advance for his approval and, presumably, his preparation.

With a producer and a sound man, who set up the recording equipment, I waited in the Duke's office, the walls of which were entirely covered from floor to ceiling with bookshelves. There was a desk, and a couple of chairs and a sofa beside a table. It was nine o'clock in the morning – which meant I had been up very early to catch the six o'clock train from Leicester – and we were the Duke's first appointment of the day. The door opened, and I could hear a muttered conversation and a rustle of paper, which sounded like an adviser showing him our questions. At last the Duke, rather stooped, walked busily into his office. Brief introductions and perfunctory handshakes followed, and he motioned me to sit opposite him for the interview. As a means of providing a sound check for the engineer, I explained what the programme was all about, and we were ready to go. I read out the first question on the sheet, which from memory asked the Duke how he first became involved with the charity. He gave a rather vague reply, of no more than five seconds. A little flustered, I moved on to the next question, which was met by an equally brief response, and on we went. After a minute and a half it was all over; I had asked all ten questions. Glancing up from the sheet of paper, I saw my producer in the background, his shoulders heaving in silent mirth. With that the Duke rose from his chair, said goodbye and left the room as briskly as he had entered only moments earlier.

A little chastened, and armed with an unusable interview, the three of us walked through the gates of Buckingham Palace and headed to the nearest underground station, only to discover that it was closed because of a bomb scare, as was my line to St Pancras. It had been a frustrating yet, curiously, rather an amusing day.

I met the Duke again in 2009, at a dinner in London hosted by the CCPR, the alliance of governing and representative bodies of sport and recreation in the United Kingdom. Tim Lamb, the former head of the England and Wales Cricket Board, is the Chief Executive of the CCPR, and he introduced me to Prince Philip, who was attending his final dinner as President after fifty-eight years in the role.

'You'll know Jonathan, sir,' said Tim. 'He commentates on *Test Match Special* on the radio.'

'Never listen,' replied the Duke gruffly. 'They never give the score.'

As he moved away, all I could manage was a disappointingly obsequious 'Thank you, sir.'

I have only pre-recorded one 'View from the Boundary'. Sir Elton John was due to perform at an enormous charity event at Battersea, which was also part of Andrew Flintoff's Benefit year. Scarily, 'Freddie' was going to sing 'Rocket Man' in a duet with Elton as some form of grotesque finale and Shilpa Patel, our fixer, arranged for me to interview Elton before the guests arrived at the function. I was one of Elton John's keenest lifelong fans, so this was going to be nerve-racking as well as very exciting.

'Would you prefer to interview Elton on his piano stool on stage, or in his trailer?' was the first question put to me by his manager when we arrived. *Elton John's famous piano stool, or his fully furnished artic trailer? Are you serious?* What a choice. Naturally I asked to inspect the trailer – purely to check the quality of the soundproofing for our recording, you understand. It was like a hotel suite in there: lovely bedroom, bathroom en suite and a large lounge which had a massive plasma television screen attached to one wall. Having nosed around the trailer, I went for my preferred option, the piano stool.

Elton joined me on the stage as I sat at his stool beside the piano. I was surprised to notice that two prompt screens had been set up for him to read the lyrics to his songs as he performed. They were showing the first few lines of 'Your Song'. Don't we all know the words to 'Your Song', and haven't we all probably murdered it on drunken karaoke evenings? It suggested to me that Elton John is seriously professional, and leaves nothing to chance.

The interview was most revealing. Elton knew much more about cricket than I imagined, and when he referred to the current one-day series between West Indies and Zimbabwe – which he presumably watched on that massive plasma screen in the trailer – he showed a level of interest and devotion exceeding that of many diehards, and certainly mine. He talked about batting at Lord's in a charity match, and of the cover of his greatest hits album, on which he is dressed as a batsman in a perfectly coached stance, albeit in pink shoes. Typical in my experience of these interviews was his ardent preference of Test cricket over the shortened form of the game. My favourite quote of his was: 'Every musician I've ever known would like to be a sportsman, and every sportsman I've known wants to be a musician. They are both great levellers, and there is a feeling of togetherness; sport and music – more than anything – bring people together.'

It fell to Andrew Flintoff later that evening to remind us exactly why it is that no matter how desperately hard a sportsman *might* want to be a musician, a measure of skill and talent is also required. The less said about his rendition of 'Rocket Man', the better. I suppose the kindest observation would be that at least it raised some money for charity, as well as for his Benefit.

Mick Jagger is another famous musician whose interview was recorded, and broadcast the following week. This was unique, in that it was the only time *Test Match Special* summarisers and rock-music lovers Mike Selvey and Jeff Thomson conducted a 'View from the Boundary' interview. The venue was the Edgbaston office of Denis Amiss, who was then the Chief Executive of Warwickshire CCC. Meanwhile I was busy on air with Jane Rossington, who for many years played Jill Richardson in the daytime soap *Crossroads*. She is also a member of Warwickshire, and found herself putting in an extended stint with me, because the heavens opened during lunch. We chatted for more than an hour, and afterwards I escorted her to Warwickshire's indoor cricket school for a bite to eat, completing a table that even by *Test Match Special*'s standards was unusual: Jeff Thomson, Mick Jagger, Mike Selvey, Chris Jagger (Mick's brother, and a great cricket enthusiast), an open-mouthed Jane Rossington and me. What a shame we only had half an hour in which to listen to the Jagger brothers eagerly asking Thommo about his time as the most feared fast bowler in the world.

Brian Johnston could easily be persuaded to enter into a sing-song with his guests, although his repertoire tended to be restricted to 'Underneath the Arches', which he performed with both Roy Hudd and David Essex. Even so, that definitely confirms Johnners' place in the 'entertainer' category, and is certainly a step too far for me, although we have had some wonderful musicians to entertain us. There cannot be too many lead singers of punk rock bands who mention cricket on the first page of their autobiography, but Hugh Cornwell of the Stranglers is a confirmed addict of the game. Watching a Test match on television during the afternoon before a concert in 1990, a troubled Cornwell was trying to muster the courage to tell his colleagues that he wanted to leave the band. Like the rest of us, he was astonished to see Devon Malcolm, one of nature's number 11 batsmen, hitting a six, and decided there and then that if Malcolm, who was surrounded by predatory close fielders, could liberate himself by striking the ball over the boundary, he could do the same thing. He told his fellow members of the Stranglers of his decision that night. Armed with Mike Selvey's guitar, Hugh played 'Golden Brown', the iconic Stranglers song, live in the commentary box, providing the sort of challenge in mixing the sound that our engineers, who usually have to deal only with speech, always enjoy. They were also in their element at old Trafford in 2010 when Tom Chaplin, the lead singer of the pop group Keane, performed 'Somewhere Only We Know' so brilliantly that our colleagues from Sky TV and Channel 5 crowded into our commentary box and spilled over into the corridor outside to listen.

The opera singer Lesley Garrett was definitely in the mood for a good time when she arrived at Lord's for her 'View from the Boundary'. Her mum used to score for the local village team in South Yorkshire, so she was particularly keen to examine Bill Frindall's complicated scoresheets, and was thrilled to meet Geoffrey Boycott for the first time when he made one of his subtle, understated entrances to the box towards the end of the interval. Not surprisingly, Lesley has an impressively strong diaphragm, which she was keen to demonstrate, and to contrast with my own feeble frame by jabbing me with her outstretched fingers.

This was put in the shade by Rolf Harris's attempt to teach me circular breathing, the technique required to play the didgeridoo. But how do you blow air out of your mouth while sucking it in through your nose at the same time? Give it a go and you will see what I mean. It seems physically impossible, yet Rolf and Aboriginal musicians can not merely do it, but make it look ridiculously easy. His demonstration of the art on the balcony of the MCC President's box at Lord's made for brilliant radio.

Eric Clapton was finally lured into the commentary box after years of trying when Shilpa devised a cunning plan involving his friend Ian Botham and a vast number of pork pies, with which she would bribe Beefy whenever the *Test Match Special* delivery from my friends at Dickinson & Morris in Melton Mowbray arrived. At last, after enough pies had been delivered to the Sky box, she secured the elusive rock star's telephone number.

Clapton seemed to offer supporting evidence for Elton John's observation that all musicians yearn to be sportsmen. 'Test cricket,' he said: 'it is the Arthurian thing featuring England, with so much romanticism and drama.' He told wonderful stories of lost weekends spent fishing with Botham. In keeping with so many of our guests, Denis Compton was his hero – surprisingly, he even admitted to wearing Brylcreem, which Compton marketed so effectively after the Second World War.

Eric Clapton was followed by Johnnie Borrell, lead singer of Razorlight and a member of Middlesex CCC. This was a valuable experience for me, in that it taught me to be very wary of information gleaned when researching someone hurriedly on the internet. Johnnie appeared at short notice, so, logging onto my trusted online encyclopaedia, I was confident that it would just be a case of quickly making a few notes to get me going, and that would be that. My eye was drawn to a paragraph that referred to a hitherto unknown predilection of Johnnie for taking evening strolls alone on Hampstead Heath. I need say no more. When I met him I decided it would be better not to mention what was being alluded to in this encyclopaedia entry, but later in the week I plucked up the courage to tell him about it. Before dialling his number I logged onto the page again to check the details. The paragraph, which had been intended to cause embarrassment, had disappeared without trace. Lesson learned.

I have fond memories of many of our visitors to the old Headingley commentary box. Bella Emberg, best known perhaps as 'Blunderwoman', the roly-poly sidekick to comedian Russ Abbott, emerged as a big Sussex supporter, and travelled all the way from Brighton to see us. Bella is a great fan of Tony Greig, the former Sussex and England captain, and after our interview I walked her to the television boxes at the other end of the ground to meet her hero. Tony, being Tony, was charm itself, but I have a recollection of Bella putting Geoffrey Boycott firmly in his place when he came out to see what all the fuss was about. Not one to be messed with, our Bella.

The actor Roger Lloyd Pack – Trigger in *Only Fools and Horses* among many other things – also came to Headingley. We all went out for dinner the night before the interview, and quite how he politely put up with the incessant 'All right, Dave?'s he encountered throughout Leeds that evening I will never know. Roger became involved in a late-night sing-song in the hotel with Mike Selvey which resulted in complaints from fellow guests and a visit from the night porter, who told them to pack it in. He then arrived at Headingley in the morning carrying a tiny old suitcase that, as Mike observed, was no bigger than that of Paddington Bear. Roger, it turned out, was busy learning his lines as Barty Crouch Sr in the latest Harry Potter film, and he told us that sitting quietly in a stand at a cricket match is his preferred line-learning environment.

Vic Marks is not widely known for his ruthlessness, but this surprising characteristic was once exposed in that old commentary box at Headingley. I was interviewing the former Chief Executive of British Airways, Rod Eddington, when he described how Victor, as captain of Oxford University, not only fluffed an easy catch offered by Tony Greig off Rod's bowling, but also dropped him for the all-important Varsity match against Cambridge, thus denying Rod a well deserved Blue. Poor Victor, who was on *TMS* duty for the game, anxiously shuffled about in the box behind us. I had promised him that I would not bring up the subject. He should have known better.

Some guests, like the actors Simon Williams, Sir Tom Courtenay and Jaye Griffiths, have become good friends. Other interviews can have a serious edge to them. Sir Ian Blair's visit came at the time that the forthcoming inquest into the death of Jean Charles de Menezes on London's Underground was a regular news item, while his predecessor as Commissioner of the Metropolitan Police, Sir John Stevens, provided us with a story that ended up leading the BBC news reports for the rest of the day. Sir John had already been on Radio 4's *Today* programme that morning, and been comprehensively grilled by that arch-inquisitor John Humphrys about the number of attempted terrorist attacks on London that had been thwarted by the police and the security services. He had steadfastly refused to give any indication whatsoever. Five hours later on *Test Match Special*, I asked exactly the same question. Without blinking he replied, 'Eight.' And he continued to elaborate with no encouragement needed from me. We concluded the interview, during which Sir John revealed that he had seen me take David Lloyd's wicket all those years ago in my debut at Grace Road.

The telephones went berserk, with the BBC newsrooms all trying to get an interview with him, but they were too late, and he had left to go on holiday. In any case, whether he had been caught off-guard at a relaxed moment, or whether he had disclosed the information quite deliberately, Sir John's answer was on tape for everyone to use in their bulletins. It was, I suppose a shame that an energetic rendition of 'Colonel Bogey' that was being played at that precise moment by the visiting Christ's Hospital Band drifted in through our window, and formed an unavoidable backdrop to that priceless soundbite.

* * *

And so to the interview that aroused more interest, anticipation and reaction than any other 'View from the Boundary' since the radio and television personality Ted Moult was Brian Johnston's first guest in 1980. Two vastly different worlds collided when the young pop star Lily Allen joined me during the Ashes Test at The Oval in 2009. The unlikely encounter was a little nervous at first, but it quickly became very entertaining, and I am still asked about it on an almost daily basis.

It all began during the Edgbaston Test, when during a break for rain I received a message from one of my trusty followers on Twitter. Lily Allen had tweeted that she was driving west along the M4, and had lost her *Test Match Special* reception. Could I help? Now, the following confession will horrify many – including Lily, I suspect – but I had never heard of her. My long-suffering producer Adam Mountford was not entirely surprised by this, because he knows only too well that I live in a virtually television-free environment at home, and often have no idea who the guests I am asked to interview are. But he smiled as he patiently explained who Lily is, and suggested that it might be a good idea to help her out. By now messages were arriving on Twitter that Lily had already been instructed to retune her radio from the 720 medium-wave frequency, which fades away approximately fifty miles from London, to the trusty 198 long wave. She was now listening loud and clear, and all was well.

But I was intrigued: a twenty-four-year-old pop star who enjoys *Test Match Special* to the point of asking for help to listen to our commentary would make a fantastic guest. After all, we are constantly trying to introduce youngsters to cricket through the programme. After the match, I tentatively sent her a message on Twitter: would she like to join me on *TMS* sometime? Her almost instantaneous reply was encouraging:

'I can't think of anything I'd like to do more. Don't you think that Onions should have got man of the match?'

Contact made, and Lily clearly had a genuine enthusiasm for cricket, even if I had to tell her that, no, I did not think Onions should have been man of the match. Arrangements were quickly put in place for her to come to the Saturday of the final Test at The Oval.

With the preamble to this encounter already in the public domain, the internet was buzzing in anticipation of Lily – who by now I was discovering through my research was a colourful character – appearing on something as traditional as *Test Match Special*. I remember talking to my daughters, Jennifer and Rebecca, to get their thoughts about their Dad interviewing Lily Allen, and they could barely stop laughing at the prospect. One evening in our kitchen I was introduced to Lily's music by Emma and my teenage stepchildren Charlotte and Thomas. They began gently enough with 'LDN' before moving on to 'Not Fair', which graphically bemoans a lover's lack of prowess in bed, and finished spectacularly with 'F— You'. I was now in no doubt why there was such massive interest in her appearance on *Test Match Special*, which was perceived as the home of middle-class good manners and polite conversation. This was going to be a challenge, both high-profile and unpredictable, and I could not wait.

Remembering Johnners' example regarding preparation, I set about burying myself in all the information I could acquire about Lily Allen. This included books, magazines, previous interviews on YouTube, and anything else I could find to help me get to know someone I had never met, and might only have a quick ten minutes with before the live half-hour interview. I jotted the fruits of my research down at the back of my current notebook, in a system that I have always used and that seems to work for me, despite much of the scrawl looking unintelligible to anyone else. Separate headings for different talking points, which are underlined, help to attract my eye during conversation, and I mark with an asterisk any reminders and additional information about that particular topic. The difficulty is to look at my notes and move the chat along without the guest thinking that I am struggling or have lost my way.

Another Johnners tool I use to compose my thoughts when I am wondering where to go next is to break off the interview for a moment to give a reminder of the score for anyone who might only recently have tuned in. It sounds natural, and it is quite straightforward to read the scorecard while at the same time scanning the interview notes and deciding what tack to take next. A quick name-check of the guest, again for the benefit of any new listeners, while looking at the notes also does the trick. I absolutely never write down a list of questions, because although that might seem to be the easiest way to get through an interview, the true art is to listen to the answer your guest is giving you, and then to embellish it in a natural, conversational manner. If you have a list of questions, the likelihood is that you will simply work through them in the order in which they are written down, resulting in a stilted and disjointed interview. (My experience with HRH the Duke of Edinburgh springs to mind.)

The morning of the big day did not begin auspiciously. Malcolm Ashton, our statistician, is a man with a great sense of humour, but he would be unlikely to choose modern pop music as his specialist subject in a pub quiz. He wanted to know all about our lunchtime guest, and I could think of no better taster than to read out the lyrics to 'F— You', the chorus of which contains several mentions of the title. As I was repeating the chorus loudly for Malcolm's benefit, and generally behaving rather boorishly, my eye was drawn to a small, unfamiliar figure standing no more than two yards away from me in the commentary box. It was with absolute horror that I realised it was a middle-aged woman – clearly one of our devoted listeners – bearing a cake.

'Hello, Aggers,' she said quietly. 'I've baked this specially for you.'

If ever there was a moment I wanted the ground to open and swallow me up, this was it. I could not have apologised more effusively or genuinely; what else could I do? Unbelievably, she claimed not to have heard anything untoward. I suspect she was merely being kind, and after we had posed for a couple of photographs she left the box as quietly as she had appeared.

Lily arrived during the morning session, with her boyfriend Sam and a bodyguard, to complete a remarkable journey. They had been at the Test on Thursday, the first day, before travelling overnight by bus to the Netherlands, where she performed in a concert during the second afternoon of the match. While there, they kept up to date with events at The Oval by listening to *Test Match Special* via a mobile phone that had been wired to a set of speakers, before starting another overnight journey on her bus, which dropped her off at The Oval that Saturday morning. What an effort she had made to get there, and little wonder she was exhausted.

By now all attempts at keeping the identity of our guest a secret were hopeless, although Phil Tufnell – one of the summarisers – kept the suspense going with a typically brilliant spur-of-the-moment quip to a question of mine.

'Our guest, Tuffers, has come by bus from Holland. Can you guess who it is?'

'Dennis Bergkamp?' (The former Arsenal and Dutch international footballer with a well-known aversion to flying.)

Finally the lunch interval arrived. Lily and I had a very quick chat outside, during which I betrayed my anxiety by asking her if she could be so kind as not to swear on air. Quite rightly, she dismissed my request with a measure of outrage: 'As if I would.' We took our seats in the front row of the commentary box, which was packed with photographers and a reporter or two. Lily was nervous, and understandably so: clearly she was new to cricket, and this was taking her right out of her comfort zone. To appear on *Test Match Special* for the first time is a daunting experience for anybody, let alone someone who has only recently become interested in the game. My concern was that if the interview went badly, we would be accused of dumbing down the programme in the interests of celebrity-chasing. In that regard I felt particularly protective of Adam, because, new to the job of producer, he had already faced unjustifiable criticism of lowering standards from some quarters, and getting Lily on the programme had been my idea.

After a gentle start, despite the intrusive noise of camera shutters and flash guns rattling like machine-gun fire in the background, we were away, and what fun it was. Gentle banter and leg-pulling while we wandered through cricket and into Lily's life as a modern-day pop star. She was bright and bubbly, and had wisely brought some prepared notes with her; another reminder, like Elton John's autocue, that you don't get to the top by accident. There were two highlights for me: her preference for Test cricket and her absolute rejection of Twenty20, and when she revealed that she disliked the ultra-white clothing that England's cricketers wear nowadays. To my delight, having ranted long and ineffectually myself on that very subject, Lily – a modern-day fashion icon – much preferred the old-fashioned creams to the shiny white kit, which would look more at home on John Travolta in *Saturday Night Fever* than at Lord's. I think it is brilliant that a young newcomer to the game from such a high-profile background can have an affection for tradition on the cricket field. If she maintains her interest in the game, Lily Allen is a future goldmine for those who administer and market English cricket.

After a snatched lunch outside, it was time for Lily to move on to her next gig – another live performance that afternoon in Essex. I was really pleased with how the interview had gone, and the feedback on the emails to *Test Match Special* was virtually entirely positive (it is never 100 per cent, whatever the subject). Many listeners said that, having tuned in expecting to hate hearing Lily Allen on *TMS*, she had won them over.

All seemed well, until the following morning. I cannot claim to be a regular reader of the *Observer*, despite having written some reports and articles for the paper over the years, and I had not preordered a copy that Sunday. However, it was not long before my attention was drawn to a particularly nasty article by the newspaper's senior sports writer, Will Buckley. The headline gave a taste of what was to come: 'When Aggers Met Lily: An Unrequited Love Affair for the Middle-Aged'.

What followed was ghastly. Buckley likened me to 'a middle-aged man panting on the edge of the dance floor', claimed that I had 'amorous ambitions' and accused me of positioning myself 'firmly on the pervy side of things'. Quotes from the interview were lifted and printed entirely out of context. The whole thing suggested that I, approaching fifty years old, had been leering all over a young girl who is the same age as my eldest daughter.

Despite my being reassured by my *Test Match Special* colleagues, and also by my wife Emma, all of whom had heard and enjoyed the interview, it was still dreadfully embarrassing that morning. I imagined that my friends at Sky, and everyone in the press box who would not have tuned in to the radio the previous day, had read Buckley's piece and assumed it to be true. I felt an absolute fool. I also worried about Lily's reaction. She had seemed fine, but had she even remotely felt that I had been behaving like an old letch? And what might she think of me now that someone had suggested I had? The whole thing was too awful for words.

But I was soon aware of a wave of protest on the internet at what Buckley had written, and at how an entirely harmless piece of fun had been so hideously misrepresented. It started, inevitably, on Twitter, where my followers left messages of support. This led to a bombardment of the *Guardian* website, where Buckley's article had appeared online, complete with an invitation to leave comments. Hundreds poured in on the Sunday alone, giving Buckley a battering. 'This is a snide, nasty, small-minded and utterly hyperbolic hatchet job, dripping in meanness,' read a typical response.

England won the Ashes that afternoon, which helped to distract me, and by evening I felt confident enough to send Lily a text message, asking if she had read the article. It turned out that not only had she read it, but that one of her friends was among those who had posted a comment, condemning it in no uncertain terms.

I telephoned Buckley on the Monday morning, while I was on the way to report on the England celebrations at their hotel near the Tower of London. He seemed surprised to hear from me, clearly had no idea about the angry reaction to his piece, and was frankly dismissive of it when I told him. I demanded an apology, and he said he would get back to me. Nothing was forthcoming during the day, despite the storm continuing to rage. By late that evening, after I had driven home, I had had enough. I posted on Twitter that I had asked Buckley to apologise and that he had not done so. I added, in case anyone was interested, that the name of the sports editor at the *Observer* is Brian Oliver, and I included his email address. (I must admit to not being terribly proud about that, and I hate to think what Oliver's inbox looked like next day.)

At ten o'clock on the Tuesday morning Lily posted to her followers, who numbered nearly one and a half million people at the time:

> *I think this Will Buckley guy should apologise to @aggerscricket* [my Twitter name]. *He was nothing but kind and gentlemanly to me during our interview. I'm sorry Aggers; I should have left you all alone.*

This was enough, finally, to extract a reluctant apology from Buckley, in which he entirely failed to grasp the power of social networking. 'The joke missed,' he wrote, 'as they so often do in the blogosphere.'

Today's journalists must be aware that there is now a means for people to react instantly to something they find offensive, and they are entirely within their rights to do so. People who use Facebook or Twitter are not 'computer nerds' or 'geeks', and it is naïve, outdated and dangerous not to recognise that. Social networking is not going to go away. It has to be understood and embraced, and we all need to remember that. I was on the right side of the Twitterstorm that day, but one small mistake in the future and it might be very different.

In the midst of the Lily saga there was one thing that still makes me chuckle today. It was the publication of what must rank as one of the most extraordinary and unlikely newspaper headlines ever, and it appeared in the online edition of the *Daily Telegraph*: 'Lily Allen Defends Jonathan Agnew Over "Pervert" Slur'.

This definitely confirmed that, for a while at least, my little world had gone completely mad. It was also the point at which I thought of old Johnners, the pioneer of 'A View from the Boundary', and what fun he would undoubtedly be having at my expense: 'Really, Aggers! I can't leave you in charge for five minutes . . .'

EIGHT

Handing Over

On 2 December 1993, Peter Baxter phoned me at home and told me that Brian had suffered a very serious heart attack, and was in hospital on a life-support machine. The details were sketchy, but it transpired that without the quick thinking of the taxi driver who was taking him to catch a train from Paddington to Bristol, Johnners would have died in the back of the cab. The driver ignored two sets of red lights and rushed to the Maida Vale hospital. There was no casualty department there, but despite his heart having stopped for several minutes, Brian was successfully resuscitated on the floor at the hospital entrance. He was then transferred to intensive care in St Mary's hospital.

Peter had spoken to Brian's family before he called me, and while everyone was being bravely optimistic, it was clear that even if Brian recovered sufficiently to be discharged from hospital, he would never be the same again. Peter kept me informed with daily bulletins, and in a bid to jog Brian's memory he was asked by Pauline to visit Brian, who by now was off the ventilator, but very confused. Peter was devastated to see his old friend reduced to a shadow of what he used to be. After Brian was allowed to return home shortly before Christmas, I rang Pauline and asked if I could see him. Kindly, she advised me not to, as I would not recognise him. 'Remember him how he was,' she said. Although I was disappointed at the time, I will always be grateful to her for that.

Again, it was Peter who rang to tell me that Brian had died barely a week later, on 5 January 1994. The final month had been a sad end to what was a magnificent innings, bursting with energy, kindness and good fun. Hastily, Peter arranged for us to broadcast a special programme on BBC Radio that evening, and he held it all together in London. Every member of *Test Match Special* was involved, with most of us making contributions from our local radio studios. Many of Brian's friends were contacted, and they recounted their favourite memories and stories of him over the telephone. I remember feeling rather detached as I sat in that tiny booth in BBC Radio Leicester. However, despite the sadness and grief on what was a really horrible day, the programme was nevertheless a happy one, and full of laughter, just as it should have been.

The funeral was a private family affair, and Brian was buried in Godlingston cemetery on the outskirts of Swanage. On 16 May, Westminster Abbey was packed to the rafters for a memorial service which was a perfect tribute to Brian's full and varied life. The members of *Test Match Special* were given our own little area in which to sit, from where we had a perfect view of the Prime Minister, John Major, and Colin Cowdrey sharing the address. Peter Baxter read a psalm, and Richard Stilgoe reduced the congregation to hysterics with a typically brilliant poem he had written specially for the occasion. Finally we processed out of the Abbey and into the sunshine to the accompaniment of the Band of the Grenadier Guards playing a number of Brian's favourite melodies and the theme tunes to his old radio programmes such as *In Town Tonight* and *Down Your Way.* When they struck up the theme music of *Neighbours* – for surely the first and only time in Westminster Abbey's history – a smile briefly wiped away the feeling of sadness and loss. Brian's family were greatly moved by the enormous turnout and the warmth of the occasion, but it was also a reminder that with the first Test of the summer against New Zealand beginning barely a week later, there was no getting away from the painful fact that the impact of Brian's death on *Test Match Special* now had to be addressed.

The programme was already precariously placed, because yet again it was being kicked about the airwaves, with no one apparently very keen to take it on. *Test Match Special* is not an easy programme to schedule. It pops up only when there is international cricket being played, but lasts for up to eight hours per day. That means all regular programming has to be shelved to accommodate cricket commentary, which – although I find it hard to believe – is not to everyone's taste. The previous three summers had seen us broadcasting on three different frequencies, which was clearly an absurd situation. Our listeners are a loyal and determined bunch, and they followed us around on our travels between Radio 3 medium wave, Radio 3 FM and then Radio 5. Politically, none of us wanted to stay on Radio 5, because that brought about the likelihood of clashes with other sports, as well as with news and traffic bulletins. Peter and I agreed that it would almost certainly spell the end for *Test Match Special* if cricket became just another part of the BBC sports output, and we were left to fight our corner against football, Wimbledon, the Olympics and everything else besides. *TMS* needed to maintain its own separate identity if it was to survive in its current ball-by-ball format.

At the end of the summer of 1993, which had been an Ashes year, the powers that be at the BBC got together to discuss the fate of *Test Match Special*. The Radio 3 medium-wave frequency had now been sold off by the government, so that was not an option, and the arrival of Classic FM meant that we would not be welcome on the BBC's only classical music station, Radio 3 FM. That left only either Radio 5, or a compromise that would allow us to use the frequency that, because of the strength and range of its signal, will be used in the event of a national emergency: Radio 4 long wave. It carries three programmes that are considered sacrosanct, and are protected by the BBC Charter and Agreement: the Shipping Forecast, *Yesterday in Parliament* and the Daily Service, which is now known as *Act of Worship*. Although it would mean some interruptions to the commentary, the choice was an easy one as far as we were concerned. We wanted Radio 4 long wave, both because *Test Match Special* would retain its separate identity and because the majority of disgruntled listeners within the United Kingdom who preferred Radio 4's usual programmes would be able to find them on FM.

In the interests of preserving *Test Match Special*, the Radio 4 long-wave argument won the day. The fact that Brian Johnston was the programme's presenter played a huge part in securing that decision, which was absolutely vital to its future. The controller of Radio 4, Michael Green, knew that any programme led by Johnners would be easier to sell to his audience, many of whom would be vociferous in their disapproval at us taking over long wave. Brian died only three months later, and never did appear on Radio 4 long wave, but the BBC's commitment to *Test Match Special* had been demonstrated. It would now be up to the rest of us to make the transition and secure Radio 4 long wave as our new home without Johnners.

The first thing Peter, as producer, had to decide was how on earth he was going to replace the irreplaceable. We were now a commentator down, but not just any commentator: in Johnners we had lost the life and soul of the programme, and the man who gave *Test Match Special* much of its profile. Whoever came in for the summer of 1994 would be under intense scrutiny, and it would be impossible for him not to be billed, in the media at least, as Brian Johnston's replacement.

We were fortunate in that the tourists that summer were New Zealand and South Africa, both of whom were bringing their own commentator with them. With Christopher Martin-Jenkins, me and one of our visitors – Bryan Waddle or Gerald de Kock – we would have three commentators at each match, which is the optimum number. But Peter reasoned very sensibly that now was the perfect time to slip in an additional commentator. He would be swallowed up as part of a four-man team, and should thus avoid unfair attention. Besides, much of the media focus would be on the historic return to England of the South Africans, after an absence of thirty years.

And so it was that Henry Calthorpe Blofeld, of Eton and Cambridge University, returned to *Test Match Special* after his brief flirtation with Sky television. Bringing him back was entirely the right decision, as the colourful Blowers would retain the programme's mildly eccentric yet friendly feel in Johnners' absence. At the same time, a genuine radio man was restored to his rightful place on the airwaves. We agreed that as I had presented the previous summer's coverage on Radio 5, complete with the dreaded eight-second 'tease' that delighted Johnners so, and was also the front man in our coverage on overseas tours, I should continue to do so. Peter decided to share the 'View from the Boundary' duties amongst all of us, and the change of network also required us to fill every lunch and tea interval. This was a new experience, and they were generally presented by me, being the cricket correspondent, and produced by Peter. It all felt very strange, but we got on with it.

The only thing I really felt uncomfortable about was continuing to talk about cakes. They were still arriving as plentifully as they always had, but they were a Johnners thing. I really did not want the listeners to think that I was moving in on his patch, or trying to take over in any way. It just did not feel right. So for years I never mentioned them. I hope those kind people who sent us wonderful cakes, buns, pastries, scones, biscuits and even meringues during that period will forgive me and understand my apparent rudeness. I am over it now; the programme has moved on, and all contributions are gratefully received.

That summer of 1994 was an emotional and trying experience. We felt an enormous wave of goodwill towards the programme from our regular listeners, who were almost universally united in their delight to hear Blowers on *Test Match Special* once again. But as Michael Green, the Controller of Radio 4, knew only too well, there was also tremendous hostility towards us from many listeners – predominately women at home – who were absolutely furious that we should be occupying their favourite radio station at the expense of their usual programmes. It did not matter how often we, and the continuity announcer in the studio, carefully described how listeners could retune to mainstream Radio 4 by altering the frequency of their radios from long wave to FM (which is hardly a taxing procedure) – the sacks full of angry letters continued to arrive in our commentary boxes. I had sympathy with some listeners, because FM is difficult to pick up in certain areas. But others were so stuck in their ways that they stubbornly refused to tune away from long wave as a silly point of principle. We battened down the hatches and made it our aim to produce the best that *Test Match Special* could offer, and to show that we were quite capable of carrying on.

Towards the end of the summer there was a noticeable shift in the tone of the correspondence. There were still complaints, of course, but they were softening. Typically, women would write: 'I was very upset when you invaded my living room in May and I could not listen to my favourite programmes any more. But even if I still have no idea what a short leg is, I have grown to enjoy the chatter and the laughter that now keeps me company instead. Please accept this cake with thanks from a new listener, and I look forward to you all returning next summer.' It was a tremendous breakthrough, and many of our loyal followers today started listening at the time that we moved to Radio 4 long wave and they unwittingly discovered *Test Match Special.*

The manner in which people now listen to the radio has changed enormously, with many of our listeners preferring digital means, either through a computer or a digital radio, while diehard long-wave listeners have become used to tuning in elsewhere for *The Archers* or *Gardeners' Question Time.* This has made life easier for everybody, even those expats in Europe who cling to the old country by listening to Radio 4 long wave, and who complained as vociferously as anybody about our intrusion. They can now listen over the internet instead. Some of our *TMS* listeners complain about the breaks in commentary for the Shipping Forecast and the like, but in the grand scheme of things these are a small price to pay, and can be avoided entirely anyway by listening through a digital medium.

The core of the team remained unchanged, and with Henry bringing his inimitable light and colourful touch to the commentary, *Test Match Special* emerged strongly from its greatest challenge. It sounded different without Johnners, of course, and it did not feel the same going to work every day, but life must go on, and there was a great determination amongst all of us that the programme would do more than merely struggle on; it would flourish. Sadly, with the passing of time we lose more of our friends and colleagues, each of whom leaves *Test Match Special* the richer for his contributions, but whose passing always reawakens concerns about the programme's vulnerability and its future. How do we maintain and preserve *Test Match Special*'s unique heritage and identity when there is precious little scope nowadays for broadcasters such as Brian Johnston, or indeed Henry Blofeld, to emerge under their own steam, free of the influence of soundbite radio, which makes all the voices and programmes sound so similar and anonymous these days. That may be fine for other sports, where the pace is faster and there is not the time for a more reflective, conversational commentary that reaches out and connects with the audience; but it is not for *Test Match Special*, and this is our greatest challenge. It is one that those of us who work on *TMS*, and truly have a feel for the programme and understand it, must confront ourselves. It is our duty to do so.

The role of Bill Frindall, our statistician, was crucial during the transitional phase immediately following Brian's death. Bill had been Brian's sidekick ever since Johnners joined *TMS* full-time in 1970, and he was always there throughout the day with a microphone, and was easy to involve if play was dull or if Brian felt short of something to say. Indeed, involving the scorer in conversation is probably the best way of giving *Test Match Special* that open, 'family' feel that makes it sound inclusive and welcoming.

After Brian's death, Bill moved up a gear. From a producer's perspective, this was not necessarily welcome, because it meant that Bill would be on the air more. Of his many great talents, controlling and editing his own broadcasting output – including his many assorted grunts and snorts – was not Bill's forte. But someone needed to step up in Brian's absence and act as senior pro, if you like, and that is exactly what Bill did. He assumed responsibility for the Primary Club on Saturdays, and dealt with many of the mentions of charitable events that we like to promote whenever we can. Because he loved broadcasting, this was also Bill's opportunity to keep the banter with the commentators going, and while it was sometimes difficult to get him to shut up, I really believe that this helped maintain the flow, as established by Brian. He also had a nose almost as sharp as Brian's at detecting unintentional *double entendres*, so just in case anyone was hankering after the trumpeting '*whoop whoop*' at such moments, one of Bill's snorts became the accepted substitute.

Bill died suddenly in January 2009, having contracted Legionnaires' Disease while on a charity cricket tour in Dubai with the Lord's Taverners. The news came as a terrible shock to us. He had been at his energetic and apparently indestructible best in India only the month before, scoring as meticulously as ever throughout the day before embarking on the terrifying journeys to his hotel by three-wheeled tuk-tuk that he would relive in exhausting detail the following morning. There was a symmetry to Bill's life that he himself would definitely have admired: he was born during the last 'timeless Test' in 1930 – a match in Durban that was finally called off after nine days to allow the England players to catch the ship home – and he was buried during the shortest Test in history, the match between West Indies and England that was abandoned after only ten balls because of the unplayable condition of the outfield.

As is too often the case, you are never fully aware of quite how special something is until it is taken away, and that is true for me of Bill's contribution to *Test Match Special*. He could be tetchy and cantankerous at times, and was driven to distraction by some of Henry's less accurate attempts at the identification of players, but Bill was the cornerstone of *TMS*, and his death was a hammer blow. Always there, and always right. The day he died, while we were on tour in St Kitts, was one of those horrible occasions on which you are required to work non-stop on a news story which is the death of a very close friend. Busily writing obituaries for bulletins against tight deadlines, and talking about Bill reflectively on the radio, I never had a chance to sit quietly and absorb the full, awful significance of what had happened.

It had been exactly the same when Fred Trueman's death was announced in 2006, during the morning session of a one-day international at Headingley, his home ground. Fred had been ill for only a short while, and like Bill's, his death hit us very hard. Again, the priority was to get the news out there, and to deal with the huge interest from all around the world. At least, as we were at Headingley, many of Fred's colleagues and former team-mates were on hand at the ground, and all of them were more than happy, despite their grief, to come on the radio and tell stories about their old friend. Naturally, our interval that day was devoted to Fred. It was all pretty much thrown together on the hoof, with messages in my earphones or scribbled notes passed to me telling me who I would be interviewing next. When it was finished and I handed over to the first commentator of the afternoon, all I could hope for was that, under very difficult circumstances, we had done Fred proud. Peter Baxter and I looked at each other and nodded; it was the best we could have done with such little preparation. Only then was it time to sit alone in quiet contemplation and shed a few tears of our own.

Of all the summarisers who have come and gone, I miss Fred the most. I worshipped him as a cricketer, of course – he was one of the greatest fast bowlers in the history of the game. And I loved his humour, which swayed wildly and unpredictably between the crude and shocking to the most gentle and old-fashioned wit that enabled him to form such a lovely and unlikely bond with the Old Etonian Johnners. For a rough diamond from a proud Yorkshire coal mining background, Fred was very warm-hearted and generous. But it is as a brilliantly colourful raconteur that I will always remember him best.

Purely from a broadcasting point of view, there was nothing better than the rain hammering against the commentary-box window, the covers over the pitch, and Fred, pipe ablaze, recounting his familiar stories with such relish that it seemed as if he was telling them for the very first time. Tales of sailing to Australia for the winter tours of years ago, and of the long train journeys between matches upcountry: 'Flies the size o' hippos, Jonathan. Flies the size o' hippos.'

Surprisingly, perhaps, Fred had a tremendous interest in and knowledge of the history of the game. This would lead to stories of some of cricket's earliest characters, like Alfred Mynn, the twenty-one-stone fast bowler from the mid-nineteenth-century 'roundarm era', and Tich Freeman, the leg-spinner who between 1914 and 1936 took an astounding 3,776 wickets for Kent, including 304 in a single season: 'Now 'e *could* bowl a bit, Jonathan.' Fred's favourite was undoubtedly Sydney Barnes, who bowled leg cutters for England in twenty-seven Tests before the First World War, and who was the only England cricketer to be selected from the leagues rather than from county cricket. He captured 189 Test wickets at an average of only 16 runs each. He loved his history, did Fred.

The only snag attached to working with Fred was his abiding wish to be remembered for what everybody already knew him to be: a great fast bowler. I am sure he never felt that he was taken seriously enough by the England management in particular, and he passionately wanted to be involved in the coaching of England's fast bowlers. But, for whatever reason, the England coaches resisted asking him, and this could make him terribly grumpy. That was what lay behind the awful row between Fred and Mickey Stewart during that infamous dinner at Pebble Mill in 1991. It also meant that before we could get on with the interesting and entertaining stories, we invariably had to put up with Fred reminding us all of what he had achieved during his fabulous career. The sad point was that we did not need to be reminded – we all knew. But Fred apparently felt very insecure and unappreciated.

This did, however, trigger my favourite broadcasting moment with Fred, which occurred one year at Headingley, when rain and bad light stopped play with the two of us at the microphone together and needing to fill time. With the players off the field, and Fred already keen to remind us of what a great fast bowler he had been, I checked the television monitor – which was behind Fred and out of his view – to see what my colleagues at the other end of the ground were going to do. It is a good rule that if the television broadcasters switch to replaying highlights, they have received word that there will probably be a long interruption. This gives me valuable guidance about how to pace our coverage during the rain break. On this occasion, as Fred was reminding us of how he used to go into the visitors' dressing room on the morning of every match and tell them how many of them he would dismiss that day, the television switched to showing highlights. And not just any old highlights either: most unusually, these were in black and white.

Fred was away. 'I used to bowl bouncers, yorkers and start t'ball on leg stump to hit t'top of off . . .'

Intrigued by the unusual highlights, I settled back to watch the television for a moment. And guess what? The first ball showed a youthful Fred Trueman running in to bowl with that wonderful, smooth approach and perfect action – and being smashed for four by a West Indian batsman. That made me sit up.

'I used to terrify them in t'visitors' dressing room before t'match started . . .'

The television picture panned out, and I could see that the highlights were of a Test match at Lord's. As Fred continued to chunter away on air, he was running in again, in black and white, on the screen behind him. Bang! Four more. Young Fred did not look best pleased as he scowled at the West Indian, who I recognised as the opening batsman Conrad Hunte. In fact, this was the 1963 Test at Lord's, at the end of which Colin Cowdrey emerged heroically, broken arm in plaster and with two balls remaining in the match, to save the day for England. It was also remembered for the way in which Hunte smashed the first three balls of the game, delivered by Trueman, to the boundary for four. Fred did not talk about it very often.

By now I was trying desperately to stop myself from bursting out laughing; the timing of this was just so perfect. Fred sensed that something was afoot, and with some effort he turned around to look at the television screen precisely at the moment that his young self was racing in very angrily to bowl the third ball of that infamous opening over. With a flourish, Hunte despatched him to the boundary a third time. As the umpire in his long white coat signalled to the scorers, I wondered what on earth I should say. So I left it to Fred, who, apparently stunned into silence, turned very slowly to face me again. 'In't it funny, Jonathan lad,' he muttered sadly at last, 'how much slower you look in black and white?'

Fred did not work on *Test Match Special* at the same time as our current strident and outspoken Yorkshireman, Geoffrey Boycott, who is now on his second stint with us. Geoffrey was working on television for most of the time Fred was on *Test Match Special*, and I am not sure there would have been enough room for both egos in the same commentary box. Typically of the Yorkshire teams in which they played, their relationship seemed to veer dramatically from being close buddies to not speaking to each other at all, although I was glad to see that they were on very good terms at the end of Fred's life.

There cannot have been a character in cricket who, both as a player and as a commentator, divides opinion as rigidly and uncompromisingly as Geoffrey Boycott; it really is a case of either loving or hating the man. Personally I love him, and always have. Like Fred and Johnners, Boycott and I are an unlikely pairing, but somehow it seems to work. Geoffrey hails from the Yorkshire coal mines, where his father worked at the coal face. He died having never fully recovered from an accident in which he was hit by empty coal carts.

'Could be worse, Jonathan,' Geoffrey often says to me as we are checking in to a distinctly unpromising hotel on the Subcontinent, or watching the rain pouring down at a Test match. 'We could be down t'pit like my old man.'

From the time that we first encountered each other in county cricket, him one of the best opening batsmen in the world, and me a young, hopeful fast bowler, Geoffrey and I always respected one another. There would never be any sledging or angry words, despite Boycott's being the wicket that everyone wanted, because you knew that if you got him out, you had *really* got him out. Geoffrey never gave his wicket away.

I first encountered Geoffrey in Melbourne, just before Christmas 1978. Aged eighteen, I was in Australia on my young cricketer's scholarship, and while I was bowling in the nets to the England captain Mike Brearley in the build-up to the traditional Boxing Day Test, a ball shot up from a good length and hit him in the face. There was a serious risk not only of Brearley missing the match, but of Boycott becoming captain in his place, which did not make me Mr Popular with the rest of the England party. I remember a lot of chuntering in corners amongst those who had been in New Zealand the previous winter, when, in the absence of the injured Brearley, Boycott had been in temporary charge. This led to one of the great stories – which Geoffrey still disputes to this day – in which Ian Botham claims that he deliberately ran his captain out for batting too slowly when England should have been pushing for victory.

My duty in the nets in Melbourne was to bowl at the England team, and there are no prizes for guessing that Geoffrey, whose life revolved almost entirely around batting, made the most of me. Hour after hour in the blazing heat I would bowl at the great man in a single net right in the middle of the vast Melbourne Cricket Ground. Just me and him. 'I've got you under my skin,' he would sing time and time again, his mouth in that lop-sided grin, as another ball thumped into the middle of his bat.

Afterwards, when I was spent, Geoffrey told me to come back with him to the team's hotel, as he had got something for me. We went up in the lift with me wondering what this might possibly be. A personally autographed Geoffrey Boycott bat, perhaps? 'Right,' he said when we reached his room. 'English Breakfast, Darjeeling or Ginseng?' That's right. My reward for all that hard work was a cup of tea.

I never played in the same team as Geoffrey, which might explain why I have such a good relationship with him. The charges of selfishness that have been made by many of those who appeared for Yorkshire and England alongside Boycott are too many not to suggest, at least, that there must be some foundation to them. As a batsman Geoffrey was a superb technician who practised day and night to eliminate any faults that might lead to him getting out, and he saw his role as being the man who had to defy the opposition. He would argue that, with a batsman's occupation of the crease, the bowlers become tired, and the runs will come in their own good time. Others would say that because Boycott only batted at one speed, it was too often left to those who came in after him to pick up the scoring rate, often losing their wickets for the greater good in the process. This led to tremendous resentment, especially at Yorkshire, where Boycott regularly topped the national batting averages, but the team under-performed. There was great unhappiness at the club during his eight years in charge, with the county split down the middle between those who wanted him as captain and those who did not.

In the middle of all that, in 1974 Boycott announced that he was making himself unavailable to play for England. He did not return to the national side until 1977. The timing of his absence gave his opponents an open goal, because he opted out of the tour of Australia in 1974–75, when the great fast bowlers Dennis Lillee and Jeff Thomson were at their ferocious best. Similarly, he missed the visit in 1976 of the West Indies, who were armed to the teeth with fear-some pace bowlers including Andy Roberts, Michael Holding and Wayne Daniel. Boycott was running scared, said his critics, although he himself forcibly rejects that claim, saying he was too distracted by his continuous arguments with the Yorkshire committee to concen-trate properly on opening the batting for England.

I saw both sides of Boycott the batsman. In 1985, when he was almost forty-five years old, he came out to bat in the second innings of a championship match at Bradford (after I had dismissed you for four in the first, Geoffrey). He scored a beautiful 82 not out, at almost a run a ball. He played every shot in the book – glorious drives, pulls and forces off the back foot – to set up Yorkshire's declaration. What a batsman he looked, even at that advanced age. He was still playing the following year when Leicestershire travelled north to Middlesbrough, where admittedly the pitch was a little lively, and batting was not entirely straightforward. Boycott scored 127 from 337 balls in six and a half hours as Yorkshire were dismissed for 309. It was his 150th first-class century. Was this disciplined batting in awkward conditions (he also had an injured hand), or a determinedly selfish exhibition of hogging the crease purely to reach a personal milestone? Either way, it condemned the game to a draw, while providing a very good example of how the great Boycott debate was fuelled in those days.

Before the BBC lost the television rights to broadcast cricket from the start of the 1999 season, I worked in the commentary box only sporadically with Geoffrey. We did some Sunday League matches together for BBC TV, and he occasionally toured with *Test Match Special* in the winter. This introduced a new side of Geoffrey Boycott to me: a man more fastidious about his clothes than any with whom I have ever shared a dressing room or commentary box. Before his first stint on air, his jacket is removed, carefully placed on a hanger which is then hooked onto a peg or a nail, and he dons a sleeveless jersey in pink, yellow or light blue. His trademark wide-brimmed hats are immaculately maintained, and his shoes always gleam. Geoffrey loves to dress well.

His attention to detail extends to the bulging Filofax he carries about with him everywhere, which contains all the most priceless information he has gleaned over years of travelling. Need a nice restaurant in Sydney? Ask Geoffrey, who will not only tell you where to go, but after consulting his notes, which table to ask for to have the best view of the Opera House. 'Got a pen? Here's the number of the man in charge. Tell him I told you to ring.' It is a fascinating insight into the precise and orderly mind of a man who leaves nothing in life to chance, and who approached batting in exactly the same fashion, making notes about the bowlers he encountered throughout his career that he could refer to when he was next due to face them.

At home, away from the public eye, Geoffrey is an entertaining and generous host. During the tour of South Africa in 2009 he invited the *Test Match Special* team for dinner at his winter retreat on a golf course near Paarl on the Western Cape. When we arrived at his house, courtesy of a page of instructions he had given us – which, bizarrely, he had autographed in full at the bottom – I introduced myself to a couple who were also present. I assumed that they were friends of the Boycotts from either England or South Africa, but it turned out that Geoffrey had never met them before: he had donated a week in his home for two people, complete with a round of golf with him and tickets for the one-day international between South Africa and England at Newlands, as an auction lot at a charity dinner in Yorkshire.

Geoffrey Boycott welcoming total strangers to his house for a week? I know him better than most, but he will never stop surprising me.

In the commentary box, he is thoroughly professional. He is never late, and he is the best I have worked with at identifying technical deficiencies in a batsman. He is a hard hitter who, having been employed for many years by the *Sun* as an expert columnist, knows the value of a headline and how to get people talking. Perhaps sometimes he can be a little repetitive, hammering a point home when he really should have moved on to something else, and he can be very intimidating to colleagues who have not worked with him before, or whose knowledge of cricket he does not rate. His outspokenness, and his unflinching ability to criticise, mean his relations with the England players and coaching staff can be rocky at times. He fell out spectacularly with Duncan Fletcher, the former England head coach, who is every bit as stubborn as him, after some of Geoffrey's critical comments.

I played club cricket with Fletcher for a season in Zimbabwe, at the Alexandra Club in Harare. This was in 1982, shortly after Independence, when the country was full of hope. There were two Zimbabwe dollars to the pound then; when I visited the devastated country twenty-five years later the exchange rate was a million dollars to the pound. Fletcher was the captain of Alex. On the field he played the game as hard as nails, but off it he was the first to have a beer in his hand, and was often to be found supervising the barbecue in a burning wheelbarrow. It is a side of Duncan that not many people see, which is a great shame. Thanks to that experience, Duncan and I have always got on well.

One day, an agitated Geoffrey approached me in the commentary box and asked me what he should do to repair his relationship with Duncan. 'No problem, Geoffrey,' I said. 'You both live in Cape Town, and you both love golf. Give Duncan a ring this winter, ask him to play a round with you, and by the fifth hole you'll be as right as rain.' I scribbled down Duncan's number and handed it to Geoffrey, who was most grateful and agreed that this was the best way forward.

Duncan caught up with me first. 'Hey, Aggers!' he shouted from across the cricket field. 'You'll never guess who had the barefaced cheek to phone me at home and ask me to play golf with him.' I feigned surprise, and even a suggestion of outrage, when he told me. 'Anyway,' Duncan continued, 'I told him to bugger off, and put the phone down.'

Geoffrey's version was similar. 'So much for your big mate,' he scoffed. 'I did what you said, and he told me t' boogger off.' I *almost* felt guilty.

The most difficult experience Geoffrey and I have ever shared in a commentary box was on 31 August 1997. We were due to work together on a televised Sunday League fixture between Hampshire and Northamptonshire in Portsmouth. As it was a pleasant place to visit, and was off our usual beaten track, I had brought Emma and her children, Charlotte and Thomas, along for the ride. We were all sharing a room, and I was woken up early on the Sunday morning by one of the children flicking through the channels on the television. I looked bleary-eyed at the screen, and immediately did a double take. There was a still picture of Diana, Princess of Wales, and underneath was written: 'July 1st 1961–August 31st 1997'.

Like everyone else in the country, we were soon watching the rolling coverage from Paris, where the Princess had died that night. As the story developed, and the sheer tragedy of it started to sink in, it seemed to me that even if that day's match were to go ahead, it would surely not be televised. When we wandered down to the ground two hours before the scheduled start of play, a small and definitely subdued crowd was starting to gather. There was great tension in the television trucks in the BBC outside broadcast area, because clearly no one had a clue what was going to happen to our programme. The coverage of Diana's death had taken over the airwaves completely, and BBC 1 and BBC 2, on which we were due to broadcast, were broadcasting exactly the same thing. By now Prince Charles had gone to Paris to collect her body, which was to be flown to RAF Northolt.

Meanwhile at Portsmouth there was an announcement over the

Tannoy that the match would continue as planned, but there was still no word from the BBC about our commentary. Geoffrey and I watched the news coverage on the monitor in the commentary box as we sat and waited for further instructions. By now I was desperately hoping that we would be stood down, as neither of us was in the mood for commentating on a cricket match.

The game finally started without any television coverage, although I am not sure anyone really had the stomach for it. The atmosphere was dreadfully flat and depressed. At about five o'clock, with the match three-quarters through, the Princess's coffin was received at Northolt, which really brought the tragedy home to everyone gathered around their television sets.

'Get ready up there in the comm box,' called the director. 'We're going on.'

Minutes later, BBC 2 broke away from the pictures from RAF Northolt with an announcement, spoken very slowly and in the most solemn of tones: 'That is where we will leave our coverage of the death of Diana, Princess of Wales, which will continue on BBC 1. Now on BBC 2, Sunday League cricket. Here's Jonathan Agnew.'

Thanks a bunch, I thought. How on earth do you follow that?

Geoffrey and I were told to avoid any attempts at humour, and just to commentate. No colour, no fun, and definitely no talk in the match context of disasters or tragedies. Through fear of saying the wrong thing, we hardly dared open our mouths. That, for Geoffrey, takes some doing. It was a thoroughly uncomfortable experience, to which surely, in retrospect, we and the players should not have been subjected. No one felt like playing or watching cricket that day, and if you cannot commentate on a game with humour and fun, it is not worth doing.

A week later, on Saturday, 6 September, I found myself strapped into a safety harness on the roof of what is now the Danubius Hotel in London, overlooking a deserted Lord's. I had been asked to commentate on the cortège as the Princess's coffin was driven from the funeral service at Westminster Abbey to her burial in the grounds of Althorp House in Northamptonshire. The procession was scheduled to travel north through Gloucester Place and into Park Road, past Lord's and along Wellington Road to Swiss Cottage before eventually joining the M1. This was obviously a very serious and solemn assignment, and one that required a lot of homework. I certainly did not want to produce a gaffe like the one Johnners made when he was broadcasting at Diana's wedding. Stationed outside St Paul's Cathedral as she arrived in her golden coach, he famously said: 'Her father, Earl Spencer, will step out and take her arm, and they will turn and walk slowly up the steps together into the pavilion . . . I mean, cathedral.'

You could get away with that at a wedding, but hardly at a funeral.

A briefing had been held for all the commentators and production staff in Broadcasting House the previous evening. I was told that my task was to pick up the commentary as the cortège drove past the Regent's Park mosque and continue until it left my sight at the top of Wellington Road. Following the meeting, I returned to the hotel, picked up my stopwatch and instructed a cabbie to drive his taxi very slowly from the mosque to the top of Wellington Road. I reckoned on the procession travelling at a stately pace, with a maximum speed of 20 miles per hour. My journey took almost three minutes. That would be my time on air the next day, and obviously I would need enough material to be able to talk steadily and calmly as the procession drove slowly past.

So at seven o'clock the next morning I was on the hotel roof, nervously making notes of what I could see. It was a beautiful day, and as I was so high up, the spectacular views over London stretched for miles. Scribbling furiously, I noted St Paul's Cathedral, London Zoo, the mosque – where the funeral service for Dodi Fayed, who died alongside the Princess, had been held earlier in the week – and an empty Lord's: the final of the NatWest Trophy between Essex and Warwickshire, scheduled for that day, had been postponed for twenty-four hours. I knew that Princess Diana's father, Earl Spencer, had died in the Wellington Hospital, a little further along Wellington Road from Lord's, in 1992, and I reckoned that by the time I had talked about the cortège and the people, many of them clutching bouquets of flowers, lining the streets below me, I had my three minutes of carefully timed and scripted commentary all ready.

My producer arrived on the roof with the hotel manager, who insisted that I strap on my safety truss. It was quite bleak up there, and I really was now feeling very anxious indeed – far more so than for any other broadcast I have ever made. This was a huge event, and with the whole country in mourning, it was crucial to strike the right tone. By now, after some very moving images of the two young Princes walking, head bowed, behind their mother's coffin, the funeral had started in Westminster Abbey. All I could do was wait for the procession to begin, while feeling somewhat ridiculous in my harness.

After the service, which I could hear clearly through my headphones, the time was drawing near. The procession departed from the Abbey, and my colleagues described the cortège as it began its final journey. One by one, each commentator handed over to the next along the route. Gripping the microphone tightly in one hand and my notes in the other, I waited for the handover to me. It seemed that my colleagues were all speaking rather fast. Then, as the fleet of black cars – one of which I quickly identified as the hearse – drove rapidly past below me, I understood why. The cortège was moving at at least twice the speed we had imagined it would. Before I knew it, it had vanished around the corner at the top of Wellington Road, and away out of my sight. What was I going to say?

'Hand straight to Swiss Cottage!' I heard the director bark in my headphones, instructing the commentator ahead of me in the queue to miss me out altogether. My producer and I looked at each other, stunned, before he kindly extricated me from the harness. And that was that; my only experience of a state occasion. I got in my car and drove home, following the cortège up the M1. Flowers lay all over the road, and thousands of people lined the bridges and service roads all the way to Northamptonshire. It was a very moving experience indeed.

The following winter, Geoffrey Boycott's world would fall apart when he was convicted in a French court of assaulting Margaret Moore, a former girlfriend. He received a three-month suspended prison sentence, and a fine of £5,100. Despite losing a subsequent appeal in the same court, Geoffrey still emphatically maintains his innocence in what he now dismisses as 'The French Farce'. In an unusual twist, Ms Moore was awarded the sum of just one franc (about 11p) in damages.

News of Geoffrey's conviction reached us in our hotel in Jamaica the day before he was due to commentate with us on the first Test of England's tour of the West Indies. Peter Baxter received instructions from the BBC in London to remove him from the *TMS* team, and I recall how awkward Peter felt as he summoned Geoffrey to his room to deliver the news. It was unthinkable that he could appear on *Test Match Special* having just been convicted of assaulting a woman, and at the request of Sky television he was also immediately dropped by TWI, whose television coverage Sky was showing back home. When his appeal failed the following November, Geoffrey was fired by the *Sun* as a columnist, and found himself a pariah.

He was rescued by Kelvin MacKenzie, the former editor of the *Sun*, who had just acquired the national commercial station Talk Radio. It was quickly rebranded as 'TalkSport', with MacKenzie, a lifelong and vociferous opponent of the BBC, effectively setting himself up in opposition to Radio 5 Live. He acquired some sports rights here and there, and signed some big names, including the unemployed Boycott, who felt no loyalty to the BBC any more, and besides, probably believed he would never be asked to work for the corporation again.

The advent of TalkSport seemed to be of little consequence until, shortly before England's 1999–2000 tour of South Africa, Peter Baxter told me that he was having terrible problems securing the rights to broadcast the series. In fact, he said, it was starting to feel as if Ali Bacher, the Chief Executive of the South African Cricket Board, was avoiding him. The reasons for this became clear with the announcement that TalkSport had secured the exclusive rights, and BBC Radio's long and proud uninterrupted tradition of commentating on Test cricket was over. The combination of Geoffrey

Boycott and Jack Bannister, who had also joined TalkSport from the BBC, convinced Bacher to sell the rights to them without even allowing the BBC to bid.

I did go to South Africa for England's tour, but it was a thoroughly frustrating trip from a personal perspective. Reduced to giving short reports on Radio 5 Live rather than commentating, I really felt as if my wings had been clipped, never more so than when TalkSport's introduction to the fray was England being reduced to 2 for 4 on the opening day of the series in Johannesburg. With Chris Cowdrey and Mark Nicholas also on board, TalkSport did a good job, but the unfamiliar intrusion of advertisements was very unpopular with listeners. The following winter, Boycott again used his influence to secure broadcasting rights for TalkSport from the cricket boards of Pakistan and Sri Lanka, where the BBC was briefly actually locked out of the Galle Test. As Peter Baxter argued with the security staff outside the padlocked gate, I retreated to the Dutch fort which overlooks the ground, along with our driver, Simmons. While he loyally shielded me from the burning sun with a colourful umbrella, I set up my satellite telephone and broadcast reports to the BBC breakfast programmes from long range until common sense finally prevailed some time after lunch, and we were allowed into the ground. Then came the killer blow: TalkSport won the bid to broadcast the Ashes from Australia in 2002–03. A pattern seemed to be forming, and one that our listeners were in danger of accepting: that the BBC commentated at home in the summer, and TalkSport from England's tours abroad during the winter.

But TalkSport had miscalculated badly with its Australian bid, which was thought to have been as much as £500,000, an amount for cricket rights unheard of in the radio world. MacKenzie bathed in the publicity for his coup until he realised that the Ashes would not draw the audiences he needed to secure the advertising revenue required to meet his enormous costs. Word filtered out from dismayed TalkSport staff that the hierarchy had not been aware that the commentary from Australia would be broadcast in the middle of the night in the United Kingdom. MacKenzie sold the rights back to the BBC at a massive loss, with enough egg on his face to whip up a very large omelette indeed.

But he remained undeterred, and TalkSport was again the radio commentary rights holder for the tour of the West Indies in 2004. This was a highly important series, because, led by Michael Vaughan, it was in the Caribbean that England started to put together the team that would win the Ashes the following year, with Steve Harmison bursting onto the scene, taking a spectacular 7 for 12 in the first Test in Jamaica. However, once again the timing of the broadcasts was a real problem for the schedulers at TalkSport. They effectively have only one national frequency, and they suddenly discovered that the cricket commentary was in conflict with their football coverage. Since the station's survival was dependent on its football content, the TalkSport cricket commentators in the West Indies found themselves silenced whenever there was any football of note at home. This happened to coincide, for instance, with Matthew Hoggard taking a dramatic match-winning hat trick in Barbados, and also, unbelievably, with Brian Lara reaching his record-breaking 400 in Antigua. To use football parlance, this was a massive own-goal. Cricket listeners were outraged, and TalkSport's credibility as a serious contender to be regarded as the home of cricket commentary was ruined.

MacKenzie sold his share in TalkSport the following year, and that was the moment I suggested to my boss at BBC Radio Sport, Gordon Turnbull, that we invite Geoffrey Boycott to return to *Test Match Special*. It was not just because he still had a large following and was one of the best summarisers in the business. I reasoned that with MacKenzie out of the reckoning at TalkSport, if we removed Boycott as well, any ambition the station might retain to continue with cricket would evaporate. Boycott was the man negotiating the rights deals for them, by using his contacts on overseas boards. If he moved to our camp, it was unlikely that TalkSport would win any more radio rights.

And that is how Geoffrey Boycott returned to the BBC. It was not universally popular, but it was the right decision. Geoffrey's incisiveness brought a sharper edge to *Test Match Special*, and when it comes to quick analytical comments on 5 Live or a lively discussion at the end of play in the *TMS* podcast, there is no one better. Additionally, TalkSport has never broadcast a Test match since.

I am constantly asked about my relationship with Geoffrey – and often praised for my apparently tireless patience when he appears to be less than full of the joys of spring. As I have playfully said many times to his face, within five minutes of listening to Geoffrey on air, you get the man. He can be rude, arrogant and selfish. But worst of all, and the thing that annoys me more than anything, he is nearly always right. And that, for him, is the most important thing. He will argue his position until he is blue in the face. Mind you, as I also remind him these days, his memory appears to be failing him. Listening to Geoffrey on the radio now, one has the impression that he really believes he used to bat like Andrew Flintoff.

I was one of only a few friends that Geoffrey invited to visit when he was suffering from throat cancer in 2002. It is a statement of the obvious that he was very ill indeed. We would sit in his kitchen and have a quiet lunch, with Geoffrey barely able to speak because of his radiation treatment. A shadow of his normal self, he struggled to walk around his garden. But gradually his strength returned, and thankfully the cancer is now in remission. The experience mellowed him, no doubt about it, and he became much closer to his family, finally marrying Rachel Swinglehurst, who is the mother of his daughter Emma. Our excellent rapport enables me to wind him up and say things to him on the radio that no one else possibly could:

'Are you still having to take all those tablets, Geoffrey?'

'Aye. Lots of vitamins and things. These ones are cyanide, actually.'

'Really? You don't fancy doing us all a favour and taking a few more of them, do you?'

I particularly enjoy digging the bear traps that he obligingly tumbles into time and again. These are even better when the audience has been tipped off, which because Geoffrey usually spends his off-air time in the roomier Channel 5 television box rather than ours, is easily done. Not many people, for example, would bother to compare the run-scoring rates of Geoffrey Boycott and Jonathan Agnew in one-day internationals, but the cricket-mad *Harry Potter* actor Daniel Radcliffe once did, and sent his findings to us by text from New York. These, as I informed the listeners, revealed that, at 66 runs per hundred balls, my average rate of scoring was faster than Geoffrey's 53 per hundred balls. Our listeners love this sort of thing, and knowing that Geoffrey was due to join me at the microphone very shortly, I told them that I would confront him with this information. I was, however, honest enough to mention that Daniel's statistics were based on my solitary innings in one-day international cricket, in which I had scored two runs from three deliveries, while Geoffrey had batted, albeit slowly, thirty-four times for his 1,082 runs.

'Welcome back Geoffrey,' I began when he returned to the box. 'You won't have heard my discussion with Victor just now, but I presume you'd agree with me that a batsman with a strike rate of 66 must be a better player than one whose scoring rate is only 53?'

I could almost feel the nation holding its breath, waiting for Geoffrey Boycott to concede that I must have been a better batsman than he was.

'Well, that's right,' he replied, and I swear I heard a loud cheer from listeners sitting in the crowd outside our commentary box window. 'Mind you,' he continued after a short pause for thought, 'I'd have to see how many times they'd batted to be absolutely sure.'

I tried for a while to argue against that obviously crucial criterion, but Geoffrey was having none of it. So, having secured what I took to be a victory of reasonable significance, I handed over the piece of paper bearing the information, and its source.

'I'll 'ave that bloody little wizard!' Geoffrey shouted, thumping the desk, knowing that he had come within a hair's breadth of months of merciless leg-pulling.

In the short term, all is well, but I do have very serious concerns about the future of *Test Match Special*. The supply line of commentators has dried up because of the abandonment of commentary on county championship matches. This was where Johnners, Arlott *et al.* cut their teeth on Saturday afternoons, and where Johnners once described umpire Henry Horton crouching at square leg 'as if he is shitting on a sooting stick'. Yes, they may have made memorable gaffes, but it was where they learned their art and honed their skills. I can still remember commentating on the old Radio 5 from Hove on the humdrum last half-hour or so of a drawn match between Sussex and the Australians in 1993. I was completely alone, sitting in a deserted stand with no summariser or scorer to turn to, just as the old guard used to be. That teaches you how to paint pictures and describe a passage of play in intricate detail, rather than adopting the modern trend of skipping over the delivery and encouraging the summariser to talk endlessly between every ball.

Commentating on Twenty20 cricket is definitely no preparation for *Test Match Special*, because the play is so fast that there is no need to have to think, and also you have to shout a lot. But there appears to be no alternative means of training the commentators, who drive the programme after all, and who are its most important ingredient. A poor commentator lowers the quality of the entire broadcast, because what should be a nice gentle and easy flow becomes disjointed and difficult to follow. The summariser then has to talk more, to cover the mistakes and hide the commentator's uncertainty.

I cannot see where the next generation of commentators will come from. Local radio coverage on Saturday afternoons is all that remains of cricket commentary that is not either Test matches or Twenty20. It is asking far too much of someone to move straight onto *Test Match Special* before they are ready for that exposure, and before they have shown that their commentary can bear the scrutiny to which a newcomer to the programme is always subjected. That is not fair on the individual, and it is not fair on *Test Match Special*, which aims to be at the very pinnacle of cricket broadcasting, the programme that others around the world aspire to follow.

I felt terribly sorry for Arlo White, who is a good friend and a very fluent and knowledgeable sports presenter on Radio 5 Live. Although he is a more than capable commentator on one-day cricket, he would agree that he is not a cricket specialist, at least not to the degree demanded to commentate on a Test match. Arlo first appeared on *Test Match Special* in 2005, and by his own admission he found it very difficult. He was savaged by newspaper critics who used his elevation as evidence of the 'dumbing down' of *TMS*, and not surprisingly his confidence took a pounding. It was not Arlo's fault; he should not have been exposed to that level of scrutiny and expectation. I hope his unhappy experience proves to the decision-makers at BBC Radio Sport that action needs to be taken urgently to invest time and money in discovering and developing a new generation of cricket commentators, and that they must cast their net much more widely than the BBC Sport Department. Most decent sports reporters can commentate on Twenty20, and I reckon I could do a reasonable job on a football penalty shoot-out if required. But that does not mean I could commentate on the next World Cup match between England and Germany, however enticing that might be, and similarly, Twenty20 commentary is no guide at all to how someone might perform at a Test match.

It is not a prerequisite to have played professional cricket in order to be a good commentator. However, because it is absolutely essential to be steeped in the game, to live and breathe cricket, and to understand it, I do think that some playing experience at a reasonable level is important for anyone commentating on a Test match. The growth of television has meant that radio commentary is much less forgiving these days, because people can see any mistakes that we make. We are the eyes and ears of those who are not present at the game, and who are relying on us entirely to provide them with an accurate assessment of what is going on. If a commentator ever loses the trust of the listener – or fails to earn it in the first place – he will not last long.

Peter Baxter's retirement as producer in June 2007, after thirty-four years, presented *Test Match Special* with a challenge to match that of Brian's death. While producing *TMS* is one of the plum jobs in the BBC, replacing someone who had been at the helm for so long would not be easy. Peter's departure coincided, more or less, with the ownership of *Test Match Special* moving from Radio 4 to Radio 5 Live, and I was not alone in worrying about the consequences of that.

Once again, I feared that the identity of the programme might be compromised. Would pressure be applied to make *TMS* sound like any other Radio 5 Live sports programme?

Adam Mountford is the lucky man who took over from Peter in 2007, after a number of years as his assistant on Radio 5 Live. I know he was very anxious not to upset the apple cart, while at the same time, like all new producers, he was keen to put his stamp on *Test Match Special*. This led to some changes to the line-up. Phil Tufnell was Adam's first new 'signing', and he has been a tremendous success. Excitingly unpredictable in what he might say in his gravelly voice, Phil has a great sense of fun, but is also a very shrewd analyst – surprisingly so, in fact.

He might have been a bit of a larrikin when he played – and he certainly drove his captains, Mike Gatting and Graham Gooch, to distraction by his less than focused attitude – but Tufnell is nobody's fool. When it was first announced that he had signed up to go into the *I'm a Celebrity* jungle, I thought he had a real chance of winning. Tuffers has a charming, definitely cheeky smile, and the television camera loves him. He is not the bravest individual in the world: I once experienced a bumpy Indian Airlines flight with him and an equally terrified Phillip DeFreitas at the end of which even I, who am now a qualified pilot of light aircraft, was scared stiff. So quite how he ate that disgusting witchetty grub, the fat, white, wood-eating larva that was his final challenge on *I'm a Celebrity*, I do not know. Mind you, the million quid he was rumoured to have made over the next year might have swung it, I suppose.

In 2009, during the final Ashes Test at The Oval, Tuffers quietly let slip in the commentary box that his next television adventure would be to take part in *Strictly Come Dancing*. I am sure he was testing the water to see what our reaction would be. Given that he has the flattest of feet and, being known to enjoy a drink and a fag, is hardly a model athlete, I was not so sure about his prospects this time, except that, once again, he does have the knack of drawing people to him. Sworn to secrecy, he was driven to BBC Television Centre for his audition in a car with blacked-out windows. On arriving at the security post, the driver wound down his window and, to Philip's surprise, told the guard that his passenger was a 'Mr Squirrel'. It turned out that this was the code name Tuffers had been given by the programme's producers, who were determined to keep the identity of the participants in the new series under wraps. Phil Tufnell – Tuffers – Tufty the squirrel – Mr Squirrel: it has some logic to it.

With Adam and Gordon Turnbull I met up with Michael Vaughan in a hotel at the end of a day's play during the first Test against Australia in Cardiff in 2009. Michael had just retired from the game, and was looking for work in the media. Adam was keen to secure his services, and it seemed likely that Sky television would also be interested, despite its commentary box being close to bursting at the seams. I had always been impressed by Michael's performances with the media when he was captain of England; I could ask him a question about anything that was of current interest in world cricket, and he would have an answer. He was always honest, and he also understood the importance of sounding interesting and lively even on a taped radio interview, because without pictures, your voice is all you have. If you sound flat and uninterested, you will come across very badly on radio.

What struck me about Vaughan at this meeting was how very ambitious and driven he is. Sitting beside his agent, 'Chubby' Chandler, he did virtually all the talking, and carefully set out his vision for his broadcasting career. He wants to report on golf as well as cricket, and is very keen to break into television in much the same way as Gary Lineker has done so successfully. We were more than happy to take him on as a summariser, and in South Africa the following winter he showed flair and a natural aptitude for broadcasting. He also does not take himself too seriously, and has an understanding of what the listeners want to know. He is definitely one of the game's more interesting gossips, and a very good team man, which bearing in mind his success as a captain, is not surprising.

It is a shame, but unavoidable, that the arrival of Phil Tufnell and Michael Vaughan meant that at least one of our regular summarisers had to move aside. It was decided that Mike Selvey – who first appeared on *TMS* on a tour of India in 1984 – should be that man. I miss Mike's droll observations and understated humour. In response, for example, to my musings during a mopping-up operation in the Caribbean, about what a small water hog (the machine that pumps the outfield dry) might be called, Mike instantly came up with 'A water piglet, of course.' It is sad when friends go, but *Test Match Special* has to remain fresh. I know that one day it will be my turn to step aside.

With CMJ, Blowers, Simon Mann and our regular visiting commentators, *Test Match Special* is in good hands for now. And Vic Marks is my favourite summariser in the world. But Adam knows that his most pressing responsibility is to safeguard the programme's future. Without an intensive, rigorous and properly financed BBC campaign to discover and develop new commentators, rather than merely something that ticks a box or two, I really do not see how he can do it. If no action is taken now, *Test Match Special* will whither on the vine, and once its unique identity perishes, it will never return.

NINE

The Legacy

Recently I spent an idle morning thumbing through a pile of old books that were gathering dust in a corner of my office. Some of them included images of larger-than-life characters with huge moustaches, strangely-shaped cricket bats and stripy blazers, and of epic contests from cricket's colourful and fascinating history. One immediately caught my eye: *Forty-Five Summers*, by Brian Johnston. Inside the cover, dated June 1991, was an inscription in black ink, written in familiar large and rather untidy handwriting:

To Aggers.
Wishing you the best of luck in your first summer with Test Match Special. May you enjoy 45 more.
Best wishes, Johnners

The subtitle to the book was rather cumbersome – *Personal Memories from 264 Test Matches Seen from the Commentary Box* – but nevertheless it got me thinking. Johnners reckoned to have seen 264 Tests in forty-five years, starting just after the end of the Second World War, when he started working in BBC television. He was the BBC's full-time cricket correspondent from 1963 until 1972, but toured with MCC and England in several of the winters either side of that period.

In 2010 I clocked up my twentieth year as cricket correspondent, and I have toured at least once in every winter during that time. Without attempting to be accurate to the very match – I have already admitted how hopeless I am with statistics – my twenty-year tally stands at approximately 230 Tests. So, continuing at the current rate, I will rack up 520 Tests if, like Johnners, I stagger on to complete forty-five summers. (It is possible: I will be seventy-five years old then, while Johnners was eighty-one when he gave his last commentary.) That would work out at almost exactly double the number of Tests in the same time frame.

Not surprisingly, the growth in one-day internationals makes a revealing comparison too. In the twenty years from playing their first ODI until Johnners wrote his book, England played in 183 ODIs. In my twenty years from 1991, they have played 345. And that does not include Twenty20 matches, or begin to reflect the explosion of one-day cricket on the Subcontinent, where India, believe it or not, played two hundred more one-day matches than England in those twenty years.

Cricket, as an industry, has grown at an astonishing rate, and with that expansion the game has changed dramatically. While Johnners and Roy Hudd were happily singing 'Underneath the Arches' at The Oval in 1993, in what turned out to be Brian's final match, the world governing body, the International Cricket Council (ICC), was run by just three people: Sir Colin Cowdrey was the President, Lieutenant Colonel John Stephenson, the Secretary of MCC, automatically became the Secretary of ICC, and a Miss S. Lawrence was something called the Administrator. The ICC was based at Lord's in those days, and did little more than act as a means of enabling contact and co-operation between the various international cricket boards and the cricket committee. The previous year, 1992, the ICC introduced its Code of Conduct, which was to be overseen and enforced by the match referee, itself a new concept. I remember interviewing Colin in the Long Room at Lord's, and his acknowledgement that it was a sad day when the ultimate power and authority for the running of a game was to be taken out of the umpires' hands. The umpire's role has since been further diminished, to the extent that even the decisions he makes on the field can be overturned by a player's referral to technology.

Today the ICC is based in plush offices in tax-free Dubai. Instead of those three people in 1993, sixty staff work there, and a further sixty are employed throughout the world. There are twelve different committees, and an Anti-Corruption and Security Unit. That alone is a sad reflection of the unsavoury recent history of match-fixing, which remains a serious threat to the integrity of the game. Cricket is already a multi-million-pound global industry, and there are serious attempts to take the game to the USA and even to China, where the interest is very promising. Based on the wonderfully artistic, convoluted and generally bamboozling table-tennis serves played in that part of the world, I cannot wait to see a Chinese wrist-spinner in action; it could be a fascinating combination of Abdul Qadir and Ma Long, the world number one ping-pong player.

The revolution of Twenty20, the quickfire format of the game in which a match is completed in only three hours, is sweeping through the game. The cricket itself is exciting but not subtle, and while the 'live' experience of Twenty20 is vibrant and great fun, it does not have the lasting appeal or depth of Test cricket. Every match is essentially the same, with swashbuckling batting and acrobatic fielding. It's all very entertaining, but because of the lack of variety, it requires something very special indeed to linger in the memory for long. That is what sets Test cricket apart: something memorable and worthy of note happens in virtually every match. A team can battle hard to earn a draw, which may sound like a dull stalemate, but in fact can be played out in an atmosphere of the most excruciating tension and drama. Who could forget the final overs of the 3rd Test in Antigua in February 2009, when West Indies' last pair of batsmen successfully hung on for ten overs to stave off defeat by England? Locals poured into the little old ground in the heart of St John's, because word had got out that their team was clinging to the match by a thread. Every ball the batsmen survived was met by deafening horn blasts and typically excitable Caribbean shouts of encouragement and advice. In rapidly fading light, we were all reminded – regardless of which country we were supporting – of just how great a sport Test cricket is.

The players enjoy Twenty20, and have worked hard to adapt to its requirements, which are very different to those of Test matches, and even fifty-over one-day games; there's lots of money to be made from it, after all, especially in the Indian Premier League. But this generation of cricketers still want to forge careers and make their names in Test cricket, because that is what they were brought up with, and they appreciate and understand it. My concern is the attitude to Test cricket of the next generation, the impressionable ten-year-olds of today. They have their eyes firmly fixed on Twenty20 cricket, and are not interested in learning the techniques that would make them successful in Test cricket as well. Many young cricketers are only focused on becoming the best one-day batsmen in the world, which would make them in great demand for the Twenty20 leagues which will soon proliferate in international cricket. Test cricket, with its demand for patience, long days in the field, damned hard work and months away from home, has little attraction for them.

While we should not be complacent about the immediate future of Test cricket, it is the long-term outlook that looks very bleak to me. It will be played by cricketers who have little grounding or interest in the skills and the mental toughness that make Test cricket so special. I certainly cannot see Test matches being scheduled over five days for very much longer, because, influenced by one-day cricket, batsmen feel the need to score faster. This makes the game more entertaining, but as well as scoring more quickly, they get out more quickly too. Test matches today move on very rapidly compared to those played in the 1960s and '70s, and that will continue to be the case. It will not be long before a team feels it will have batted well to complete one hundred overs. It might have scored 400 runs in that time, but Test cricket will have become an extension of the one-day game, without the ebb and flow that is the ultimate challenge of technique and resilience.

The way in which cricket is reported now is also very different to how it was when Brian was BBC cricket correspondent in the 1960s. The relationship between the players and press is still much better in the cricket world than it is in football, and we are fortunate that the ECB continues to encourage the rapport between them. I do not know how football correspondents can report on the characters of the players they watch, with whom they have virtually no informal contact. Cricket correspondents, by contrast, often stay in the same hotels as the players, where they will share a drink or two with them in the bar, and can even find themselves sitting amongst them on an aircraft. We get to know each individual's character, while from the players' perspective, common sense and human nature dictate that a correspondent is less likely to criticise somebody he likes. I suspect there is a difference in the mentality of footballers, who are so wealthy and live such cosseted lives that they do not feel they need to have any sort of relationship with the media. Many cricketers, on the other hand, have half an eye on working on television or radio when they retire.

Even so, today it is nothing like the way it was in Johnners' time, when he seemed to be virtually one of the team. He was sunbathing with the players in the Caribbean in 1968 when Fred Titmus lost four toes in an accident with a motorboat, and he was dining in a restaurant with the captain, Colin Cowdrey, in Barbados when a waiter told Colin that he was a good fast bowler, and wanted to bowl at the team in the nets. Without further ado, tables were cleared to one side, an ice bucket was set down as the stumps, and Colin took guard with a large serving spoon. The waiter weaved his way in to bowl between the tables and the other diners before unleashing a rapid yorker with a bread roll which hit the ice bucket without Cowdrey getting a touch. Needless to say, he was invited to bowl in the nets next morning. I often wonder if his cricket career took off from there. I suspect that an incident like that would quickly find its way into the tabloid press these days, disapprovingly reported as demonstrating an inappropriate lack of seriousness. But it is still possible to arrange dinner with the England captain on a one-to-one basis if you go through the correct team channels and, importantly, if you are in the good books at the time. Of how many other sports can that be said?

Television has been cricket's driving force for both good and bad.

From those very early, pioneering days after the Second World War, when Johnners and his fellow commentators were watched by virtually nobody, the game is now beamed from far-flung cricket grounds straight into our homes. Cricket has never been more accessible, followed more keenly or better explained and publicised. Kerry Packer's World Series Cricket introduced the game to commercial television, with its aggressive marketing, ratings wars and advertising revenue. In exchange for effectively promoting cricket within Australia, Packer's Channel 9 paid the Australian Cricket Board £600,000 for the first three years of a ten-year deal. It was a vast amount of money at the time, and it was looked upon with great envy by the rest of the cricket world, which had supported the ACB in its battle against Packer and WSC. How could other nations compete with an Australian team that was now being bankrolled so spectacularly by the board's old adversary? And the administrators were doing nothing more for their money than simply selling cricket to the highest bidder. It was not as though it was even a particularly successful product: in the first ten years post-Packer, Australia lost four Ashes series and won only one. But still the cash rolled in from Channel 9.

The Packer revolution brought about a sea change in the manner in which cricket is financed. No state broadcaster has exclusive rights to the game any more; it is commercially driven everywhere. Here in England and Wales, the bar has been raised even higher by allowing only satellite television, with its comparatively small subscription-paying audience, to show the sport live in exchange for close to £300 million over four years. Even this staggering amount of money is dwarfed by similar rights deals in India, where Sony Entertainment Television paid US$1.94 billion over ten years to broadcast the Indian Premier League. Those massive figures explain the global stampede to stage more televised one-day cricket, because obviously, the more televised tournaments there are, the more money cricket boards and players can make. Television finances cricket and broadcasts the game around the world in an instant, but in doing so it has also fostered greed, kickbacks, encouraged corruption through illegal betting, influenced bad decisions such as the Stanford deal, and threatens the overkill of Twenty20.

Mind you, I wonder if there has ever been a time throughout cricket's rich, varied and fascinating history when a correspondent would have felt able to state with confidence and honesty that in his opinion all was well with the game. Even in what is known as the 'golden age', in the years before the outbreak of the First World War, when the majority of cricketers in the fledgling county championship played within the spirit of the game, as well as within its laws, there would have been arguments about how cricket was defining itself, and the direction it was taking as its popularity grew. There might have been debates about the standard of pitches in 1878, much as there is today – except that the current concern is that batsmen are able to score runs too easily. With more Tests finishing without going the full five-day distance, administrators find themselves losing money on gate takings and corporate hospitality. Groundsmen, therefore, are now 'encouraged' to produce pitches that make the game more likely to last the course.

Back in 1878, the hugely anticipated three-day fixture between MCC and the first Australians to tour England failed to live up to expectations by finishing in a single day: MCC 33 and 19; Australia 41 and 12 for 1. Australia won by nine wickets. However, the correspondents of that era had less cricket to write about than today's generation, and would have created rather more of an outcry about the swift conclusion to the match than they would do if it happened today. In the midst of our crammed fixture lists of Tests, ODIs and Twenty20, we might wish for something similar every now and then, to give us an opportunity to get our lawns mown.

Ethical arguments about the conduct of the game are nothing new. In the Bodyline series of 1932–33, England's fast bowler Harold Larwood deliberately aimed short deliveries at the Australian batsmen's ribs, with fielders strategically placed to take a catch as they defended themselves. This was considered wholly unsporting and against the spirit of cricket, by the Australians at least, to the extent that it seriously strained diplomatic relations between the two countries. The moral question of South Africa's apartheid system, which was reflected in the selection of its sports teams, split the game, and it would be twenty-one years before the reformed Proteas were admitted to world cricket. But it was not until World Series Cricket was set up in opposition to the establishment in 1977 that cricket faced the first crisis created by its rapidly growing ability to generate enormous sums of money.

Whatever one might have thought of WSC at the time, there is no question that everyone involved in the game has benefited from cricket's newfound wealth. Today's players, administrators, umpires, coaches, commentators and correspondents are paid much more than their predecessors ever were. A career in cricket, be it playing, administering or reporting on the game, is now seen as highly desirable. More people have been encouraged to get involved, and this improves standards. But as with everything, a balance has to be struck between generating enough revenue to invest in the future of cricket, and flogging it to the point of over-exposure. We are already at that point with Twenty20.

In May 2010 I embarked on a trip to the Caribbean to commentate on the ICC's World Twenty20 tournament, the second identical series in less than twelve months. It was won by England despite it being their third tour of the winter. I followed England's group, and commentated on nineteen matches in a fortnight. That tournament came hard on the heels of the Indian Premier League, which had ended the previous week, meaning that Twenty20 cricket was the only top-class cricket played anywhere in the world in more than two months. There was no other cricket shown on television during that time. Goodness knows how many sixes were heaved into the packed stands to excited screams from the embarrassingly overhyped commentators. There was a healthy number of exciting and dramatic finishes to savour too, Mike Hussey's remarkable innings in which he scored 18 from the last over to enable Australia to beat Pakistan in the semi-final being one of the best ever. It is little wonder that the cricket world ground to a shuddering halt when England then played two Tests in near-empty grounds against Bangladesh. What chance does Test cricket have when it is juxtaposed as cruelly as that? No wonder there is a drive to play floodlit Test cricket, the aim being to jazz the game up a bit and get people in the grounds after work. But for me, this would be one of the craziest and most dangerous moves I can imagine, because it would threaten the integrity of Test cricket.

In order to remain the supreme challenge between the finest players in the world, Test cricket has to be played in the best conditions possible. Thirty years of floodlit one-day cricket has demonstrated how the atmospherics alter virtually everywhere in the world once darkness falls. The atmosphere becomes damp, and this makes the ball swing more in the air and creates sideways movement off the pitch. In some countries heavy dew accompanies nightfall, which makes gripping the ball almost impossible for spin bowlers, and the hitting of boundaries very difficult for batsmen. Perhaps surprisingly, Geoff Boycott is an advocate of day/night Test cricket, because he believes that more people will come to watch. But I would love to have been a fly on the dressing-room wall if he had ever been dismissed cheaply by a pink, yellow or orange ball nipping unpredictably about under unsatisfactory floodlights. Test cricket must remain sacrosanct, with the conditions being the same for both teams, rather than matches being decided by which team has the misfortune to be batting under the floodlights. The outcome could simply come down to the winner of the toss. Once a sport's integrity is compromised, it is a damaged product. The records and statistics would become meaningless.

I also feel that the inclusion of Bangladesh and Zimbabwe – which will return from political isolation one day – has created a problem for Test cricket. They simply are not of a high enough standard to demand equal status alongside the other eight Test-playing nations. Two divisions of five teams is often mooted as an alternative, but that is not the answer, because it would be impossible to negotiate and maximise television rights if there was uncertainty, say, about England and Australia being in the same division. Could we really do away with the Ashes? Similarly, it would be tragic if India and Pakistan did not meet regularly in Test matches. Such wildly anticipated encounters bring the Subcontinent to a standstill.

There is a good argument for a first division of nine teams. There could be a one-up, one-down promotion and relegation system to a second division comprising improving teams like Ireland, Scotland, the Netherlands, Kenya and Afghanistan. They could host regular tours by teams such as the England Lions, effectively the England second XI, and play against each other to determine who earns the right to a four-year period in the first division. Bangladesh and Zimbabwe could continue to play one-day internationals and appear in World Cups, but it does nothing for the image of Test cricket to have two very obviously substandard teams playing in front of tiny crowds, and being barely able to compete, let alone capable of winning matches. Bangladesh did record two victories in the West Indies in 2009, but only because the hosts' front-line players were all on strike at the time. A first division of nine would eliminate one of the lesser teams, and create an element of context and interest for Test cricket as a whole. After all, lose a Test series to Bangladesh and you might be demoted.

Johnners would have enjoyed Twenty20, of that I am certain. Fast and fun as it is, he would have loved the tension, the drama and the excitement as the matches reach their climax, and he would also have recognised the importance of taking cricket to a new audience. He would certainly have had no time to chortle on about chocolate cake. He would also have known that Twenty20, with its emphasis on hitting sixes and fours, is no substitute for the subtlety, complexity and depth of Test cricket.

When Twenty20 was introduced to county cricket in 2003, crowds flocked to watch. Suddenly, grounds that had been attracting little more than the proverbial two men and a dog were bursting at the seams. Such was the hype surrounding this bold and brash new form of the game that to sound like anything other than a total convert from Test cricket led to accusations of being old-fashioned and out of touch. The tournament was short and sharp, and gained momentum because it had its own uninterrupted slot during the season. There was a colourful finals day at the end, complete with a live band.

And that is how Twenty20 should have remained. A quick, exciting midsummer hit that would finance county cricket for the rest of the year, allowing the main focus to remain on the county championship, which by grooming and preparing Test players of the future, is the bedrock of professional cricket. But the administrators wanted more, and produced a Twenty20 competition that stretched from June to July, interspersed randomly with a few championship matches. Counties struggled to sell tickets, the gate numbers dwindled, and surely it was evidence of overkill. We also saw the earliest ever start to a cricket season, with spongy pitches and frosty outfields, to accommodate the most important format of our domestic game. That is the extent to which the priorities have been lost sight of. Yet, believe it or not, the counties want to find room for yet more Twenty20, despite the indisputable evidence that its attendances are dropping.

There is a great deal of talk about the setting up of a franchise-based tournament in England, based on the IPL format, which would involve the amalgamation of the existing counties into regional teams: Northamptonshire, Derbyshire, Leicestershire and Nottinghamshire might together form the East Midlands, or something similar, and have Trent Bridge as their base. But would people really feel any affinity for these teams, and travel regularly, say, from Northampton to Nottingham, or from Taunton to Cardiff, to support them in a game lasting just three hours? I do not think so. The Indian model works because each team is based in a huge, cricket-crazy city, every one of which is crying out for its own identity in the massive country. England is very different. I believe it is a great shame that our administrators were not satisfied with what they had, a highly successful and exciting tournament, making money, attracting large crowds and giving the flagging image of county cricket a much-needed shot in the arm.

It does not help that the majority of individuals who run our game have no genuine cricket background. They are businessmen and entrepreneurs – some more successful than others – who urgently need to heed the warnings about overkill they are receiving from players, the Professional Cricketers Association and the media before the damage they cause the game becomes irreparable. The £300 million the ECB receives from television rights and the income generated by a successful Twenty20 should be more than enough to finance a structure that produces the best Test team in the world, and that should indisputably be the main priority of the ECB. Instead, I fear we will see a further reduction in the amount of county championship matches played by our aspiring Test cricketers, and no let-up in flogging Twenty20 to death. This will end up not only killing the golden goose, but also producing a mediocre Test team consisting of impatient batsmen who lack the necessary grounding to succeed in the ultimate examination of skill, technique and temperament. That will lead to falling standards, declining numbers of spectators attending Test cricket, and less paid by broadcasters for television rights. The current balance between Twenty20 and championship cricket is already worryingly out of kilter. It threatens the long-term success of the England team, and with that the future of cricket in this country.

India came to Twenty20 very late. In fact the Indian board was decidedly sniffy about it at the beginning, presumably because it assumed that because the shorter game has fewer commercial breaks, it would not generate the same television revenue as the standard fifty-over one-day match. This led to the setting up of a rebel, unauthorised Twenty20 league called the Indian Cricket League, which stung the board into unveiling the Indian Premier League. The IPL has quickly become cricket's most financially lucrative competition, but after only three seasons it has become mired in controversy and allegations of corruption on a massive scale. Lalit Modi, whose brainchild the tournament was, was suspended from his position as IPL Chairman and Commissioner while investigations into his financial affairs were instigated. Comprising eight franchises, the value of the IPL has been estimated at US$4.13 billion, with players from all over the world being auctioned off for as much as $1.55 million. It brought new ideas and an exciting concept to cricket, but the world will be watching to see how the Indian board regains control of the IPL and repairs its tattered image.

Despite the enormous sums of money on offer, the IPL remains a domestic Indian competition, and this has caused huge scheduling issues. International cricketers such as England's Kevin Pietersen can only be released to take part in the IPL with the ECB's blessing, and he picks up his $1.55 million only if he actually plays. If England are involved in a Test or ODI series at the time, Pietersen would not be able to appear in the IPL; therefore he would not be paid. I doubt whether the necessary administrative overhaul and the inquiry into the running of the IPL will put players off participating in future, but it is in the interests of all international cricketers to be free of Test commitments during the spring, when the IPL is staged. This is not simply a case of cricketers being greedy: they have short careers, with no guarantees attached. Almost overnight, the IPL has become the international cricketer's pension plan.

Inevitably, the Indian board was not content with the huge sums of money generated by the original format of the IPL. It was during the negotiations for a planned expansion for the 2011 season, in the form of a further two teams, or franchises, and an extension of the tournament from sixty to ninety-four matches, that the first serious allegations of fraud arose. If the IPL is enlarged still further, it will place even more of a strain on the scheduling of international cricket, and increase the likelihood of more cricketers like Andrew Flintoff retiring from Test cricket altogether and becoming Twenty20 free-lances. What is easier: spending six weeks bowling four overs a match and fielding for no more than twenty overs for your million dollars, or playing for at least two years for the same amount, with months spent away from home? Even I can work that one out.

Another unsavoury aspect of Twenty20 cricket is that it is a match-fixer's delight. Not only is it possible to bet on the outcome of the game, there is also spread betting on individual players' performance, and almost limitless opportunities for what is called 'spot betting', on small movements or single incidents within a match – how many runs are scored from the ninth over, for example, or how many wides are delivered. It was in this connection that two Essex players, the Pakistani leg-spinner Danish Kaneria and the twenty-two-year-old fast bowler Mervyn Westfield, were arrested at the start of the 2010 season in connection with a forty-over game against Derbyshire the previous September. The range of wild and unpredictable shots that are played in Twenty20 makes it almost impossible to tell whether a batsman has been genuinely dismissed through attempted innovation and urgency, or has got out on purpose because he was paid to make a particular score, or to lose his wicket at a certain point in the game.

It was in 2000 that the game was finally forced to accept that illegal gambling and betting had taken a grip on a number of international players. I had watched a one-day series the previous year featuring England, Pakistan and India in Sharjah, United Arab Emirates, during which I was as certain as I could be that I had witnessed a fixed match. This game, between Pakistan and England, featured in the Pakistan Board's inquiry into match fixing in 2000, headed by a senior judge, Justice Malik Qayyum, as a result of which two Pakistan players, Salim Malik and Ata-ur-Rehman, were banned from cricket for life, and a number of other well-known Pakistan cricketers were fined. During the inquiry Pakistan's coach, the legendary batsman Javed Miandad, testified that he had received a telephone call telling him that five of his players had been paid to throw the game. It was the reckless manner in which Pakistan batted that had alerted my attention, but at the time I did not have the confidence to say anything publicly. There had already been rumours of match-fixing during the 1999 World Cup, but it was only the following year, when Hansie Cronje, the South African captain and Mohammad Azharuddin, his Indian counterpart, were charged with corruption and banned from the game for life, that cricket realised the full extent of the problem.

It was so easy. There was far too much one-day cricket played, much of it in Sharjah, which was not monitored properly by the authorities, and if a series had already been decided, there were a lot of 'dead' matches on which nothing depended. Players could be persuaded to get themselves out for less than their batting 'spread', a score based on their batting average, on which punters chose to bet either above or below. Put very simply indeed, if a batsman's average is 33, his spread might be set between 30 and 35. If he is then bribed to get out for 10, everyone who has bet that he will score more than 35 that day will lose. The beauty of it is that the batsman's team could still win the match, assuaging any feeling of guilt he might have at giving his wicket away in exchange for a brown envelope. This sort of fixing is very hard to detect, even by the trained eye. And needless to say, betting on cricket has become much more intricate and involved than this very basic example.

Cronje and Azharuddin were undone by evidence the Indian police had secured by tapping their mobile phones, which was corroborated by their largely unsuspecting and innocent team-mates. The involvement of these fine cricketers and seemingly decent men in illegal gambling shook the cricket world to the core. The ICC formed an Anti-Corruption Unit, headed by the former Commissioner of the Metropolitan Police, Paul Condon, and there are now tight restrictions governing the movement of people around dressing rooms, and banning cricketers from using mobile phones during a match. The players know that to be found guilty of corruption or match-fixing will end their careers, but still it goes on. The rewards are so great, and Twenty20 provides such a perfect cover, that vulnerable cricketers will always find themselves tempted. 'What's the harm in just doing it once?' they might think. But as Cronje discovered, once he was on the bookmakers' hook, no amount of struggling could set him free, although he claimed to have tried. In his day it was estimated that £16 million was wagered illegally by Indian bookies on every one-day international. Now it is many times that, and with the advent of Twenty20 there are many more matches to interest bookmakers and their punters. By flooding the calendar with cricket, the administrators are inadvertently encouraging corruption.

I do not have a downer on Twenty20 cricket, but it does frustrate me that it has been pushed so hard as representing the future of cricket by people who really do not know what they are talking about. If managed and controlled properly and responsibly, Twenty20 cricket is very much a part of the game's future, but only alongside Test cricket and one-day internationals. It is a revenue-raiser, providing short, sharp entertainment, and it has a role in encouraging newcomers to cricket, but please do not try to convince me that Twenty20 is anything more meaningful or enduring than that.

Where Twenty20 does have an advantage over other formats of the game is that it is played almost exclusively in self-contained tournaments. With so many one-day internationals being played, it is essential that some sort of fifty-overs league is introduced to give the matches context. Between 2009 and 2013, England will play a staggering thirty-one one-day internationals against Australia (not including the World Cup or the Champions Trophy). Twenty-four of them will be played in England in four series which have no relevance to anything apart from winning the latest sponsor's cup. These matches are played purely for television money. The ECB will say that it is taking cricket around the country, but the reality is that it is swamping the summer with an unnecessary number of matches.

The prospect of watching the Australians every four years used to be tremendously exciting for England cricket-lovers, who packed into the grounds, and still talk about the first time they saw the visiting Aussies. Now they drop by almost every summer. I am sure the Ashes will continue to be popular, but will people really continue to buy expensive tickets for these fifty-over games, which are in danger of becoming little more than exhibition matches? Even a man with the enthusiasm for cricket of Brian Johnston would have found his appetite tested by the prospect of the seventh one-day match in 2009, which was played at Chester-le-Street with the Australians already 6–0 up. Thankfully England managed to win the final game of what had been a terribly tedious and one-sided series – a description that really should never be applied to one-day cricket, which is supposed to be spontaneous, compelling and thrilling.

The subject of using technology to help the umpires make accurate decisions was steadily moving up the cricketing agenda while Johnners was commentating on *Test Match Special*, and we discussed it many times. He was a supporter of introducing slow-motion replays for run-outs and stumpings, and it was difficult to argue against that. Commentating regularly on Tests and one-day matches, we see umpires make mistakes, and also give batsmen the benefit of the doubt, as they are supposed to do. Umpiring is a very difficult job, and we always try to remember that when passing judgement on a questionable decision. But as the quality and the speed of the technology available to television improved at an alarming rate in the early 1990s, it became increasingly difficult to justify glaring errors in the middle which would have been eliminated by referral to technology.

The cricketers themselves were becoming increasingly irritated by poor umpiring decisions, which after all can have a serious impact on an individual's career. I had a good friend in my early Leicestershire days called Martin Schepens. He was a good young batsman, but the renewal of his contract at the end of each summer was always nip and tuck. His career ended with a poor LBW decision against him in his final championship match, and he was released from the staff almost immediately afterwards. To his great credit, he accepted the whole business with remarkable stoicism. As the technology improved, and with slow-motion replays able to show that a batsman should not have been given out long before he returned to the dressing room in high dudgeon, the pressure grew steadily for some sort of review system that would help to eradicate glaring umpiring errors.

But when the ICC eventually brought in such a system for run-outs and stumpings in time for England's tour of South Africa in 1995, I was concerned that it would be the thin end of the wedge, and that once cricket started to venture down the route of introducing technology, there would be pressure to increase its use. Replays were extended to include low catches claimed by fielders, which because of the two-dimensional image on the television screen, and the depth of field of the camera, proved impossible for the third umpire to give out. Some genuinely brilliant catches were overruled because the batsmen declined to walk, forcing the umpires in the middle to refer the decision to their colleague in the stands. On every occasion the television picture made it appear as if the ball had landed just in front of the fielder's outstretched fingers, so without exception, and after an interminable delay, the batsman was given not out. This ought to have been sufficient proof that television technology is not yet good enough to control the adjudication of the game, but nevertheless the umpires' Decision Review System (DRS) is now up and running. This enables all decisions, even LBWs, to be reviewed by a third umpire who can overrule his colleagues in the middle, based on television replays that we can all see, and, in the case of LBW, the predictions of a computer using ball-tracking technology. In many ways it is inevitable that the game has taken this course, but the procedure for reviewing an umpire's decision flies in the face of the spirit of cricket, and will I believe have very damaging consequences. Rather than the umpire asking for his decision to be reviewed, the batsman must challenge the decision, which is in absolute defiance of the laws of the game.

Every cricketer has been brought up to respect the game's traditions. We often hear about the spirit of cricket, and this is not some unspoken, intangible code of conduct; it is enshrined within the laws:

> *Cricket is a game that owes much of its appeal to the fact that it should be played not only within its Laws, but also within the Spirit of the Game. This involves showing respect for 1) Your opponents. 2) Your own captain and team. 3) The role of the umpires. 4) The game's traditional values.*
>
> *It is against the Spirit of the Game to dispute an umpire's decision by word, action or gesture.*

This could not be spelled out more clearly, and every batsman knows when an umpire raises his finger, you walk. You might not like the decision; it could very well be wrong. But, based on the assumption that the umpire is an honest and honourable sort of fellow, you accept that any error he makes is not deliberate or malicious. You must take it on the chin. That is cricket; and dealing decently and sportingly with a bad decision is a valuable lesson in life.

That, apparently, is a thing of the past, in Test cricket at least. The batsman now stands his ground and gestures that he wants the decision against him reviewed. The fielding captain can do the same if he believes that the batsman should have been despatched. Either way, the players are challenging the umpire's authority. How long will it be before this is repeated on village greens and school playing fields? There will be no Hawkeye or third umpire to call upon there, but once cricketers, including impressionable children, see their heroes on television refusing to accept the umpire's decision, it is naïve to assume they will not copy them. You only have to see how the high-five celebration of the fall of a wicket is now as commonplace in village cricket as it is at Lord's to appreciate the power of television, and the very serious ramifications of this review system. Never has the precious spirit of cricket been so threatened.

The ICC refuses to consider altering the system to enable the umpire to call up assistance in making his decision. This, they say, would make for weak umpires who would check the technology before every decision, and there is some substance to that argument. But the ICC must consider the impact the current system is having on the image of cricket. I would prefer to see an umpire check with his colleague before giving a ruling than a batsmen standing his ground, or the unseemly spectacle of the fielders gathering round to discuss whether or not to challenge a decision. 'It's not cricket' may sound like a very old-fashioned observation these days, but never has it been more necessary. It is worth noting that most of the players and umpires I speak to are very uncomfortable with the whole business of challenging an umpire's authority. Cricket was not designed to be played this way, and its enviable reputation for decency and fair play must be protected.

I am also frustrated that commentators have not been consulted to establish the effect that the frequent stoppages caused by the review system have on the coverage of a match. Speaking as a radio broadcaster, I believe that the DRS has a profoundly damaging impact on the flow of the game. It destroys the impact, the drama and the description of a wicket being taken, because unless the batsman's stumps have been flattened or he has spooned a gentle catch, he might well ask for the decision to be referred – or at least have a conversation with his partner about it – which means the moment falls absolutely flat. Is he out, or isn't he? It kills the commentary stone dead. Certainly the overwhelming response we receive on email is strongly opposed to the DRS, which listeners regard as an unwelcome intrusion. But the ICC would prefer not to know that, constantly reiterating that the umpires are in favour of the technology – but of the several I spoke to over a quiet rum punch in the Caribbean during the World Twenty20, not one spoke up for the system. The ICC appears to have an agenda to drive in the DRS, regardless of what the majority feel about it.

I would prefer to do away with the use of technology in umpiring altogether, except for line decisions. Unfortunately, the success of adjudicating run-outs and stumpings with the aid of two fixed side-on cameras has influenced the powers that be into thinking that all technology will be an improvement. The problem will not go away, because television broadcasters use these various gizmos very successfully to enhance their coverage. They display ball-tracking technology like Hawkeye to determine whether or not a batsman is LBW, and infra-red cameras to produce Hotspot, which detects whether the ball has made contact with the bat. Super-slow-motion cameras record at up to a thousand frames per second, while microphones beside the stumps provide Snickometer, which also helps to detect whether or not the ball has touched the bat. These combine to make the commentators and the viewers in their armchairs apparently better-equipped to make umpiring decisions than the two men wearing white coats in the middle. Originally introduced as entertainment, this technology is now part and parcel of the modern game.

It has not helped the case of those who argue in favour of the Review System that the early attempts to use it have hardly been a roaring success. In the West Indies in 2009 there was an incident in the first Test in which the West Indian number 11 batsman challenged a decision for caught behind against him. All attention immediately focused on the third umpire's room, where the Australian Daryl Harper was on duty. The catch had been taken down the leg side, and would have been reasonably straightforward for Mr Harper to adjudicate had he been able to see the ball in the replays he was shown. Time and again he called for the director to give him a slow-motion replay which showed the ball, and each time the director replied that he was doing so. Harper was apparently the only person in the world who could not see the ball on his screen. Eventually the players simply walked off the ground while the recriminations started. It turned out that Harper's television screen had been mistakenly put onto a zoom setting either by a technician or a cleaner doing the dusting, so his 'tightened' picture excluded the ball. You could not make it up.

Poor old Daryl was also on duty in Johannesburg in 2010 when England appealed confidently for a catch by the wicketkeeper, Matt Prior, against South Africa's captain and leading batsman, Graeme Smith. It was a key moment in the game, with Smith's wicket crucial to England having any chance of avoiding defeat. The commentators on Sky television clearly heard the sound of an edge and announced that Smith was out, while next door, on the South African Broadcasting Corporation, Matthew Hoggard told his audience that he could not hear a thing, and that Smith was not out. The SABC feed was the one sent to Harper, sitting in a room about sixty yards away, and to the disbelief of the England players and the Sky commentary team, Harper ruled not out on the not unreasonable grounds that he could not hear anything. Clearly there was a technical issue which enabled Sky's commentators and viewers to hear the noise, but not the SABC or the third umpire Daryl Harper, who was pilloried for incompetence, but again appears to have been unlucky. It is difficult to justify using technology when it does not work, and when rather than simplifying the game, it makes it even more confusing and complicated.

Umpires are not trained to be technicians, and they pride themselves on the quality of the decisions they make out in the middle. That is where they are tested, and the majority of those I speak to want to keep that challenge, and to rise to the top of their profession through their own skill, rather relying on technology which is entirely out of their hands, and being reduced to little more than counting the number of balls in an over.

I was invited to moderate a fascinating meeting at the ICC headquarters in Dubai shortly before the 2010 season. This was a gathering of everyone involved in implementing technology in Test cricket, from the designers and creators of this wonderful equipment to the television producers and directors who use it. Also present were the chief executives of the Test-playing countries, which would have to pay for it all: from England and Australia, which have plenty of money available to install a belt-and-braces system, to Bangladesh, which could not afford even the most basic review system. This, combined with the preference of India's players not to use the Decision Review System, has created the crazy situation of some Test series being played with the DRS while others are not. The aim of the meeting was to find a way to make technology work better, and it was very clear to me that the ICC, having introduced that technology, is absolutely determined for it to succeed by hook or by crook.

These observations might seem like gripes from an old traditionalist stuck in his ways. But they concern matters that cricket-lovers are arguing about in clubs all over the land. There are other issues too, like the presence of so many South African born and raised cricketers in the England team. This is an issue the ECB desperately tries to ignore, but I regularly hear complaints about it when I am out and about. The identity of the England team is important, but even more so is the incentive of playing for one's country, that drives our professional cricketers to perform at their very best in county cricket. Perhaps I feel more strongly about it than most because I was one of those borderline cricketers throughout my career, one who usually had at least a chance of being selected for the next Test match. Of course I was disappointed when I heard on the radio that I had been overlooked, but if Graham Dilley, Neil Foster or Norman Cowans had been preferred to me, that was entirely acceptable. They were all fine products of our county system. But what on earth Liam Plunkett, Matthew Hoggard and Sajid Mahmood felt when Darren Pattinson was parachuted in to play for England at Headingley in 2008, I can only imagine. To be fair, it was no fault of Pattinson's: he was simply using the system. He had lived virtually his entire life in Melbourne, where he was a roof tiler by trade, but having been born in Grimsby, he was entitled to play county cricket for Nottinghamshire as an Englishman. That was all he intended to do, but within four months he was called up to play for England.

'Tell me, Darren,' I asked him immediately after he had been handed his cap, 'when you were tiling those roofs in Melbourne, did you dream about this?'

'No, mate!' he replied in a broad Australian accent. The honour of representing England took a knock that day; and the integrity of county cricket too.

Playing for England is the dream and aspiration of every English sportsman. Millions of pounds are poured into academies and coaching systems in order to help the best young cricketers rise to the top. Adil Rashid, James Taylor and Ajmal Shahzad are three fine young prospects in whom a great deal of time and money has been invested. But they would be entitled to wonder what the point was when, after so much hard work and personal sacrifice, and just one step away from finally reaching their goal, they are leapfrogged by someone who is the product of another country? South African politics, and the quota system that was imposed on first-class teams there in order to encourage the participation of non-white players, have not helped our situation. When cricketers like Jonathan Trott and Craig Kieswetter, who were both good enough to represent South Africa Under 19s, choose to earn a living in English county cricket rather than play for their own country, clearly there is a very serious problem for Cricket South Africa that needs to be addressed urgently. It simply is not right, in my view, that barely a fortnight after serving his qualification period, Kieswetter was chosen for England ahead of Steven Davies, James Foster, Chris Read and indeed any other player whose childhood dream and motivation it has been to keep wicket for England one day. I once asked Craig White, the Yorkshire player who represented England in Test cricket despite having been born and brought up in Australia, if it is possible to adopt another country, in his case to feel as thoroughly English as he did Australian. With admirable honesty, he replied that he does not think it can be done, no matter how hard you try.

It is a passion for cricket that drives us all – players, commentators, umpires, scorers, writers and supporters – every day. Cricket is a wonderful game, and I only hope that in twenty-five years' time, when I produce my own *Forty-Five Summers*, *TMS* will still be a place for intelligent debate and conversation. By that time I hope to be rather as Johnners was when I first walked through that battered old door at Headingley, comfortably ensconced as the old man in the commentary box, the correspondent's baton having been passed on to my successor long ago. Gone will be the serious issues and the thirty-second reports, and I can simply enjoy the commentary, the company and the spirit of *Test Match Special*.

For our listeners, *TMS* is a place where there is no nastiness, no moaning, and nothing unpleasant ever happens. Everyone sounds cheerful and everything appears to be great fun, even if the reality can sometimes be a little different. The programme provides escapism for its audience whose mental picture of our apparently perfect world conjures a smile and offers a distraction from everyday life. It is the sound of summer.

Johnners would love the modern *Test Match Special*, because the atmosphere which he created continues today. He gave *TMS* its soul, and with a few colleagues created a quirky, welcoming and unique radio programme that is much more than just commentary on a cricket match. It is something very precious; it is the legacy of our friend and my mentor, Brian Johnston.

Index

(the initials BJ and JA in subentries refer to Brian Johnston and Jonathan Agnew)